ACTION PRIEST
The Story of Father Joe Lauro

ACTION PRIEST

THE STORY OF FATHER JOE LAURO

By

Rev. Joseph Lauro and Arthur Orrmont

With a Foreword by Richard Cardinal Cushing

WILLIAM MORROW and COMPANY, INC.
New York   1971

Printed in the United States of America by
American Book-Stratford Press, New York, N.Y.

Library of Congress Catalog Card Number 75-118269

To Regina Coeli
(The Queen of Heaven)

Teach me to soar aloft, yet ever so,
When near the Sun, to stoop again below.
Thus shall my humble feathers safely hover,
And, though near Earth, more than the Heavens discover.

SIR THOMAS BROWNE, *Religio Medici*

CONTENTS

FOREWORD

IT is a measure of the man and priest that not until now, reading Father Joe Lauro's life story, did I learn of his bitter trials in achieving the priesthood. I knew of the much-decorated bomber pilot in World War II; of the parish priest with Chicago in his mouth who fought his way into the hearts of the reserved and sometimes hostile people of the Arkansas hill country; of the priest of the Ecuadorian poor who has done such compassionate and masterful work among them. But I did not know that it took Joe Lauro fourteen years to reach the priesthood at the age of thirty-eight, when the average seminarian is ordained at twenty-four.

He has suffered, sometimes terribly, for his vocation, as few priests are obliged to do. But then he is not an average man. Much of his story underscores this fact, not by what he and his collaborator, Arthur Orrmont, write—Joe is too modest for that—but by virtue of the mere telling of what has happened to him. He was always behind, or sidetracked—somehow out of step with the usual, the conventional, the easy. This despite his distinction as a schoolboy and college athlete, his excellence as a pilot with the RAF and AAF, his great popularity wherever he has gone. This dislocation in his life was fate in only an incidental sense; it developed from the simple fact that he lacked a signature to a certain piece of paper.

The man who denied him that signature was a priest, and thus, because of the intricacies of Canon Law, it was also the Church that for so long denied Joe Lauro his vocation. Yet never once in these pages is there a trace of real bitterness or self-pity. Joe loves too much; he knows only one language, that of the heart. Like his Master, there is no condemnation in him.

And since he loves he also laughs. There is pain in this book, as there is pain in any life that is truly lived, but of sourness there is nothing. Joe's humor is as genuine as his toughness in the face of want and injustice. His hilarious vignettes of hill country life and people will remain with me as long as the account of his ministrations to "God's poor," as one of the one hundred and thirty-five priests of the Society of St. James the Apostle, in the *barriadas* and *campos* of the Latin American Missions.

I remember how, during my trip to Latin America in the summer of 1964, while I was preparing for ceremonies at his parish seat of Boca de los Sapos, Joe said to me, "Your Eminence, these people would be thrilled if you gave them the full treatment." I turned to my secretary and said, "All right, Monsignor Rossiter, bring out the red." Joe threw back his balding head and roared, and his laughter was with me warmingly throughout a long and fatiguing day.

This is the way Joe Lauro affects people. They cannot but take on some of his vitality, his energy, his passion to help, to succor, to understand.

He is a good priest. I cannot pay him a higher compliment. Reading his story, I am not sure that all who do so will be inspired by it, but I do say that no one who reads it will be indifferent. For this book is not confined in its interest to a Catholic audience. What it says of hope and faith and love is for all men.

> ✠ Richard Cardinal Cushing
> Former Archbishop of Boston
> Founder of the Society of
> St. James the Apostle

PART I

THE CLOSING OF A DOOR

CHAPTER

1

I READ the letter Abbot Lambert Burton had just handed me. I was twenty-three years old, and big and healthy, but my hand shook.

The shock was too overwhelming to register immediately. Like a man riding a hencoop in a flood who notices that his shoelace is untied, only a single trivial detail from the general welter of disaster penetrated my mind: I would lose my deposit on the black Benedictine cassock the Abbey tailor had measured me for two weeks ago today.

Automatically I reread the letter from the Chicago Chancery: "We cannot excardinate you from your Chicago diocese so that you might be incardinated into the Benedictine Order. Henceforth your case will be in the hands of the Bishop of Chicago. In future please communicate with the Bishop and not this Chancery regarding the same."

The cool finality of a Chancery rejection. My request to enter the novitiate of the Benedictines had been refused without explanation, the door to the Holy Priesthood slammed in my face. Suddenly my shock and disappointment were grief.

The Abbot looked at me with sympathy; he knew my bitterness and would not condemn it. "Joe," he said, "some bear a cross of sickness, others a cross of loss. You have endured much for your calling. God cannot be unmindful."

I didn't believe He was unmindful. I felt that in His wisdom He was denying me the call. But why? I couldn't conceivably understand why. Was it simply obscurity that was my enemy?

My question was in my eyes, and answering it with his amazing perception, Abbot Burton smiled: "You may never know. God gives answers, but never at the questioner's convenience."

Somehow his smile was balm, reducing my grief again to a manageable disappointment. "When, Father Abbot?" I asked. "When can I hope for an answer to my difficulties I can live with?"

"In His good time. That's cold comfort, I know, but there is better to come. I'm convinced of that, despite all the evidence to the contrary."

I mulled on this. Certainly there was evidence to the contrary, stretching back seven years to 1927, when I was a boy of sixteen and already determined on the priesthood.

In 1927 my father, Nicholas Lauro, was a warden of Assumption Church at 60th and Marshfield Streets, on the Southside of Chicago. The great bubble of optimism for paper holdings still had two years before it was to burst, but already the parish church was having financial difficulty. One day, at a meeting with Pastor Stukel and his fellow wardens, Nicholas Lauro suggested that Father Stukel take a cut in salary. The pastor was from the old country and not used to interference. Angrily he ordered my father from the room.

The following Sunday, when I appeared as usual at Assumption Church to serve as altar boy at mass, Father Stukel ordered me to leave. After that I served at St. Raphael's Church, where I attended grade school. My father worshipped thereafter at St. Theodore's, to which he brought his fine tenor voice. The rest of the family, my mother and her six other children, also left Assumption parish to worship at St. Theodore's.

Father Stukel's grudge against my father followed me like a storm cloud that grows larger and more threatening the

farther you move away from it. That fall I entered Quigley
Preparatory Seminary to study for the priesthood. It was an
hour and a half trip each way on the streetcar. At the end of
the first three-month grading period I got my report card,
which had to be signed by both parents and pastor. Father
Stukel refused to sign and I told my teacher I had lost the card.

Nicholas Lauro died in the spring of 1928. Things were
bad at home, and I got a job as a water boy and weekend
watchman with a Chicago construction outfit working on the
new Holy Name Cathedral Rectory. In September, with the
financial help of my Jewish brother-in-law, Harry Davidson,
I entered St. Viator's High School, where I played fullback
on the football team. After two years I applied to study for
the novitiate at St. Viator's Seminary.

Father Stukel's recommendation was required for acceptance, and he refused it. My only course was to continue in
high school and accumulate the credits necessary for the seminary, hoping that he would eventually relent. I graduated
from St. Rita's High, run by the Augustinian Fathers, in 1931.

It took me two years, working at various jobs in Chicago,
to save enough money for my first two years of college. In
the spring of 1933 I entered St. Benedict's College in Atchi-
son, Kansas, hoping to prepare for the Benedictine Order.
There I met Father Damian Glenn and Father William Mott,
who were faculty members at St. Martin's College in Olympia,
Washington, but taking further studies at St. Benedict's. They
encouraged me to transfer to St. Martin's, where opportunities
for campus employment were good.

I entered St. Martin's the following fall with the intention
of carrying on studies to become a Benedictine monk. To that
intent I was enrolled in what was then called the Classical
Course. During the fall, winter and spring quarters I accomplished a record of better than average and the completion of
sophomore standing.

Normally I would have applied for the novitiate at St. Martin's, and the Community would have voted to accept or reject my application. I did apply, and Abbot Burton gathered the necessary documents to present my application to the assembled monks for their discussion and approval. That approval would have been mine; I had many friends at St. Martin's. (I learned later that several of my teachers had gone so far as to call at the Chicago Chancery, in person, to plead my case for the novitiate.) But the one necessary document was missing; the recommendation of Father Stukel, and by Canon Law it was essential. Again he summarily refused to recommend me.

Abbot Burton had told me there was better ahead. But how in the face of these facts could I continue to hope I would one day achieve Holy Orders? Only if I believed that God wished me to continue, and I so believed. I had no choice not to, for I knew I had a vocation.

"It's obvious we can do nothing here," Abbot Burton said now. "We desire you as a candidate but our problem rests with the Bishop and the pastor in Chicago. Perhaps you'd best return home and go to school, and work out your problem there. We'll keep your vocation in our prayers."

I didn't want to go home to Chicago. In the past eight months St. Martin's Abbey had become my home. Here I had hoped to fulfill the end for which my nature was credited—to please God by a love which responded to the love of God with a love equally pure and disinterested. Here, ignoring the thundercloud, I had looked forward to the novitiate, the time of trial spent in prayer, work and study to determine whether one had a vocation to be a Benedictine priest or brother, after which one continued his college course and, after five years, was professed in the Order.

I believed utterly in the Benedictine idea: to love God in such a way that one could fulfill every obligation which in Christian charity one owed to his neighbor. Sometimes, chanting the plainsong of Palestrina in chapel with my fellow Scholasticates, I had been lifted above myself to a Community

of fellowship in which the absoluteness of my joy was a revelation of my fitness for that Community.

"Joe," Abbot Burton said, "I have one last practical suggestion. Call on the Apostolic Delegate in Washington. See what
he says. I'll write Archbishop Cicognani in advance so he'll
have the facts before him when you arrive."

"I will, Father Abbot."

The Abbot rose from behind his desk. "Come see me again
before you go."

I shook his hand, wishing that some of the strength in that
clasp could communicate itself and give me the power to
overcome my disappointment. For I couldn't believe that a
few minutes' conversation with the Apostolic Delegate could
solve a problem whose roots extended back seven long years,
and were entwined with the uncompromising law of the
Church.

Maurey Schafer, a fellow student and my best friend at St.
Martin's, watched as I packed my battered valise. Through
the dormitory window I could see the snow-capped top of
Mt. Rainier and the notched peaks of the Cascades, henceforth to be landmarks of the mind only.

"So you're hitching to Washington, and then home?"

I stuffed three clean but threadbare handkerchiefs into a
corner of the valise. "That's right, Maurey."

He cleared his throat. "You need a couple of bucks?"

I did, but I wasn't going to borrow from Maurey, although
his father owned half the timber in the state. I'd get by somehow; I always had. "No thanks," I told him.

"They'll miss you at KGY."

"The feeling's mutual." I'd enjoyed work at Station KGY,
one of the first in the Pacific Northwest, even though Father
Sebastian, the director, had been obliged to make me an an-
nouncer because I was the "worst engineer" he'd ever seen.
Nor had I minded putting in a couple of hours every day at

the post office, sorting the mail. These two on-campus jobs had made it possible for me to survive at St. Martin's.

"Joe, why hitchhike?" asked Maurey. "It's tough on the road. Borrow a hundred—I can spare it."

"How does a rich man's son like you know how tough it is on the road?" I kidded him, and tugged on a mildewed strap. It broke.

I almost never swore but this time the temptation was overpowering. Maurey whistled, eyes trained innocently on the ceiling, till the storm passed. Then he said, "You could use a new suitcase. That one looks like it came over with your father on the boat. They've got some nice cowhide ones in town, reasonable."

I reminded Maurey that Brother Augustus, the Abbey custodian, was famous for his collection of rope and twine. Early next morning, before breakfast, my suitcase roped securely at one end, I left the Abbey. In my pocket was a ten-dollar bill I'd found under my pillow after Maurey had left, together with another fifteen, the last of my nest egg. Wanting to avoid the embarrassment of a public farewell in the dining hall, I'd said my other goodbyes individually the night before.

I met a lot of different people in the next five days. A couple who had lost their farm to the bank. Young hoboes fourteen and fifteen years old. A man wanted for murder in Idaho. A college boy in gray flannel bags who turned out to be a leader of the American Student Union. A matron who was reading Hervey Allen's best-selling *Anthony Adverse*. And at least a half-dozen other hitchhikers with signs on their backs reading "En route to New York to appear on Major Bowes!" Once, from necessity, I borrowed such a sign, and it worked, though it was no fun confessing my deception to the inquisitive Methodist clergyman who picked me up.

I arrived in Washington with six dollars and the conviction that although the people of America felt that Roosevelt had given their country back to them, they still didn't know what to do with it. In every city of any size I'd passed through—Yakima and Boise, Omaha and St. Louis, Cincinnati and Baltimore—there had been queues outside the employment offices and "No Help Wanted" signs in the stores.

At St. Martin's I hadn't been completely insulated from the depressed world; we Scholasticates were no strangers to the town, nor was its grim air of hanging on lost upon us. But for almost a year I hadn't set foot in the larger cities, and what I saw now was disturbing. When I entered a Boise lunchroom and headed toward the proprietor to ask him a question, he shook his head and pointed to the door before I could tell him what I wanted wasn't a job but directions to the washroom. In St. Louis a well-dressed man handed me a quarter on the street. Making a beeline for the nearest Y, I quickly shed my travel-stained clothes for the blue serge at the bottom of my suitcase.

To this world in which there seemed as little hope as there was sunlight, in which a rainy day seemed an appropriate symbol of the national mood, I was returning, with my way to make. I had no illusions it would be easy. But there was one last chance I could bypass the workaday world for a way of life whose attraction was not its relative security but its rightness for me, my rightness for it.

I got my suit pressed, put on my last clean shirt and presented myself at the Washington residence of the Apostolic Delegate, the Pope's representative in the United States.

Archbishop Cicognani, later to be Vatican Secretary of State, was out of town, but one of his secretaries heard me out and I left with assurances that the Archbishop would be in touch with the Chicago Chancery about my case. I should be hearing from him shortly.

In two and a half days I was in Chicago.

The trip home through the Southside took an hour by bus and trolley. I got off the streetcar at Wood and walked up a block to 60th. Wood Street, with its small brick and frame houses, all on postage-stamp lots, was a typical respectable working-class street. It was changeless; Wood Street would still be the same, with its philodendron in the windows and its lace-covered radio consoles glimpsable beyond, when Roosevelt had licked the Depression and a new car sat in every garage.

The door, as usual, was open. I came into the severely clean parlor and called out, "*Mika!*" My mother emerged from the kitchen, her mouth round in surprise. I hadn't written I was leaving St. Martin's—it had come to the point where confessing my failures in person was less painful than announcing them in advance.

But she knew what had happened. There was only one thing that could have brought me home. "The novitiate, *Josiçu*, you were refused permission?"

"Abbot Burton did all he could." I told her about my visit to Archbishop Cicognani's office.

My mother could neither read nor write English, though she spoke it well enough, but she had too much old-country wisdom to expect miracles, except from God through the intercession of the saints of the Church. My way had been hard. In the logic of things it would be harder still; let me persevere. One day as a priest, God willing, I would offer her funeral mass.

"You are dirty, *Josiçu!* And your shirt! You go lie down for a while and I start your tub."

The rest of the family were home from school or work by six thirty: my sisters Ann, Helen and Rose; my brothers Walter, Nick and Frank; my brother-in-law, Harry. Dinner was eaten in a series of silences and sudden bursts of conversation. Nobody wanted to talk about the reason I was home, least of all me; but the effort to avoid the question was more of a strain than if I had stood up suddenly from the table and shouted, "All right, it's happened again! I'm no closer to the priesthood than I was seven years ago! I'll never be a priest! Say it!" I kept my eyes on my plate.

I went to bed early, pleading 7 o'clock mass at St. Theodore's next morning.

The letter from the Apostolic Delegate arrived two weeks later: "I regret to inform you that we must uphold the decision of the Cardinal in Chicago."

I went for a long walk and it was dark when I came home. I sat down on the side of the bed and took off my shoes. The leather had worn through on the sole of my right foot. There was a neat round hole in the center of my sock, and around it a clotted crust of blood. Precisely in the middle of my foot was another hole, less neat and scraped to the raw. I touched it and winced, glad of the pain, glad to be alive again and feeling.

CHAPTER

2

NICHOLAS LAURO arrived in the United States from Krasica, Yugoslavia, in 1904 and settled in the Croatian community on the Southside of Chicago. As a master carpenter he had no trouble finding work at seven dollars a week with Swift & Co. at the stockyards.

The family followed him to the U.S. a year later. Mother's telegram announcing her arrival at Union Station was garbled in transit, and Papa met the wrong train. Mother, pregnant with my brother Walter at the time, loaded sister Rose and brother Nick into a horse-drawn wagon and set off for the prairieland outside Chicago—the word *suburb* was unknown. It was the dead of winter and very cold. The wagon arrived three hours later at Wood Street and 60th, the children sniffling and chilled to the bone.

Four-year-old Nick died three days later. The doctor said that Rose must be taken to the hospital immediately, but Mother refused. If she was to lose her infant daughter she wanted her to die at home; this was how they did things in the old country. Of the $4000 she had brought with her from Krasica, Mother spent half to save Rose's life. Neighbors thought a private hospital had been opened on Wood Street, there were so many doctors and nurses coming and going for the next few weeks. Several complaints were lodged at City Hall and an official showed up with a summons. Mother drove him off the doorstep with her broom.

Next year, in 1906, my parents bought a six-room house and adjoining lot at 6004 South Wood Street with the $2000 that remained from their savings. Here the rest of us were born: Walter in 1908; Nick the following year, myself two years later; Ann in 1915, Helen in 1919 and Frank, the baby, in 1924.

The neighborhood was Croatian, Irish and German. Before my father caught them at it, the German and Irish kids would crouch, giggling, at the basement window to watch him treading grapes in his bare feet. They thought remarkable the goats and chickens he raised in the lot. But aside from a disposition on the part of the non-Croatians to find outlandish any old-country customs different from their own, the three ethnic groups got on well together. They had in common frugality, morality and religion in what has been called the only completely corrupt city in America.

I was troublesome from the start. Mother couldn't get to church because there wasn't anybody at home to take care of me; Papa was always at Father Sorich's Assumption Church, doing painting, carpentry and repairs, singing in the choir or ushering at mass. Mother asked Father Sorich, my godfather, why her husband couldn't usher at one mass instead of two. Let *him* take care of Little Joe for a while. Father shook his handsome, graying head and said, "No, I need your husband."

Mother set her chin and took me, three months old, to Sunday mass. She sat in the first row. I was quiet till the sermon, and then I let out a howl that could be heard outside on Marshfield. Nor did I stop. Father Sorich looked up reproachfully at my father in the choir and asked him to take his son home. Later he told mother not to come to mass for a while, till "Little Joe got church broken."

Father Sorich came to dinner once a week. When I was seven or eight and old enough to run errands, Papa gave me ten cents to go to the corner for Father's after-dinner cigar. I came back and handed Father Sorich his cigar. He lit up, puffed and scowled. Then he noticed the disappearing bulge in my cheek. "*Sporco!* Pig!" he shouted. "This is a five-cent cigar! The other five cents is in your stomach!" Papa sent me back to the store for a real ten-cent cigar.

Somehow Father Sorich happened on the scene of all my derelictions. When I refused to go to first grade at the Catholic grammar school because it meant leaving my kindergarten friends behind at Earl Public School, it was Father Sorich who found me hiding in the basement. "*Sporco*," he accused, "to-day you are a rabbit?" One afternoon Tony Gates, Vince Maurovich, Ray Mathys and I were caught sneaking into the fire exit of the Avalon Theater and put to work mopping floors. Father Sorich, natty in his derby and chesterfield coat, just happened to drop by that day to visit Mr. Fields, the theater manager. Once, when the gang was playing street hockey and I, playing forward, inadvertently drove the heavy tin puck into the windshield of an approaching car, Father Sorich had to be strolling by.

"This boy," he warned my parents, "will wind up in jail."

In vain Papa reminded him that I was an altar boy, had a paper route, that my grades in school were better than average. I already spoke of wanting to be a priest. "A priest!" Father Sorich grunted. "He'll be lucky to end up a ballplayer!"

Father Sorich, soon to be replaced by Father Stukel, didn't realize that it was precisely the sports-mindedness of the South-side boys that kept them out of serious trouble. We lived and breathed sports: football, baseball, basketball, hockey. A pickup street football game—tackling permitted—had attractions that a crap game, however profitable, couldn't match. Given a choice between throwing rotten eggs at streetcar conductors and nine innings at the playground against a good pitcher, we chose baseball almost every time. A girl was not so interestingly shaped as a pigskin. And how easy it was to avoid tangling with the cops when you could beat them with the System.

The System worked this way. Across the Lauro backyard were strung several lengths of heavy clothesline. Unknown to my mother, she owned three sets of clothesline, not one. We'd painted these in three colors; gray, green and black. In the afternoons after school we took down the gray, or regular, clothesline and put up the green. After nightfall we took down the green and put up the black.

An alley ran between the backyards of Wood and Honre Streets. Chased by the cops, we fled down the alley and across the Lauro yard, expertly ducking the clothesline. Swiftly we emerged on Wood Street while the cops rose gingerly from the grass, rubbing their rope-burned necks and searching for lost caps. Since precinct patrolmen were constantly being transferred, probably to discourage graft, none of the cops felt familiar enough with the neighborhood to knock on my mother's door and ask why she owned a green or black clothesline.

Once at the dinner table Mother turned to Papa and said, "There's something wrong with the clothesline, Nicola. It turns green. Then it turns white again."

Papa shrugged. "It holds up the clothes. What more can you expect from a clothesline"—he paused—"in Chicago?"

The cops chased us for throwing rotten eggs, parking garbage cans on the streetcar tracks, shooting off pipe-lengths primed with sulphur and potash that traveled a quarter-mile or more. Or for shooting craps. (We even shot craps for marbles.) Usually they broke up our crap games after confiscating the take, but on one occasion they pushed five of us into a squad car, whereupon we merely exited out the other side and ran. Next time we were ready for them—every coin they picked up and dropped into their pockets had been carefully dipped in skunk oil. That was the last time the cops broke up a crap game on Wood Street.

One Saturday afternoon, with a dime between us, the gang

was shooting dice at the corner of Wood and 60th. The bread man, flush with his weekend receipts and unsteady from a couple of whiskeys, stopped to watch. He asked what we were doing and we told him, "Just practicing." Within fifteen minutes we had relieved him of more than thirty dollars. We returned it because he had four kids.

The bread man was putting away his money when a black Packard touring car pulled up at the curb. Three frozen-faced, flashily-dressed young punks from 69th Street stepped out and challenged the bread man to a game. Their leader wore an orange tie.

"He's finished playing," Vince Maurovich said, not too loudly. It was well-known in the neighborhood that two of these boys had already served time at Joliet.

Orange Tie didn't bother to reply. He took a five-dollar bill from his pocket, plucked another from the bread man's wad, and let both flutter to the sidewalk. Then he knelt and rolled his pair of dice. A seven. He was about to roll again when somebody said, "Let's see those cubes."

We looked up. It was my brother Nick. People called him The Cat because you seldom heard him coming.

"Who wants to see them dice?" said Orange Tie, in soft menace.

"I do," said Nick. He picked up the dice, hefted and returned them to Orange Tie. "They're loaded," he told him. "Get out of here with your crooked dice and don't come back."

The other two hoods exchanged glances. Orange Tie looked at Nick. Maybe he'd heard of Nick Lauro, who wasn't big but who could kick a football sixty yards and run the hundred in ten seconds; who once had taken two Irishmen apart and put them into County Hospital. Orange tie hesitated. Then he shrugged his shoulders in his cheap suit and turned back to the car, leaving the ten bucks on the sidewalk. The henchmen followed.

Two days later we read in the *Tribune* that the police had picked up the 69th Street bunch in their black Packard near Jackson Park. In the back seat they found five revolvers and two sub-machine guns.

In the old country Nicholas Lauro had been something of a rebel. He left the seminary although his family wanted him to be a priest. He studied opera by listening to recordings and developed a fine tenor voice. He knocked around from job to job until he settled on carpentry, not the most appropriate trade for the son of an educated man. He told his prospective father-in-law that he planned to take his daughter to America whether or not Mr. Soich, a well-to-do merchant with servants, approved. And he saved his money and did just that.

In America he ceased rebelling; it was as though becoming a citizen of a country born in revolution had exhausted his radical potentialities. He joined lodges, groups, fraternal organizations. He instructed the altar boys at church. He started a collection for the old people of the Croatian community who wanted to go home to die, and he was always ready to help the sick, the troubled, those in bad with the law. Many newcomers to America stayed with the Lauros on Wood Street till they found their sea legs in the New World. One, a walleyed woodworker, slept on a cot in the hallway for more than a year.

My father liked to entertain. From the market at Blue Island he brought home great sides of beef, veal and lamb, and chickens by the dozen. This was Mother's signal to prepare for a party of at least twenty-five. Wooden horses were put up in the living room and covered with boards and tablecloths. People sat down to dinner at 5:30 and got up at midnight. My job was collecting the empty bottles of homemade wine Father produced in the cellar.

In the late 1920's, when he became an independent contractor, Papa insisted that we boys help him Saturdays on the job.

Walter was a willing worker, but Nick and I had more important things on our minds, like a game against the 62nd Street
football team. Nick thought of a way to get us off the hook.
"Don't saw the plank at the pencil mark like Papa tells you,"
he advised us. "Saw it *short*." I did and Papa came after me
with a 2 by 4. Naturally I ran, with Nick ahead of me. That
night we came home at seven thirty; on Saturdays Papa always
left the house for a lodge meeting at seven o'clock sharp.

Next Saturday morning Nick sawed the plank short. "These
boys can't see a pencil mark," Papa said, and arranged a visit
for Nick and me to the oculist. We didn't show up.

There were times, not many, when my parents did not
speak. We children were used then as a go-between for essential communication. It was "Tell your father this," and "Tell
your mother that" until the situation had deteriorated to the
point where Papa moved downstairs to keep house for himself
and cook his own meals. We could hear him stamping around.
Since he practically lived on jacketed potatoes, baked on the
furnace coals, we welcomed these interludes; they meant that
upstairs we could gorge ourselves on Mother's meats and pastries, then run downstairs for Papa's baked potatoes. Hostilities
ended when it was noticed how much weight we were putting
on.

Mother might make peace for the children's sake, but in
other ways she was rock stubborn. Every afternoon she walked
three miles to church, St. Jude's at 18th and Ashland, and
three miles back again, merely because she refused to ask the
streetcar conductor on the Ashland route if he continued north
or turned off at Archer for downtown. To make sure she got
off at Ashland and walked the rest of the way to St. Jude's.

One winter she fell getting off the streetcar. A claims adjuster came to see if Mrs. Lauro would settle for $100. She didn't
want anything, so she told him "no." The adjuster upped his
offer to $200. Mother shook her head. He went to $600, and
finally, just to get rid of him, she said, "Well, all right." When

the check arrived Mother returned it. Another check for $750 arrived. She cashed it "to save the company postage."

She was as proud as she was stubborn. After my father's death in 1928 we moved upstairs and rented the bottom floor. For the next fourteen years my sister Rose, working as a Postal Telegraph supervisor, gave Mother her weekly salary. Yet in referring to the arrangement Mother never said, "I'm living with Rose and her husband Harry." It was always "Rose and Harry are living with me."

In 1921 Rose had accepted an engagement ring from the Yugoslav Consul General in Chicago, whom she had met through Papa. The romance was doomed when her fiancé told her he was being transferred back to Europe and Rose would have to go to school to learn Croatian "properly." It received its death blow when Harry Davidson came to work at Postal Telegraph and he and Rose fell in love.

Harry Davidson was a Jew, and when he refused to turn Catholic, Mother and Father vetoed the marriage. Desperate, Rose decided on an elopement and confided in Nick and me. We told her we could manage it for her if she paid us two dollars a week for as long "as the marriage lasted." She agreed.

Early one morning we helped Rose move her bags out of the house and carried them down to the streetcar. At City Hall we lugged them up to the marriage license bureau where Harry was waiting. The only problem was that Rose didn't have a birth certificate. She and Harry decided to take separate rooms at a Crown Point Hotel until she could produce proof of citizenship and Nick and I went home to tell the family the news.

Although at nine years old I was two years Nick's junior, Mother somehow held me responsible for the elopement. "Judas!" she raged at me. "You sold your sister for two dollars!"

"One," I corrected her. "Nick got half."

A month later the folks relented and Rose and Harry were

married in church by Father Sorich. In over thirty years of marriage I never heard a harsh word pass between them.

When I was eighteen, in '29, the gang chipped in and bought a Nash touring car for eight dollars on the East Side. It was yellow with a black band around its middle and looked something like a bilious bumblebee. And it was not popular in the neighborhood. When we took off, the cracked carburetor made a terrible wailing sound that made crap shooters mistake it for an approaching patrol car.

We hadn't bothered to get license plates, but that wasn't the Nash's most serious disability—it had no brakes. One of us had to ride on the front fender and jump off at intersections to stop traffic so that the car could get through. The front seat could accommodate only the driver, because on turns the man at the wheel, to prevent the car from turning over, had to swing his feet to the other side while simultaneously keeping both hands on the wheel. Neither Tony Gates nor Ray Mathys was allowed to drive the Nash after Tony ploughed up a flower border on Wood Street and Ray overturned the car negotiating the corner of Damon and 60th.

In our egg wars the Nash saw honorable service. Discovering that rotten eggs affected a new paint job better than acid or lye, we toured the neighborhood peppering the bigger fellows' cars with decayed eggs whose stunning odor temporarily incapacitated them for pursuit. Streetcar conductors learned to speed up when they saw the Nash approaching in their rear-view mirrors. To test our courage we liked to drive on the Outer Drive of Chicago's Lake Front, where the traffic was heavy. On one occasion we accidentally rammed a man driving a brand-new Ford with 924 miles on his speedometer. When he broke down and wept, our eyes moistened in sympathy.

Once the cops stopped us on Ashland Avenue, pointed out that we had no plates, and demanded our names. The sergeant was writing down the false names we gave him when Tony Gates commented that the patrol car's radiator was steaming, although curiously it was not. Tony went over to the patrol car, lifted the hood, and with one deft tug put the engine out of commission. "Hey, you've got some real trouble here," he said, and motioned the cops over. While they gathered around the engine we piled into the Nash and roared off down the street. Ray Mathys said thoughtfully, "From now on they'll be looking for us. We need a new paint job, solid color. What about red?"

We painted the Nash red. A short time later the same sergeant and patrolman caught us climbing the el pillars at Loomis Street. "You kids look familiar," he said. "What kind of car yez got?"

"Red Nash," said Walt with confidence.

"It ain't yellow with a black band?" the sergeant persisted.

We swore it was red.

"Your car the one parked over on Loomis?" the sergeant asked, and we allowed it was, hoping he hadn't noticed the Nash was plateless.

The sergeant bit his lip, and we could see he was considering taking us over to Loomis and checking on the car. But the patrolman reminded him they were overdue at the station house, and the two cops left with a warning on sneaking into the el.

"Maybe we need another paint job just to be on the safe side," Tony said, but we voted him down. The Chicago cops just didn't belong in our league.

Summers we were accustomed to swimming in the lagoon at Ogden Park. One Saturday afternoon a passerby reported us and the Blue screamed up in a patrol car. They found our clothes, so there was nothing to do but get dressed and go along to the field house.

One of the cops asked Bill Lynch for his name. "Joe Lauro,"

he said. The cop turned to Tony Gates. "Joe Lauro," Tony said. The cop turned to me with hands on hips. "I suppose you're another spaghetti juggler, eh? You tell me your name's Joe Lauro and it's jail for the lot of yez."

I said my name was Bill Lynch, and the cop nodded. "All right, that's an improvement. Is yer father a cop?"

I knew better than to fall for that one. "No," I told him, "my father tried for the force but he couldn't make it."

The cops grinned warmly. Then, ritually, they gave each of us a hard kick in the backside and turned us loose, saying, "Better a kick in the rear than a wallop in the ear from yer father."

It was still another victory over the law, if you forgot that two of us caught bad colds from putting on dry clothes over wet skin.

Ogden Park also had a pool which closed at 5 P.M. sharp. Naturally we were interested only in swimming at night. All we had to do was climb the fence, but we had not anticipated the park putting on a night watchman. One night, undressing in the locker room, we heard him approaching. All of us were dressed except Bill Lynch, who was still shoeless, so I told Bill, "You swing when he comes around the corner, and the rest of us'll make tracks." I ran then, but toward a dead end rather than the exit. Backtracking, I came around the corner where Bill was waiting and got a beautiful punch in the jaw. Bill took off and left me to the mercies of the night watchman. He turned out to be a decent guy; he helped me to my feet and let me go with a warning that in this world of ours you never got something for nothing.

We didn't believe it. That fall we developed a scheme to get into the high school football game at South Park without paying. The field was well-protected; no one to our knowledge had ever succeeded in getting inside free. But we thought it was possible if you could make your way into the railway yards north of the field. What we failed to anticipate was the railway

dick who, at gun point, locked us into a decommissioned refrigerator car.

Tony was sure we'd end up in California. Ray Mathys didn't
mind that so much, except that we'd have a six-day trip without water. "Pray for us, Joe," Bill Lynch begged me. The boys
knew I was going to be a priest.

The railroad dick let us out after the game was over. "Nobody ever got into South Park without he paid for it," he told
us. Once there was some daylight between the dick and us we
threw some rocks at him and ran.

In the winter of 1918 a major flu epidemic swept Chicago.
The whole household came down with it, but I was worst hit.
Dr. Kline, the family physician, suggested that the best place
for a child in my condition was the TB sanitarium, where he
was staff doctor and could keep an eye on me. I agreed to go,
but only if brother Nick came along.

We were there in Ward B for the better part of a year.
Homesick, Nick ran away periodically. His favorite method of
escape was to hide in Reilly's, the undertaker's, hearse whenever Reilly came out to the sanitarium to pick up a corpse.

I graduated from St. Rita's High in June, 1931. Shortly before graduation Mother asked me when I was getting my diploma. The following week, I told her. On graduation night I
went to the movies with the gang. That evening Mother was
sitting on the porch when Mrs. McWilliams, our neighbor,
whose son Tom was also graduating, came by. Mrs. McWilliams said, "Mrs. Lauro, I'll go with you to graduation."

"What graduation?" asked my mother in surprise.

"Why, Tom and Joe are graduating from St. Rita's tonight,"
Mrs. McWilliams said.

"Joe told me graduation wasn't till next week," my mother
replied grimly, and went inside to dress.

At midnight, when I came home from the show, Mother
was waiting for me.

I explained. We were in the Depression. A cap, gown and ring would have cost thirty dollars, and we didn't have it. "I don't need a cap and gown for seminary," I told her, "only my transcripts."

But she didn't understand. "They called your name three times, *Josiçu*," she kept saying sadly. It took all summer for her to get over her disappointment.

CHAPTER
3

JUNE, 1938, I sat in the waiting room of Bishop Bernard James Sheil of Chicago. It was six years since I'd come home from St. Martin's College. I was twenty-seven years old and no closer to the priesthood.

I had been waiting for more than thirty minutes, shifting my hams in the hardwood chair, leafing through the diocesan magazine, getting up to look at the chromos on the walls. The waiting didn't bother me—I knew the Bishop was a busy man and felt fortunate to have an appointment. I'd written him outlining the facts of my case and he had agreed to discuss it with me. The Bishop had been born in Chicago, like me; like me had gone to St. Viator's. Known for his anti-Establishment tendencies, he thought meat packers should make more than thirty-nine cents an hour. I did, too. That, I told myself, was hopeful.

But for ten years now I'd been living on hope, and it was wearing thin.

After returning from St. Martin's I'd gone to work for the gas company and entered night school at De Paul University, majoring in philosophy for credits that would be acceptable to a seminary. What with the gas company and an extra Saturday job in the Montgomery Ward stockroom, about the only time I had for studying was on the streetcar going to and coming from work. Often I fell asleep and passed my stop.

Though my grades were good, a full-time job and night school proved too much for me. For my third year at De Paul I decided to quit the gas company and go to school days. I made the football team. The swimming and baseball coaches approached me but I told them I didn't have the time. I was working four-hour evening shifts and Saturdays at Monkey Ward's and, on Sundays, helping District Attorney John Boyle with his athletic program for the youth of the 16th Ward.

At the end of my junior year I ran out of money. Harry Davidson offered to stake me but he and Rose were having a hard enough time. I went back to night school and worked days for the gas company.

During these years I'd returned to the Chancery office several times. I had asked the Chancellor, Monsignor Ryan, to meet with Father Stukel and me. If, during this meeting, I suggested, in the Chancellor's judgment Father Stukel gave sufficient reason for his withholding of a recommendation, I would abandon my efforts for the priesthood. The Chancellor told me such a meeting was impossible. I asked him to arrange an appointment for me with Cardinal Mundelein of Chicago. He refused. "We are sorry," he said. "This is our final decision. You must look elsewhere." Where, I wondered. Rome? In my last conversation with a Chancery official he had told me, "A vocation comes from the Bishop." I had answered: "I don't believe that. A vocation comes from God."

One raw winter day in 1936, while reading a meter in a cellar on Ashland Avenue, I suddenly got to my feet and walked three blocks to Father Stukel's rectory at 60th and Marshfield. I knocked, and he opened the door. When he recognized me he shut it in my face.

A year later I met Mrs. Jeremiah O'Brien, a sister of Bishop O'Brien of Chicago. She sent me to her brother, but the Bishop said he could do nothing; Canon Law was Canon Law. Then Mrs. O'Brien went to see Father Stukel. He told her to write him a letter. When she said that obviously such a letter was useless, he ordered her out of the rectory.

The door to Bishop Sheil's office swung open. His secretary, an Irish priest with a cheerful smile, said, "Mr. Lauro, the Bishop will see you now."

The Bishop sat at his desk. He looked up from a letter he was reading and asked me to sit down. When he put down the letter I saw that it was mine.

"Mr. Lauro," the Bishop said, "you write convincingly."

I cautioned myself against outrageous hope—as yet he had said nothing. "I'm finishing college, Bishop Sheil," I said. "I want to go on to seminary. Can you do anything for me?"

"I would, except that you come under Father Stukel's jurisdiction. And I am an auxiliary bishop, not the Ordinary."

The familiar dull pain had settled into my chest again. Despite it, I felt anger. "I'm sorry, but I don't come under Father Stukel's jurisdiction. My father is dead. It's ten years since his death, and all this time I've been a communicant at St. Theodore's, whose pastor is Monsignor Kerns. He tells me he'll recommend me. I'm getting no closer to the priesthood and there's nothing wrong with my appealing. I'm appealing now to your Christian charity. I'm also appealing for a final answer, so that if the word is against me I can give up, try to forget my vocation."

The Bishop smiled. " 'My vocation?' That's a slip of the tongue that would interest Doctor Freud. Your logic is somewhat at fault. It seems to me you have already received your answer, from the Apostolic Delegate"—he consulted the letter—"in 1933."

"Have I, Bishop? The Apostolic Delegate told me the matter was in the hands of the Archdiocese of Chicago."

"And the Archdiocese finds, has found, that you are under Father Stukel's jurisdiction. I'm sorry. You have zeal; you must also have the strength of character to accept a disappointment."

My appeal had failed. I got to my feet. "Thank you," I said, and left the Bishop's office.

That evening, as usual, I went to work at Monkey Ward's. A problem came up—five missing boxes of jewelry, among the store's more expensive items. I tracked them down and the relieved stockroom manager called me in to pat me on the back. He saw I wasn't listening. "Something the matter, Joe? You don't look so hot."

"There's nothing the matter," I told him truthfully. There wasn't; I'd made my decision and felt much better for it. Going home on the Cottage Grove streetcar I would fall off the front platform in such a way that the car wheel would sever my right hand at the wrist. The right hand was indispensable to a priest in the Holy Sacrifice of the Mass. Nothing else would end my craving unless it were death itself, and I had never thought seriously of suicide.

At midnight I boarded the streetcar and took a seat near the front platform. Except for the motorman there were only three other people in the car, a man and two women.

When the car arrived at the long stretch between 47th and 55th, where it reached speeds of 30 miles per hour, I got up to move out to the platform.

Someone touched my arm. It was a young, attractive girl with frightened eyes. "Please," she said, "that man back there—he's been bothering me. He says he's going to get off when I do. Will you see me home?"

I couldn't refuse her. We left the car together at 55th. The man didn't follow and I walked her home.

Then I went back to the stop. It was another thirty minutes before another Cottage Grove trolley came along. I took a seat in the middle of the car. The crisis had passed. I knew God had saved me for some purpose of His own.

Terence Moran, Alderman of the 16th Ward and a well-oiled cog in the Kelly machine, had been in office for the last twenty-one years. For the youth of the eastern part of the ward he threw dances, provided football uniforms, organized bus trips to Jackson and Ogden Parks. For the West End young people he did nothing.

John Boyle, an assistant U.S. Attorney with a fine record, was running against Moran in the Democratic primary of 1939. A few years before, when we had formed the Panther A. C., John Boyle had come forward and bought uniforms for the football team. With his help we had built a softball league with sixteen teams and over three hundred players. The league had taken a lot of boys off the streets. At every football game John Boyle's car stood by for use as an ambulance to take the injured to hospital, and he had paid for X-rays out of his own pocket. Under John's coaching Boyle's Blackdevils had been good enough to play and beat some of the best semi-pro teams in Illinois, Indiana and Michigan. For many of us, the penniless sons of immigrants, Boyle's Blackdevils meant our only opportunity to travel out of the state.

People said John Boyle had no chance against Terence Moran's dollars and hoodlums. The Panther A. C. meant to prove them wrong.

We had saved some money for Panther windbreakers, and the boys agreed to spend it instead for campaign trucks and sound equipment. When the sound equipment was paid for we had $175 to be used as a campaign fund for the home precinct.

We got to work. Outside the city we printed up several thousand brochures that would have cost five times as much had they been produced in Chicago. A club member who worked for Chicago Cardboard provided a few hundred feet of cardboard. On Lake Street we bought bulbs, electric wiring and onionskin paper. For twelve cents apiece we made dozens of electric signs saying, "John Boyle for Alderman" to be hung up in the back windows of cars and lighted by an attachment to the dome light. They were the first electric political signs in Chicago and perhaps in the nation. When the opposition copied the signs they were made from metal and cost twenty dollars apiece. Moran's precinct captains were the only ones to get them.

We knew Moran was in the habit of buying votes at five and ten dollars a head. When people came to tell us they needed the money, we advised them, "Take the money and vote for John S."

When Terence Moran realized he had a fight on his hands, his hoodlums started getting rough. They tipped over our sound trucks and smashed the equipment. They invaded fund-raising dances at the Panther A. C. and broke them up. It got so bad that Chicago newspapers began to call the 16th "the bloody ward." The publicity did John Boyle no harm because everybody knew who started fights in the 16th.

In the February election John Boyle ran only a few hundred votes behind Moran. A runoff was called for May.

On election eve at the A. C. we got a frantic call from precinct headquarters at 57th and Peoria. Moran's hoods were breaking up the place; come over as fast as we could. Since most of Boyle's precinct captains were with us that evening I thought it might be Moran strategy to get the cops to arrest us at precinct headquarters so we'd all be locked up over election day and unable to prevent ballot-box stuffing and other skullduggery. I said as much, but was overruled. Thirty of us took off in three cars for 57th and Peoria.

When we got there Moran's men had broken up the furniture and were busting heads. We posted guards outside and waded in. Somebody had yanked out the telephone wires and it was the neighbors who called the police. We got away just in time.

I was driving the Nash, with Vince Maurovich, Tony Gates and four other precinct captains piled in the back. One held a handkerchief to a bloody nose, another moaned softly from a kick in the groin. We were on Ashland, heading toward 64th, when a black Packard filled with Moran henchmen caught up and pulled alongside.

"Pull over!" the driver yelled. He had Jimmy Cagney's snarling mouth.

Walt shouted an insult as I gunned the Nash away. Shots rang out. At the clubhouse we examined the car for damage. There were eight bullet holes in the back and tonneau.

Three days before the election Walt dropped in at Monkey Ward's. "Joe," he said, "there's a woman at the hospital who needs blood."

I looked at him.

"It's a vote, Joe."

"What's the matter with your blood, Walt?" I asked him.

"Not the right type."

"How do you know mine is?"

Walt looked at his watch. "You've got an hour for lunch. Just enough time to get you over to the hospital and back."

Walt drove me over to the hospital and I gave two pints of blood to a young woman with an unpronounceable Polish name. It turned out I had the right type.

At nine o'clock at the clubhouse that night there was a pounding at the door. Tony Gates answered it and came back grinning. "Guy asking for you, Joe. Better watch out, he's mad."

I went out to the main room. Waiting for me was a huge man in overalls with bloodshot eyes. He seized me by the lapels and I winced at his whiskey breath. "Listen," he said in broken English with a strong Polish accent, "I hear you give my wife blood. What else you give her, hah? This is last warning. You stay away from her or I kill you! Understand?" He shook me hard and my teeth rattled so much I was speechless. Then he shoved me into a spring-sprung chair and left, slamming the door behind him. From the next room came screams of laughter.

On election day Boyle captains were stationed in every pre-

cinct to guard against fraud. Moran had thoughtfully provided
five-pound boxes of chocolates with a sign reading, "Compli-
ments of Alderman Terence Moran." We charged campaign-
ing and in most precincts managed to get the signs removed. It
wasn't easily accomplished, but every sealed ballot box that
went to City Hall was accompanied by a Boyle precinct
captain.

John Boyle won by 3 to 1, the first victory of several that
would eventually make him Chief Justice of the Cook County
Circuit Court.

He took me aside during the victory celebration. "Joe," he
said, "there's no man more responsible for this than you.
You've got real organizational ability. What about taking up
politics as a career? I can fix it so you could quit your gas
company job, leave night school and finish up days at De Paul."

It was a generous offer. I was no closer to the priesthood
and I felt tempted; moreover, I appreciated John's confidence
in me. But what had happened on the Cottage Grove streetcar
was still fresh in my mind, and I remembered that later this
week I had an appointment with Father Lux of *Catholic Extension* magazine. Father Lux had connections in the Church
and a reputation for getting things done. Maybe I wasn't
licked yet.

I thanked John Boyle and said no.

Father Joseph Lux reminded me of descriptions I had read of
Cardinal Merry del Val. He was elegant and cosmopolitan
with a sophistication perhaps more appropriate to Rome or
New York than to hog-butchering Chicago. His clericals had
been cut by a State Street custom tailor and he smoked cigarettes in a long black holder. He was a handsome man with
black hair going prematurely white. His turn of mind was fig-
urative and literary, yet he spoke with surgical precision. You
could have predicted that this humane and able man, as editor-
in-chief of *Catholic Extension*, would discover many of today's

outstanding Catholic writers and bring the magazine to its present success and half-million circulation.

I told him my story. He lit a cigarette. "I'm amazed at your lack of bitterness and that you haven't committed murder in this city so well-known for its homicide rate. Have you heard of St. Camillus de Lillus, dates 1550-1614?"

"Wasn't St. Camillus a Benedictine monk?"

Father Lux shook his head. "Three times he tried to become a Francisan and three times sores broke out on his leg, so the order refused to take him. Finally he formed his own order, that of the Camillus Fathers, to tend the wounded and sick on the battlefields of Europe. He antedated the Red Cross by several hundred years."

I nodded.

"Evidently God didn't wish St. Camillus to serve as a Franciscan," said Father Lux.

"Are you suggesting, Father, that I give up my search for the priesthood and try to serve God some other way?"

"Not necessarily. I mean that all too often we don't know what God wants us to do. Sometimes, like Camillus, we may come to think God has forgotten us. But He doesn't. Now I have two suggestions, Joe. One, maybe Father Stukel has to be approached in a different way. I'm going to see him and ask that if he doesn't feel like recommending you for the priesthood, will he write me a letter to that effect that if anybody wants to ordain you, he won't object."

"I'd be very grateful for that."

"My second suggestion is that I write to Bishop McGuiness in North Carolina and ask if he'd be interested in accepting you for his seminary in Raleigh. The Bishop needs candidates for ordination and his home missions. What's your address and phone number?"

He took them down. "You'll be hearing from me." He shook my hand. "Remember St. Camillus."

Father Lux called a week later. "It didn't work out with

Father Stukel, Joe. I went to see him and all he'd talk about was your father. I said that had nothing to do with you, that you were a good boy. He said, 'Oh, he's not such a good boy. He went to mass every day in the summer, but do you know what he did afterward? He gathered up all the young people in the parish and took them down to the beach.'

"I thought that was pretty good apostolic work, but I knew by this time that no amount of argument would change the old man, so I asked him if he'd write a letter of no recommendation but no objection to ordination. He said he'd think it over. That was Wednesday. Yesterday I got a letter from him saying that his conscience wouldn't permit him to write the letter I was asking for."

I told Father Lux I was sorry he'd gone to all this trouble.

"No trouble," he said sharply. "Now I should be hearing from Bishop McGuiness in a couple of days. Don't give up. You're not giving up, are you?"

"No, Father," I told him, but he'd already hung up.

Four days later he called again. Bishop McGuiness had written that he was taking no seminarians from outside the home diocese. But Monsignor Gaffney, Rector of St. John's Seminary, in Little Rock, Arkansas, was in town looking for prospective seminarians. He would interview tomorrow at two o'clock.

My interview with Monsignor Gaffney was successful. I was accepted at St. John's for the fall term. The next day Hitler invaded Poland.

When I went to thank Father Lux I brought him a box of Turkish cigarettes. They didn't fit his holder.

CHAPTER

4

AT the end of the third quarter of the Theology League basketball game, the Hodcarriers led my Boilermakers by 50 to 41.

Nothing too surprising about that. Joe Quinn's Hodcarriers stood at the top of the League standings with five victories and no defeats. The Boilermakers shared last place with the Plumbers, our dismal records an identical single win against four losses.

It was too much to expect the Boilermakers to come from behind to beat Joe Quinn's boys. Not only were they the inferior team, but Joe's men were tricksters of the most shameless sort. Quinn was a master with the elbows under the basket, Danny Silk and Pat Newell adept pants-tuggers, and Charlie Diamond almost as good a blocker as Arkansas U's famous Muscles Campbell. Add to this the fact that Deacon Jim McDonnell, the referee, had poor eyesight and the Boilermakers didn't stand much of a chance today. Of the six personal fouls called in the game so far, Deacon Jim had called five of them against my team. I had three fouls, and my fellow forward, Barney Loughrey, two.

Deacon Jim had failed to catch my irony when, at half time, I'd presented him with a pocket-handkerchief to wipe his glasses clean with. Now, at the third-period break, he stood talking on the sidelines with Monsignor Smith, St. John's Seminary's athletic director. Deacon Jim took out the handkerchief to wipe his glasses again, and it gave me an idea.

"There's only one way to win this game," I told my team. "By fast-breaking them all over the court."

Jerry McKenna shrugged doubtfully. "Joe, a fast-breaking game means fouls."

Buck Johnson agreed. "You've got three fouls against you already," he reminded me. "Suppose Deacon Jim calls a fourth, and boots you out of the game? This is a five-man team with no substitutes. We'd be finished."

The other boys, Ed Baltutis and Barney Loughrey, nodded.

"It's you four guys who are going to make with the elbows and the pants-tugging," I told them. "When Deacon Jim isn't looking. And I'll play the angel."

Deacon Jim blew the fourth-quarter whistle and we trotted out on the court. Monsignor Smith, in cassock and biretta, nodded at me gravely. He was as much as saying, "Joe, let's see something happen out there."

Luck had turned in our favor. The Hodcarriers were overconfident and sloppy, and we caught fire. With Buck and Barney getting in some fancy elbow work, and Jerry sinking three sensational long shots, we came within two points of evening the score. Twice Joe Quinn protested to Deacon Jim, but Jim waved him aside. There was a light in his supposedly neutral eye and he sensed an upset.

With five minutes to go Bujarski screened for Quinn on a 20-foot set shot and the ball rimmed the hoop. Ed Baltutis barged in from deep position and snagged the rebound. He passed to Loughrey, who dribbled to mid-court and passed to McKenna. Jerry made a successful one-handed jump shot. Buck Johnson sank a lay-up—53 to 50, our favor. Charlie Diamond of the Hodcarriers threw me a dirty look.

The Hodcarriers came back with two points, and then disaster. Danny Silk nudged me in the seat of my pants, and then claimed I'd hit his knee with my backside.

"Four fouls, Joe, out you go!" shouted Deacon Jim.

"Silk nudged me!" I yelled.

"You hit Silk's knee," said the Deacon, and jerked his thumb. He wasn't too enthusiastic about it, but I was out of the game, and from now on until the final whistle the Boiler-makers were a four-man team. The vision of a win posted on the Morris Hall bulletin board faded. "McDonnell," I yelled at Deacon Jim, "you're blind as an Arkansas bat!" and threw the ball at him.

He ducked, the ball sped on, rebounded off the wall and hit Monsignor Smith in the shins. He bent with the pain. The cassocked Theology student who had just come in fussed over him solicitously.

I hurried over and asked the Monsignor if he was hurt.

He straightened and shook his head. "A nice game, Joe, you almost had them. But a bad temper." He indicated the Theology student. "Albert here just came in with a message. Monsignor Gaffney wants to see you in his office. Better get your shower quickly."

I wasn't breathing right. This could mean only one thing: Monsignor Gaffney had heard from Chicago on his request that I be excardinated from the Chicago diocese to that of Little Rock, in which case Little Rock would confer upon me the Minor Order of Tonsure, with or without Father Stukel's recommendation. After seven months at St. John's I had gotten that far.

How far that was, in practical terms, was uncertain. After midterms, at the end of January, Monsignor Garrity, who was in charge of credentials for Minor Orders, had called me in to say there was still no word from the Chicago Chancery on Monsignor Gaffney's request. Did I want to write again as a reminder? I had gone to my room and written to the Chancellor of the Archdiocese of Chicago and also to Bishop William D. O'Brien, President of *Catholic Extension*, sealing both envelopes with a prayer. Monsignor Gaffney had written again, too.

Now, a few days before Holy Week, he had finally heard. The ball game forgotten, I hurried through my shower and half ran to his office in Morris Hall.

Monsignor Gaffney motioned me to a chair and began to pace from desk to door. His look was somber and I knew the news was bad. My mind flashed back to St. Martin's and Abbot Burton. This scene had happened once before; only the players were a bit older. Was I doomed to be a squirrel in a theological cage, eternally running a treadmill?

"Joe, we've heard from Chicago, and the word isn't favorable. We can't give you tonsure. The Chicago diocese refuses to excardinate you on the basis that your pastor will not recommend. This is logical hair-splitting. Beyond that, I don't know what to say. For almost eight months we've examined your fitness to serve, and you haven't been found wanting. Last January I asked you to serve after ordination in the Arkansas missions; I was that certain of your fitness. You have the recommendations of myself, Bishop O'Brien of Chicago and Bishop Fletcher of Little Rock. I believe in your vocation."

I said nothing; there was nothing to say.

"Joe, you know you're welcome at St. John's as long as you want to stay here."

"Thanks, Monsignor, but four years of Theology with no priesthood in view seems pointless. I'll be leaving the sem."

He nodded. "What are you thinking of doing?"

"Enlisting in the Canadian air force. I'd feel more useful in the service. And then I have the crazy idea that being in service might make it possible for me to plead my case in Rome."

He smiled; perhaps the picture of an ex-seminarian landing

by parachute on St. Peter's dome amused him. "I hear you have relatives in Yugoslavia."

"Yes. My aunt's been sent to a concentration camp."

"A bad business. We'll be in it eventually, I feel." He paused. "Joe, I'm not saying enlisting with the Canadians is the wrong decision. But no candidate for the priesthood I've ever known has struggled toward his vocation under such a strain. You've been trying for more than a dozen years. Now this business of the service—mightn't that add immeasurably to the strain?"

"That's the chance I'll be taking, Monsignor. But if my vocation does survive the test then maybe Our Lord will see fit to grant me ordination."

Monsignor put his hand on my shoulder. "Sleep on it, Joe, and pray for guidance during Holy Week. You'll be in my prayers."

That night I wept, and had no sleep, and asked God to help that I might do His will. The next I prayed, and weighed my problem. It resolved itself into a number of questions, moral and practical. Could anything as antithetical to the priesthood as a war be the way to it? I had read of an ace in World War I, a Frenchman, who had later taken Holy Orders. This man had not lost his vocation, though he had been directly responsible for the deaths of at least five men. Could I kill a single human being, even in the name of country? And if I survived, would my health be such that I could qualify for Holy Orders? A man must be physically fit to assume the heavy duties of the priesthood. Of course this was assuming that my way to it was finally cleared.

It took me three days to finally make up my mind. Then I wrote airmail to the RCAF in Toronto. The answer came a week later. My application had been approved pending a physical examination in Windsor, Ontario. I was to report to the induction center there as soon as possible.

That evening I sat watching a First Theology student trim

a Second at table tennis in the rec room. A classmate sat down
at the table with a Coke.

"British troops moved into Athens today," he told me. He
seemed depressed out of proportion to the news until I remembered that he was half-Greek on one side of his family.

"You think Yugoslavia has much chance against Hitler
once he decides to attack?" I asked him.

"The hell with Yugoslavia," he said, and left the table.
Everybody these days was edgy, it seemed.

Early on Good Friday I dropped in on Monsignor Gaffney
and told him about my letter from the RCAF. I asked his permission to leave the seminary while the rest of the boys were
at mass at St. Andrew's Cathedral in Little Rock. It was
hard, I said, to say goodbye.

"You have it, Joe. You'll write?"

"I'll write, Monsignor."

Knotting my tie at my fourth-floor window, my bags all
packed, I looked down at the seminary grounds with eyes that
saw everything in preternaturally sharp detail. A group of
black-suited seminarians, a little late for mass in town, hurried
along the diagonal toward the main gate. One's suit fitted him
badly, another needed a haircut. They would catch the next
trolley and I the one after that, thus avoiding questions as to
why I was leaving the seminary for Easter vacation on Good
Friday.

I picked up my grips and stood with them foolishly for a
moment in the center of the room, looking around at the iron
bedstead, the scarred wardrobe, the bookshelves, the desk.
They were not beautiful; they had the Spartan look of a barracks, but at this moment the associations of this room were
so rich and strong and happy that I knew I had to leave it
quickly or I might not leave at all.

I left the door open behind me and took the empty stairs.
In the downstairs hallway a cassocked figure spoke to me. I
answered briefly. Whether between the steps of Morris Hall

and the main gate anybody spoke to me again I didn't know. There was a haze before my eyes that made it hard to distinguish voices and faces.

I stopped outside the main gate and set my bags down for a moment. My faculties were clearer now; no longer was I an iron filing within the seminary's powerful magnetic range.

I started down Tyler Street. Pretty, six-year-old Junior Finley was standing on the Finley lawn, in her hand a stone, as usual. She threw it, and as always she missed.

I stopped. "You missed, Junior."

"I meant to. Birdhead, y'all coming on the porch for coffee?" Not "inside"; seminarians were forbidden to enter the homes of townspeople except on major holidays.

"Can't today, Junior," I told her. "I've got to catch a train."

"That's a Birdhead thing to do, not stopping in to say goodbye when y'all going Nawth on vacation."

I hadn't known how much I was going to miss Junior and the Finleys. Catholic Southerners, they had treated me, a Chicago Yankee, like a prince of the Church. The least I could do was tell Junior I was leaving the sem.

I motioned her forward and dropped to one knee on the grass. "Junior, there's something I want you to tell your mother and dad for me. There won't be any more stone-throwing and Birdhead stuff for a while because I'm leaving St. John's to join the Canadian air force. Would you tell them that?"

She nodded solemnly. "Why you joining their old air force?"

"Tell your folks I can't explain just now, but that I'll write them, and you." I hugged her and got to my feet. "Before I go do you want to throw a stone? Real up close?"

"No," she said, and hung her head. Then she began to cry.

I picked up my bags quickly and started off. When I'd reached the corner she called out, "Joe!" I turned. She waved and I waved back.

Pulaski Heights had terraced lawns, hedges, evergreens and curved drives. Higher and cooler than the rest of Little Rock, it attracted homeowners who liked the suburban atmosphere of pine-studded hillsides and ravines. In spring the sidewalks were bordered by violets and yellow jonquils; in summer a profusion of roses, azaleas and honeysuckle.

The trolley whined its way toward town. Passing now the pillared houses, the gingerbread Victorian mansions, the trim, blue-roofed bungalows, I thought of spring nights sitting at my desk over Aquinas or Latin or Canon Law while the scent of honeysuckle hovered outside like a presence. I'd miss that too, much as I had railed against it as a distraction.

"What's that you said?" I asked the motorman. He had spoken to me in the empty car, but we were passing the Country Club drugstore, where seminarians went for Saturday afternoon milk shakes, and I'd been thinking of how Joe Quinn, nervous about his midterms, had once spilled a milk shake in Danny Silk's lap.

"I said y'all must be goin' home for vacation."

"Well, yes."

"Bet you can't wait to get back. All the seminary boys I've spoke to, they love that place like it was a college." He clanged his bell at a dog crossing Kavenaugh Street.

"It's a great place," I said.

"But pretty strong on the discipline, ain't it? I mean you boys don't get out much. Just Saturday afternoons. And you can't go to the show."

"We see movies up at the sem."

"But they're picked for you, ain't they?"

Did I detect some anti-Catholic feeling here? It was rife enough in Arkansas, especially in the back country. I didn't answer his question.

"Well, those boys sure do love the place. Rode one once who'd flunked out, and he was crying."

I got off at my stop near the railway station and watched

the trolley disappear down Kavenaugh. After I'd bought my coach ticket to Chicago on the Missouri Pacific and checked my bags through, I had almost an hour's free time, enough to walk to St. Andrew's Cathedral and see a few minutes of Bishop Fletcher's mass.

St. Andrew's was in the English Gothic style. Completed in 1882, it had succeeded a small frame building at 2nd and Center Streets which, since 1845, had been the seat of the Arkansas diocese. The history of the Roman Catholic Church in Little Rock dated back to 1830, when Father Donnelly said the first mass in a temporary chapel over a store at 2nd and Main. Interestingly, Chicago Diocese, founded the same year, had since become the largest in the nation.

I took a seat in the last pew. Since it was Good Friday the altar was bare, without flowers or candles. The tabernacle was open, the Blessed Sacrament absent.

One of Bishop Fletcher's acolytes, I noticed, was a snub-nosed kid with freckles I'd seen tossing a football on Country Club Road near the seminary.

In the first pews sat my classmates, black-cassocked and white-surpliced, and behind them the non-participating semi-narians. I had witnessed many ordinations in St. Andrew's sanctuary. It was here I had hoped to promise God my entire life.

As I knelt for the Offertory the woman beside me glanced curiously at my dark suit and tie. If I was a seminarian what was I doing here at the back of the church? I belonged up front with the others. Or did I? I wondered. My leave-taking had already worked its dissociations; only the mass was real. The back of Paul Bujarski's head, with its cowlick, seemed no longer familiar but something in a dream.

I left before the Pre-Sanctified Mass and walked back to the station through the traffic of Louisiana Street.

The 3:15 pulled out on time. The walk had tired me, and no sooner had I leaned my head against the window than I fell asleep. I woke to see two china-blue eyes staring into mine.

The man stuck out his hand. "You going to St. Louis?" He was plump and round with thinning sandy hair, and poured into a chocolate brown suit. I took him for a circus advance man or a drummer.

"Chicago," I told him.

"My name's Chuck Wellington. I sell crop insurance. Didn't do so good in Arkansas; the farmers're so poor they can't afford it."

I introduced myself and he asked, "You go to school in Little Rock?"

I nodded.

"Took you for a student at that undertaker's college on Main."

I muttered something noncommittal and looked out the window. Two little colored boys, standing in a junk-choked yard, were watching the passing train, shielding their eyes from the sun.

Wellington started reading his newspaper. "That Roosevelt," he said with distaste. "I think he means to get us into war."

"Don't forget the Neutrality Act," I told him.

"Don't mean a thing. We're sellin' arms to the British, ain't we? And what about this Lend-Lease Congress is considerin'?"

I didn't want to argue the question, but Chuck Wellington did. Though a sign directly ahead warned against smoking except in the lounge, he nipped a cigar between his teeth and began to hold forth on America First. He was a member of the St. Louis chapter. Last month the St. Louis chapter had had the honor of being addressed by Senator Nye. "You can't get away from the fact that France and England brought the war on Germany," Wellington told me.

The conductor stopped and pointed to the No Smoking sign. Wellington got up and without excusing himself went to the lounge.

Ten minutes later he was back. What about the fifty destroyers? he wanted to know. Everybody knew the eight naval bases we'd gotten in exchange for them were worthless. This business of the U.S. being an "arsenal of democracy" was all very well, but when you built an arsenal you eventually used it. The American people didn't want war.

I asked him if he followed the Gallup polls and he looked at me suspiciously and said, "Sometimes."

"Well, just after Munich a Gallup poll showed only 37 percent of the American people were in favor of military training. But when Hitler took Paris, just last year, the figure rose to 65 percent."

I could see he didn't care for figures that had nothing to do with crop insurance. There was a trace of red now under his collar. "You college fellows," he said in disgust. "If you college fellows are so all-fired up against Hitler, why in hell don't you join the Canadians or the British and fight?"

We got into Chicago that afternoon. I'd had plenty of time to think about how I was going to explain to my mother, who didn't expect me home. In the last year she'd developed heart trouble and the doctors had said any bad or startling news would be dangerous. I planned to tell her that Monsignor Gaffney had agreed that my financial situation was such that dropping out a year to work was advisable. There were good construction jobs in Canada. If she asked me why I couldn't take a job closer to home, I'd say there just wasn't any well-paying construction work in Chicago. Walt and Nick would back me up on that.

Next morning when I got back from church, Father McCarthy of St. Theodore's, who had brought communion to Mother daily during the worst of her illness, was coming down the front steps.

He shook my hand. "Joe, your mother's upset about your leaving the sem. I've been delegated to get the real story."

Father McCarthy was used to getting results with his bluff Irish charm, but today he was in for a disappointment. "I can't explain now, Father," I told him, "but thanks for taking care of Mother," and brushed past him into the house.

After Easter dinner the working members of the clan began making preparations to leave. My sister Helen was driving back to Kalamazoo, Michigan. Since Kalamazoo was on my way to Detroit, I arranged to do the driving.

I'd told Mother I'd be writing regularly to Helen. Since Mother couldn't read English, Helen would read her my letters over the phone. She didn't question this roundabout method of communication.

"*Josiçu*," Mother had told me, "you be careful on these construction jobs. Promise me you won't climb too high."

I'd promised.

On the way to Michigan I told Helen the true state of affairs. She didn't see how I could have stayed on at St. John's under the circumstances, and I was feeling better when she let me off at Kalamazoo bus station. From there I took a bus to Detroit and another from Detroit to Windsor. The RCAF recruiting center was closing for the night, and an NCO directed me to a nearby college gymnasium in temporary use as a barracks. He noticed the missal I carried and warned me, not unkindly, "You won't have much time for reading that."

Three men sat on cots in the huge room. It turned out they were all Americans in their early twenties. One was a garage mechanic, the others college students from Michigan. The students were determined to be fighter pilots. I felt a little ancient in their company.

We all had two blankets, but somebody had forgotten to close two of the gym windows, which were unreachable from the floor. We froze that night, and I was glad I'd brought my winter overcoat from Chicago.

"They didn't tell me Canada was going to be so damned cold," one of the boys complained next morning. It was something I was to hear often in the next thirteen months.

A couple of days of shots and physicals and I had signed my enlistment papers and was on my way to Manning Depot in Brandon, Manitoba. It was a two days' trip of a thousand miles. I saw a great deal of open prairie country, more desolate and less populated than our own.

At Manning we were quartered in a huge field house that must have held a thousand double-decker bunks. It reminded me of the field house at De Paul. The group of men was a mixed one: American college boys, Hudson's Bay Company trappers, hulking lumberjacks from the west, bond salesmen, a couple of Mounties, a gold miner from Kirkland, a university professor. To my knowledge I was the only ex-seminarian, a fact I was careful not to advertise.

My bunkmate was Bill Lawrence, ex-Kansas State Teachers. Bill, an open-faced boy with limitless enthusiasm, had logged some flying time as a civilian and was a master of "bunk flying," in which you lay on your back and "flew" with arms and legs. His slow-rolls and snap-rolls were impressive.

The Manning noncoms teamed us up quickly into basketball quintets. On my team were Lee Usher of Iowa State, Gil Miracle of Kentucky, Bill Lawrence and Ed Holmsicourt of Saskatoon, Saskatchewan. Either we had a lot of luck or the opposition was very mediocre, for in two months of organized play we dropped only a handful of games. All this glory was lost upon the Canadians, who looked down on basketball as an American sport inferior to ice hockey.

Manning was uniform-fitting, lectures, indoctrination and drill. Afternoons were devoted to sports or calisthenics. There was much KP. And where there's KP, I found, there is the "college man" trick.

The mess sergeant, a short, bullet-headed man from the northern Provinces, was named Fox. Fox hated all mankind, but his worst hatred was saved for college men. Bill Lawrence told us he'd heard from well-wishers that Fox asked for col-

lege men volunteers and then took pleasure in assigning them
to the most unsavory details, like garbage-loading and pot-
washing. We were well prepared. When Fox asked the college men of my KP group to put up their hands, Gil Miracle
and I kept ours in our pockets.

Fox grinned with pleasure. "Men who raised their hands on
dishes and silverware!" he snarled. "Men who didn't on pots
and garbage." He shook a finger in Gil Miracle's face.
"Fooled you college cutup Yanks, didn't I now? Think you
outfox Fox, do you? He'll outfox you every time!" Most of
the time he spoke in the third person.

Seven hours later we staggered back to our bunks, exhausted. Grease had soaked its way into my pores up to my
elbows, and Gil stank. When we taxed Bill with his bad advice, he barely managed to hide a grin. "What do you expect?" he said. "Fox is crazy."

"Like a Fox," Gil said. We stopped talking to Bill Lawrence.

Bill got KP two days later. He came back at four in the
afternoon and collapsed on his bunk, groaning. The stink of
his garbage-soaked fatigues hit us simultaneously.

I said, "Lawrence, you don't smell like silver or trays."

"Fox outfoxed me," he said dully.

"Poor Bill," Gil said with relish. "It must have been boring,
hauling all those garbage cans up on the lorry. How many
were there? A hundred?"

"Leave me alone," Bill mumbled drowsily. "I've got to get
some sleep." He stretched, releasing a new nosegay of odors.

Gil and I attacked. We stripped Bill of trousers and shirt
and dropped them into a tubful of soapy water in the latrine.
Then we scrubbed them. Then we scrubbed them again and
hung them up to dry.

Bill got KP again next day. His fatigues being damp, he
borrowed mine. He outfoxed Fox at the guessing game, but
my fatigues were too big for him and aroused Pilot Officer

Quinn's suspicions. For wearing another man's fatigues Bill got three days' CB, confinement to barracks, in which the confinee is required to drop in at the guardhouse every hour on the hour after his day's work is done. Getting up every hour on the hour after lights out to report to a guardhouse a quarter-mile away is no fun. Gil and I considered ourselves decently revenged.

That Saturday we had drill parade and a two-hour route march. Sergeant McCall took me aside and said he needed two men to carry the big drum. A sinecure, he assured me; as soon as the formation passed the Wing Commander at the reviewing stand and cleared the drill field, the band would be dismissed while the rest of the outfit continued on the march. I promptly volunteered Bill and myself for the job.

When I told him about it Bill was doubtful. "So you volunteered me, eh?"

"Cancel out if you want to," I told him. "It sounds good to me."

"All right, I'll go along. But if it turns out nasty, Joe, you've had it."

It turned out nasty. We passed the reviewing stands and parade grounds and found ourselves leading the platoon on the long route march. With every step Bill rammed the big drum into the small of my back. "This is for you, Joe (ram)," he kept saying. "For volunteering my services (ram). Next time I do not choose (ram) to volunteer (ram). Do you understand? (ram). Clearly?" (ram)

During a break I got permission from Sergeant McCall to change places with Bill on the drum. When we got back to quarters both our backs were black and blue. That was some consolation.

Next morning Bill and I got KP. Fox had outfoxed both of us.

*   *   *

At Manning I'd grown close to Bill and Lee and Gil. It was a wrench being separated for No. 7 Initial Training School at Saskatoon, Saskatchewan. Of the Manning bunch only Ed Holmsicourt was assigned to No. 7.

At ITS, over the eight-week course, we studied mathematics, map reading, aircraft recognition, Morse and the Aldis Lamp, armament, meteorology, airmanship and navigation. After the first month I knew that although I might forget the rest I'd always remember navigation, if only because of Flying Officer Saunders.

Saunders was a slightly built man in his thirties with his eyes too close together. He was a fanatic who believed that navigators would win the war. He was contemptuous of bombardiers, disdainful of gunners, and he hated pilots. Especially American pilots. As an American who had let it be known that in the course of things I hoped to fly a plane, I was warned about Saunders by a number of men in his navigation class. Because I wasn't in Saunders' class but in Flying Officer Battles', I didn't give the matter much thought. I should have.

The afternoon of the day that our first grades in navigation were posted, Saunders came up to me in the mess.

"Lauro, I understand you're number two man with Battles."

"So far, sir," I told him.

He eyed me narrowly. "How about going on to navigation school?"

"Sir, I hope to go on to elementary flying."

"And be a fool truckdriver?" His eyes narrowed a bit more. "That's all pilots are, you know. Truckdrivers."

"That may be, sir," I told him. "But flying a plane appeals to me."

"Fighters or bombers?" he shot at me.

"I don't much care. Probably I'm better suited to bombers."

"No doubt," he said pleasantly, changing his tack. "But it's the navigator who brings the plane to target and brings it back. Nothing more important than that. He's got responsibility for the entire crew."

That seemed to be overstating it a bit, but I nodded.

He slapped me on the shoulder. "Well, you think it over."

That evening Holmsie told me that Saunders had taken Goldstein, No. 1 man in Battles' navigation class, to town for drinks. I was slightly resentful before it occurred to me that this might have been strategy on Saunders' part to make me jealous.

A few days later Saunders caught me coming out of Aldis class. "Lauro," he said, "how'd you like to go to town and hoist a few? Pleasant little roadhouse on the north road I know of. I'd like to talk over a few things." He regarded me narrowly.

"Thanks, sir, but I don't drink."

He rocked on his heels. "Well, wouldn't you like to get off the station for a bit?"

I told him they kept us so busy that all I wanted to do at night was fall into bed.

"Um, yes. Well, how's that decision about nav school coming along?"

"I still want to go on to elementary flying."

He exploded. "You damn Americans are all alike! Want to be glorified truckdrivers! It's the low-class in you! No sense in the important things! No appreciation of the beauty of pure mathematics! Tell me, Lauro, how do you Americans get that way? Are you all born as well as conceived in automobiles? Are you weaned on petrol?"

"Sir, if you don't mind, I'm due for meteorology."

He glared at me, his eyes narrow. "Lauro, do you realize Guderian has encircled the Russians at Smolensk?"

I shook my head.

"That's a disaster. And when we have disasters, we need navigators. Navigators, understand? Not pilots!"

I excused myself and escaped.

That evening I discussed my problem with Holmsie. He had a solution. "Slip in your navigation grades, down to seventh or eighth man, say. Then Saunders'll lose interest."

"That's a pretty negative way of handling it," I told him.

We heard that Goldstein had given in and agreed to go to nav school. Since I'd kept my grades up that made me Saunders' chief target now in Battles' class, and as we approached the end of training at Saskatoon he stepped up his recruiting campaign accordingly.

Saunders was everywhere I went. When I slipped my hand into my pocket for change to pay for a cup of coffee, Saunders' thin arm would snake past me to deposit a coin on the counter. Protests were useless; if an officer wanted to pay, he paid. I'd come out of class to find him waiting near the door, brushing lint from his uniform or looking at his watch. He was getting me very nervous.

One afternoon he joined me in the canteen. "Read about the Germans taking 600,000 prisoners at Kiev, Lauro?"

"Yes, sir."

"Things don't look good at all." He cleared his throat. "I hear you're having trouble with the Winco, getting lorries for church in town."

"Well—" I began.

"Don't think it's right we have no Catholic chaplain at No. 7. Always been attracted to the Catholic faith, simply marvelous sense of ritual. The least Winco can do is give you a lorry for Sundays. Now I'm going to speak to him in your behalf. I'm going—"

"Sir, forgive me for interrupting, but that business is all straightened out. The Group Captain called me in this morning and said I could have a lorry."

"You mean you went over Winco's head?" He grinned wolfishly. "You'll need somebody to fix things for you with Winco now, won't you?"

"Not quite, sir. The Winco passed on my request to the Group Captain."

"Oh," he said with disappointment. He stirred his tea. "How do you feel about nav school?"

"Still negative."

He looked at me with narrow concern. "Well, think it over carefully. I haven't given up on you yet."

I decided I'd better have a talk with Flying Officer Battles.

"Don't worry," he told me. "All you've got to do is wait Saunders out. Or if the going gets too rough, mention the name McAllister."

"McAllister?"

"McAllister left here last March for elementary flying. Saunders almost broke him down; for a while it was touch and go. McAllister developed the shakes and went to see the doc. The doc went to Winco, and Saunders got properly eaten out. He hasn't pressed so hard since."

"I have slight indentation marks all over me, nonetheless. Sir, are you suggesting I may have to see the doc?"

"Not at all. You're made of sterner stuff than McAllister. Just keep those stars and stripes flying when Saunders makes his final pitch."

Saunders chose a strange place to make it, the YMCA pool in town where Holmsie and I went to swim a couple of times a week. I had no idea Saunders had followed me there until one day I drew myself out of the pool, dripping, and found myself looking at his polished shoes.

He smiled falsely and handed me my towel. "Nice crawl you've got there, Lauro. Did you swim for your college back in the States?"

"No, sir." I began to towel myself off. On the other side of the pool Holmsie sat drying his toes with great deliberation.

"Danny Ferguson, one of the best boys I ever sent on to nav school, swam for McGill, y'know. Held the Canadian record for the 440."

"Did he, sir?"

His eyes narrowed. "Lauro, I want you to know that any man I send on to nav school gets favored treatment, wherever he is. Manitoba, Quebec, Saskatchewan, it doesn't make any difference. He gets better quarters and superior grub. He gets the best squadron assignments. I've got a lot of friends, you see. Now I want to hear your final decision. I can't wait any more. I know it's in favor of nav school. No man in his right mind wouldn't want to be a navigator and bring his ship in."

"Sir, I may not be in my right mind, but I intend to be a pilot, probably in bombers. I'm sorry."

He took a deep breath. "That's your last word, Aircraftsman?"

"I'm afraid so."

Saunders took it well. He straightened his shoulders, as though facing a firing squad that had just clicked its bolts. He touched the knot of his tie. Looking straight ahead, he wheeled smartly and marched off toward the pool exit. He slipped once in the wet, but regained his balance. Then he disappeared through the swinging doors.

Holmsie whooped with laughter, but somehow I couldn't join in. You had to respect Saunders' single-mindedness, his fanaticism, even. It was, after all, in a good cause. And I was glad he'd gotten Goldstein.

In the natural course of events I would have left No. 7 ITS in mid-July for one of the dozens of elementary flying schools scattered around Canada. But things didn't work out that way. My orders, when they arrived, were a single sentence saying: "Course concluded satisfactorily. Await further orders."

I sat on Holmsie's bunk while he happily packed his gear. "There must be some mistake, Joe," he told me. "Why on earth would they want you hanging around Saskatoon?"

"Maybe Saunders is getting his revenge."

"Well, he *is* pretty social."

I paled. "Do you mean Saunders has real influence?"

"That's what I hear. There's an Air Marshal in the family."

I got up quickly. "I'd better see the Winco."

Winco was very busy, his adjutant told me. Could he help?

"Sir," I told him, "I'd like to know why I haven't received my orders."

"I'll look into it and let you know."

I stamped, saluted, and left the office. It seemed to me he hadn't quite been able to meet my eye. I asked around, trying to establish whether the adjutant was a friend of Saunders, but it seemed he wasn't, particularly.

That night, alone in the empty barracks, I couldn't stand the quiet and went to the rec room to write a letter home: "It looks like I'm going to be here in Saskatoon a little longer than I thought. The man I'm working for just got a new contract to put up an elementary school . . . The foliage here is really breathtaking . . . We read, with what feelings you can imagine, of the German successes in Russia."

The new class came in next day, a bunch of Brandon-fresh youngsters, few of them over twenty. At least nobody had been assigned to my bunk.

As a holdover I was a target for puzzled questions from officers whose classes I had passed. When my throat went dry from explanations I set up headquarters in a corner of the rec room. My time was my own and I didn't like it.

After another few days I dropped back to Administration. Had the adjutant been able to check on my situation?

He looked at me blankly. "What's your name and number, Aircraftsman?"

"Lauro, J.W., 1886163, sir. I was in the other day."

"Oh yes, wait a moment."

He returned from the files. "You've concluded your course

satisfactorily with especially high marks in navigation. You're to await further orders."

"But why, sir?"

He gave me a cold stare. "Aircraftsman, are you questioning the efficiency of the RCAF?"

"No, sir, but I'm naturally curious as to—"

"Aircraftsman, I doubt if you're aware of the magnitude of the British Commonwealth Air Training Plan. Approximately 40,000 aircrew personnel are being trained this year. Fifty new airfields are under construction. We're establishing more than a hundred and twenty new schools, and training nearly seventy thousand officers and men to operate them."

"Yes, sir. Still—"

"Loring, you miss the point. You haven't been sent on to EFS because there isn't room for you yet. There will be, eventually." He saluted. "Dismissed."

I dropped by to see Saunders. At first he didn't recognize me, and I knew he'd had nothing to do with my situation; when he'd given me up for nav school I'd literally ceased to exist for him.

A few days later I was reading a letter from Holmsie, at an EFS in Manitoba, when a Squadron Leader came in the barracks door.

"Why aren't you in class?" he snapped.

I explained and he said, "We'd better look into this. Come along to Admin."

The adjutant, with some prompting from me, filled the Squadron Leader in. "Well, we can't just let him lounge about," said the S/L. "Bad for morale. See that he sits in on classes; a good chance to brush up." He left.

The adjutant regarded me with distaste. "Laurel, is it? What's your number again?"

I came out of Administration with passes admitting me to five classes. One was with Flying Officer Saunders.

Somehow the weeks passed. My only bright spot was getting the Catholic boys into town for Sunday mass. Holmsie wrote that he was flying Tiger Moths. Gil Miracle wrote from Ontario that he'd soon be flying Tiger Moths. Lee Usher wrote from Prince Edward Island that he was having some trouble with his instructor, a madman who didn't think he could fly a Tiger Moth.

The classes were boring but at least I didn't have to retake the exams. Saunders never once called on me for recitation, and on at least two occasions he bumped into me as though I wasn't there. His current No. 1 was a tall boy from Moose Jaw named Donahue.

I was beginning to feel seriously invisible when finally, towards the end of October, my orders came through. I'd been assigned to No. 19 Elementary Flying School in Virden, Manitoba, and was to arrive there "without delay."

I wrote Father Lux in Chicago: "My experience in the RCAF tells me I'm a born anomaly, fated to be perpetually out of step with the others. This raises a question, not so much theological as philosophical, about my vocation. Can it be that God hasn't been testing me, as I have thought, but merely that this anomalousness has extended to the priesthood as it has extended to all other things in my life? Could I be out of step with Our Lord, too? Of course I'm only joking."

But was I?

CHAPTER
5

VIRDEN at first sight was unimpressive: a small ops hutment and flying field with hangars, a few barracks and a line of rondeled yellow Tiger Moths parked on the apron. The flying field was a small lake, and only sandbag walls prevented the water from invading the campsite.

"They won't need to put in a swimming pool," a fellow new-arrival commented to me.

Squadron Leader Andy Madore, cordial and vastly competent, was Chief Flying Instructor. He quickly corrected any notion we might have had that Virden was a second-rate way station on the route to Wings Parade. "Take your Tigers seriously," he warned us. "A Tiger can wash you out as quickly as a Cessna. And it can kill you twice as fast."

The schedule was rough: reveille at 6 A.M. and formation twenty-five minutes later. A half-hour of calisthenics in the biting October wind that howled in from Bosshill Creek, followed by breakfast. A full day of Link Trainer, engine classes, aerodynamics, navigation and—when you were ready for it—flying.

Virden was a Civil Flying School, like all but one of the other Elementary Flying Training Schools in Canada. In the years before World War II Canadians needed encouragement to be air-minded, and in 1927 the Dominion Government offered to assist in the organization of flying clubs and in the training of beginners working toward private and commercial pilots' licenses. The Dominion gave each flying club two aircraft, and added another for each aircraft the club bought for itself.

In 1939 there were twenty-six flying clubs in operation across Canada, and hundreds of their graduates were in the RAF and RCAF. When the Commonwealth Air Training Plan was proposed that year, the flying clubs volunteered to undertake elementary flying training for the BCATP. The airlines assumed operation of the Air Observer Schools. Relieved of this preliminary training, the RCAF was free to concentrate on specialized service training. No. 19 EFTS at Virden was one of the first flying schools established.

Its flying instructors were civilian bush pilots, a breed of men who could fly anything anywhere, under any conditions.

Bush pilots had conquered the Canadian wilderness, flying in cargoes of hay, dynamite, oxen, flour, machinery and medical supplies. They had flown prospectors, mining engineers and midwives. They had introduced forest reconnaissance; in protection of Canada's forest, bush pilots had turned their planes into fire engines, carrying equipment, chemical bombs and fire-fighters into the blazing woods. Bush pilots had had a hand in Canada's important fishing industry, transporting by air spawn from the government's salmon hatcheries to places where fish shortages existed.

Mr. White, my instructor, was a bush pilot who'd had the seat of his pants singed by an Alberta forest fire, but he looked and spoke like a college professor. The shelves in his quarters were crammed with books: Huxley and Orwell, Mann and Proust.

My first time up, in a dual-control yellow Moth, I handled the controls for five minutes; the second, I practiced spins, some steep turns and then bunk flying maneuvers, slow rolls, snap rolls and the loop. I did them poorly, but I did them.

Then Mr. White took over and did them as they should be done.

"Pretty good, Joe," he told me. "You should be soloing in under seven hours."

The third day White had me shooting landings, and then I did a series of takeoffs and landings. I was a bit rough, but after the fourth series he jumped out of the back cockpit and said, "She's all yours. Give me another takeoff and landing."

I licked my lips. "Solo, Mr. White?"

He smiled and walked away.

I revved up the Tiger, gave White the thumbs up signal, pushed the throttle forward, and taxied off. Once the ship was moving directly into the wind I put the throttle forward and watched the airspeed build to 55. At 65 she was lifting. I held her down for a gradual climb to 70, then roared the Moth skyward, thinking, If only Bishop Fletcher could see me now.

At 1000 feet I started my slow turn on the circuit, completing 180 degrees. On my downwind leg I checked the field and traffic pattern and saw I was approaching the end of the field.

I flew the downwind leg a little longer to give me ample time for approach and landing. Turning, I began to lose a little altitude and took my base leg. I could spot Mr. White standing on the edge of the field, in a puddle.

I lost altitude gradually, checking airspeed, altitude and field position. A little bubble of fear burst when I was down to 400 feet. But I had airspeed of 65 and was losing altitude well. At 50 feet I was in good position when the engine sputtered. I gave her a little throttle and she cleared. At 10 feet I brought her nose up a little and, flaring out, flew in for a fair landing. I had soloed.

When I taxied in Mr. White waved me around for another circuit. Absolutely without fear now I took off from the wet field for my circuit.

Throttling back at 100 feet, I started a shallow climb, and

at 500 turned to the left and looked down at the field. Mr. White, a small tan dot, waved.

At 1000 feet I began to make corrections for a landing. The motor sputtered at 800 feet. I tried to clear it, and turned toward the field, pushing the Moth's nose down slightly. The motor sputtered again and died.

I was faced with a deadstick landing. I prayed "Oh God, help me!" Losing altitude rapidly now, I flared out at 100, eased the plane down, and onto the field. The ship's wheels fanned spray from the puddles and the Moth came to a stop.

Looking over toward the tower, I saw Squadron Leader Madore's jeep barrelling down the taxi strip toward me. Mr. White was running across the field.

They reached me simultaneously, shouting, "Good job, smashing good landing."

Madore listened closely while White threw questions at me. Then the Squadron Leader got into the cockpit while White turned the prop. No dice. Madore ordered the plane towed into the hangar.

One of the ground crew was shaking his head. "What's the matter?" I asked him.

Another erk, or mechanic, a small man with very red hair, pointed to the sky. "A lot's goin' to happen to you up there."

"That so?"

"Solo and you conk out? Oh my yes, a helluva lot's goin' to happen to you up there. It's *fated*."

As at Saskatoon, there was no Catholic padre based at Virden, and for some weeks now I had been taking the Catholic boys to town for Sunday mass. One very cold Sunday morning in November I picked up my lorry at the motor pool a few minutes before six o'clock.

I looked at the open truck without enthusiasm. "It's fifteen below," I told the NCO on duty. "Sergeant Baker promised me closed transport."

"No closed lorries available, yer Highness," the corporal said with sleepy sarcasm. "Take it or leave it."

I knew the sergeant wouldn't take kindly to being wakened this early to hear my problem, especially since he was a firm agnostic. I held out my hand for the key.

When I honked my horn outside the barracks twenty-two men came out. Thirty had guaranteed their presence, but for so cold a morning the percentage was good. All the men wore parkas and fleece-lined gloves, and not a few of the wiser ones had blankets.

There was some grumbling when they saw the open lorry. "Who's going to ride with you in the cab?" asked Stockton, a thin Albertan. He shivered.

"There's room for two of you. We'll draw lots."

Lots were drawn by match-length, and two boys from Vancouver won. The rest settled themselves in back and we rode off toward Virden, a small farming village fifteen miles away.

Six miles out of town the rear left tire went flat. I went around to the back. The boys sat huddled on the wooden seats, faces blue and expressionless. From Stockton's nose hung a tiny icicle.

"Lauro," he said, "I didn't join the RCAF to freeze to death on the *ground*. If I want to cop my packet on the ground I could have joined the army."

"No spare and no jack," I told them. "We'll have to get out and walk."

The already half-frozen men groaned. Bollinger, an Ontarian, said he wanted to stay in the truck. "If we walk we'll freeze to death in discomfort. If we stay we'll just freeze to death." He got a ragged cheer.

"We've got a nice warm church to head for," I told them. "Let's pile out of there and help me get the lorry off to the side of the road."

An hour later we staggered into the small wooden mission

church. We had missed the mass but were in time to interrupt
the sermon.

The Father smiled. "Lorry trouble, boys? You people in the
pews near the stove kindly give these men some room."

Huddling near the potbellied stove, we gradually thawed
out. Bollinger whispered to me that he almost certainly had
a bad case of frostbite. Could frostbite get you out of the air
force? I told him no; they'd probably put him in the motor
pool, taking jacks and spares off trucks.

The sermon was titled "The Cold in Heart," and the boys
enjoyed it.

Next day I was waiting for Mr. White in the students' room
when Squadron Leader Madore came in. "Joe," he said, "I
want you to do me a favor."

"You mean quit taking the boys to mass?"

He grinned; by now the story of the lorry breakdown had
made the station rounds. The lorry that had been sent out to
pick us up in Virden also came down with a flat, and as a
result the sergeant in charge of the motor pool had been de-
moted for inefficiency. It was rumored that he held his demo-
tion against "certain religious types" at Virden.

"No, something else," said Madore. "Tom Evans, one of
the twins, isn't doing so well with Mr. Spinney. I—"

Noting my sudden pallor, he hurried on. "Joe, I want you
to exchange instructors with Tom. He'll do better with Mr.
White."

"Sir, everybody does better with Mr. White. I feel *confident* with Mr. White."

"That isn't the point. You're older, and you can take what
Spinney dishes out. He's probably our best man, Joe. One of
the great bush pilots of North America."

"He also washed out two men last week."

"They would have washed out sooner or later."

"Sir," I protested, "can you honestly tell me these men
would have washed out with Mr. White?"

He evaded my question. "I feel you can handle Spinney. All I ask is that you give him a try."

At eight fifty-five next morning I was waiting in the students' room. Promptly on the dot of nine in walked Mr. Spinney—a short, burly Bostonian with the set of a bulldog.

"Come on, Lauro," he snapped, "let's go."

I hitched up my chute and followed him toward the line of Tigers. Even his walk was hostile, I thought. Was I in a movie about an apprentice pilot in conflict with a hardnosed instructor who was riding him for his own good? Or was Spinney really that mean?

I got into the front seat and began the cockpit check.

It wasn't fast enough for Spinney. He barked from the backseat, "Let's go, boy. We've got flying to do, not ground school."

The movie feeling faded. I felt Spinney didn't like me personally. If he didn't like me personally I was likely to wash out. No washout of Spinney's lasted more than four weeks. I was determined to last five.

I taxied out and lined up for takeoff. Although he said nothing, somehow Spinney made me feel as though I'd made a rotten job of it.

"Any time you're ready let's go," he called over the interphone.

I cleared the throttle and jockeyed the plane into the wind. Pouring the throttle, I reached 55, then eased back on the stick. She sailed along smoothly and at 65 was airborne.

So far no word from Spinney. I started a climb. Suddenly the throttle slipped out of my hand. The engine idled as Spinney reduced power from his instructor's seat. We came down and landed from ten feet.

The interphone crackled: "What in hell do you call that, a takeoff? That's no takeoff! Now taxi back and give me a Navy takeoff, a takeoff that's a takeoff."

Taxiing back I wondered what a Navy takeoff was. Such was Spinney's spell that I never thought to ask him.

Into wind again, I started down the runway, easing off at 65 and taking off more gradually, trying to keep the nose down in order not to gain excessive altitude in too fast a climb. Spinney chopped off the throttle and curtly ordered me to land.

After I'd taxied in Spinney whispered over the interphone in martyred tones, "Lauro, how many air hours you logged?"

"Twelve," I told him.

He exploded in disbelief. "Twelve hours, you baboon, and you call that a Navy takeoff?"

"Sir, what's a—"

"Back for takeoff," Spinney interrupted coldly. As I lined up, the interphone crackled again: "Follow me through on the controls and watch the horizon as this damn plane gets airborne!"

I followed him through, and as we eased off he told me to put my nose slightly above the horizon and start a gentle climb. I followed orders without abuse. Spinney made a 100-foot pattern, brought the plane in, and positioned it for takeoff.

"She's yours now," he said gruffly. "Now for God's sake give me a Navy takeoff."

A Navy takeoff, I concluded, was a *smooth* takeoff. At a hundred feet Spinney chopped the throttle back, and I pushed the Moth's nose down for an emergency landing. At twenty-five feet he gave me the throttle again and told me to take her up.

I climbed, and at 150 feet Spinney ordered me to shoot some landings. After the fifth my hour was up, and silently we walked to the students' room. Spinney turned to me at the door. "Not so good, Lauro. You've got a lot to learn, and I'm not so impressed by those reflexes."

That hurt; reflexes were the one thing you couldn't improve on. Without speaking I left him for the canteen.

The Evans twins, John and Tom, were there. Although Tom looked the other way, I made a point of joining their table.

"Pretty cold out," I said, beginning to feel again that a camera was grinding somewhere behind me.

"Sure is," said John. Tom grinned weakly.

"Going down to fifteen below, I hear," I said.

"Joe," Tom said, "I'm sorry. It was Andy Madore's idea to exchange instructors, not mine."

I drank my tea. "Sure is cold out," I said.

Tom got up, ostensibly for another cup of tea. He didn't come back.

"You think it's going to get still colder, John?" I asked.

"Joe, it's not my fault I'm the kid's brother."

"Pretty cold here in Canada, you ask me," I said, and John picked up his mug and left. I felt a little better.

Next morning I shot three takeoffs and landings with Spinney and flew instruments for the rest of the time. Walking to the hangar, Spinney said, "Lauro, you've got fourteen hours flying time. Do you think you'll ever solo?"

"Sir," I said mildly, as the cameras began to grind again, "I soloed that plane in seven hours and I can solo it again."

He stopped, gaping at me. "You *soloed* in *seven hours?* Nobody here's ever soloed in under eight."

"Ask Mr. White," I told him, and he left me, scowling.

Next morning Spinney came into the students' room two minutes early, scowling. "Well, Lauro," he said, "you think you can fly it alone. I hate funerals, and I wouldn't get a kick out of seeing you break your neck, but it's your neck, not mine. You can fly it alone this morning, but watch the King's property, you got that?"

"You talk to Mr. White?" I asked him.

He scowled and stalked off toward the field.

When I took off Spinney and two other instructors were watching from the apron. I flew the pattern at 1000 feet and gave myself a good approach leg. Down at 500 my final check showed me well-positioned with not too many puddles in my lane. I flared out at fifteen feet and with a little throttle eased her down. It was one of my better landings.

Spinney was waiting for me at the hangar. "Not so bad," he grunted. "Nice if you'd do as well every time. Now let's have a few more circuits and landings."

I tried to keep my tone casual. "No, thanks. I've had enough for today. Sorry you can't come to my funeral."

He turned red. "Now look here, boy, you get it and you get it straight. I'm rough and I'm a rider, but it's riding that keeps you guys alive. This isn't a Hollywood movie where it all turns out roses; this is real life. You make a bad mistake and it's curtains. You don't get a chance to make another—what the devil are you staring at me for?"

I was staring at him because his mentioning the movies had made it impossible that we were in one. He was right: we were in real life.

"Sorry," I said.

"You do a helluva lot of staring," he said, and stalked off, kicking through a mud puddle and spattering his boots.

The two-month course was over December 8. I passed and was assigned to No. 10 Service Flying Training School, Dauphin, Manitoba, about 100 miles from Virden. Dauphin was Bomber Command, and some of the boys ticketed for it were disappointed they wouldn't be flying fighters. I had other things on my mind: news of Pearl Harbor had come over the radio on the 7th. When Andy Madore asked me if I'd be transferring to the U.S. Army Air Corps I said I didn't plan to, not with only two more months of service flying school before going overseas.

I put in a long-distance call to my sister Helen in Kalamazoo. Mother was holding her own but worried I'd be drafted now that we were in the war. "Tell her I'll be building airfields in

Canada—that gives me draft proof status," I told Helen. Looking down at my Aircraftsman's stripes I felt doubly the anomalous fraud: an American in Canadian uniform with the U.S. now at war.

At the testimonial dinner in the mess hall they gave me the honor of toasting the King in front of the Canadian Jack. That meant that Spinney had named me his best student. Up to the last he hadn't said a pleasant word. When I thanked him he frowned and said, "Now for God's sake don't disgrace me at Dauphin."

Pearl Harbor had intensified RCAF training schedules to the breaking point. In eight weeks at Dauphin, with classes night and day, we were expected to learn how to fly a twin-engined plane, the Cessna, discipline a crew, carry a payload to target and get the crew safely home.

Ed Holmsicourt and a Virden buddy, Brian Campbell, were in my hutment. Ed had broken a leg and lost enough time for me to draw abreast of him. There were others who were to become close friends: George Hertel from the Eastern Province and Chuck Harbottle of Manitoba. Our instructor on the twin-engine Cessna Cranes was Bob Hemmons of Manitoba. Bob badly wanted to go overseas and resented his instructorship.

The Cessna was a reliable ship with one bad characteristic. In the strong Canadian winds she would float a long way before touching down. You had to swallow your pride and "pour the coals on" to make her go around again before landing.

Dauphin was even colder than Virden; it was usually five or ten below, and outside you always wore a parka and fleece-lined gloves. The hutment stoves were kept blazing hot. The snowfall was so heavy that they didn't bother to clear the runways; they just hooked rollers to tractors and rolled the snow down hard. We took off and landed on skis from a strip that was a foot above the ground. It was all right till the sun came out, and then landing became a real hazard.

The cold was worst on night flying on cross-countries. One week, with the temperature a steady 35 below, we drew a blisteringly cold night for a 10 P.M. to 1 A.M. flight. I finished my plotting in the briefing room and went out on the runway to check the plane.

An erk was adjusting tarps over the engine. He looked at me strangely when I started my cockpit check. "Sir, you ain't flying in this weather?"

"Orders. Get those tarps off, will you? And I'll need some ground crew."

I ran through the check and gave the signal to the ground crew for contact. The engine spluttered a little and then set up a steady purr.

I flipped on the heater switch and taxied out to the end of the runway. No heat yet; the vent was stone cold. Was the heater on the fritz? I should taxi back for another plane with an operational heating unit.

The green Aldis light flashed for takeoff. I decided to take my chances and took the Cessna down the runway. In a moment I was airborne over the cold white fields.

It was half moon with good visibility. The cockpit seemed warmer. I circled the field and set my course for the first leg.

Ten minutes in the air, at 3000 feet, I tried the heater again. Cold as Himmler's heart. The cold was getting worse now and I found I couldn't hold the stick with both hands; if I did the fingers of the outside hand lost all feeling. I tucked the fingers of my left hand under me and flew the Cessna with the right. Holmsie and Brian had been scheduled to take off a few minutes after me, and I wondered how they were doing. Brian hated the cold with passion.

My first leg to Lanigan, 225 miles and an hour and a half flying time, was off by about half a mile. I made corrections and started on the second leg to Regina. Lauro was a-cold. My thoughts kept drifting to last week's fatal accident at Quill Lakes when one of the men on a cross-country had been forced down near the shore and froze to death before help could reach him. The same thing could happen to me.

To avoid the cold and the thought of Quill Lakes I tried to concentrate on navigation, but it was no use; I had to keep my hands and feet from freezing. I stamped one foot at a time and rubbed my gloved hands together. The rubbing didn't work; it was better to sit on the fingers of one hand. Meanwhile my nostril hairs were freezing.

My second leg was on the money, and using the same winds I headed for home. ETA (Estimated Time of Arrival) was an hour and ten minutes away. I kept thinking of hot chocolate and warm beds and the blessed warmth of hutment stoves red in darkness. I remembered how comfortable my room at St. John's Seminary in Little Rock had been in the cold winter of '40, how the steam heat had hissed faintly from the radiators. The cold now was worse, if that was possible. Even the moonlight was frigid. I found myself worrying about Brian and Holmsie; maybe their heaters were on the blink, too.

The worry shaded into blankness and minor hallucinations: the world below had frozen into ice, and back at the station I'd be greeted by ice men whose touch was death.

Then, in the distance, amazingly, our beacon. I'd made it; I was in. It was a tough job bringing the plane down with one numbed hand and chattering teeth. The Crane floated and bounced, but I managed to put her down without a "go around."

The crew chief came up as I was making my final check, and I told him about the heater.

His jaw dropped. "You was up there in that cold with a busted heater? My God, man." He was so shocked he forgot to apologize.

Holmsie and Brian were in the briefing room, reading comfortably near the stove. All solicitude, they rushed up to me, took off my shoes and gloves, and examined my fingers and toes. "Blue," said Holmsie, shaking his head, and went outside for some snow to rub me down with. Brian left to pick up some coffee at the canteen.

"How come you guys look so good?" I asked Holmsie suspiciously.

He gave me a tentative smile. "Our heaters conked out on us, Buddy. We circled around for twenty minutes or so and then came in."

"But what about your flight plans?"

"We ducked back here, waited the time out, and then told the timekeeper we'd just come in."

I stared at him, speechless.

"Now take it easy, Joe. Nobody goes on cross-countries on a night like this, especially with a busted heater. Not unless they're crazy."

I was about to crown him with an ashtray when Brian came back with the coffee, which was cold. "Bad news," he told Holmsie. "The Squadron Leader caught me outside the canteen and asked where I was going with the coffee. Like a fool I told him it was for Joe. He happened to remember his departure time, and he'd just heard from the crew chief about the heaters. So he asked me if I'd gone on the trip. I hemmed and I hawed and he left me to go into Ops. He's bound to check our plans."

"Oh no," groaned Holmsie. "This could mean our wings."

I bundled up and smugly left the briefing room for the hutment.

The boys had a sleepless night. Next morning the Squadron Leader called them in. They got off with a stiff reprimand; Canada needed men with wings.

I drew Bob Hemmons as pilot for one of my last assignments at Dauphin—towing target sleeves for gunnery practice from Fairy Battles, obsolete fighters that were blind from one wing.

The Battle had a floor hatch from which you released the

target drogue. Sitting at the hatch, I could see the ground 4000 feet below.

Bob asked over the intercom, "Drogue out?" and when I answered in the affirmative said, "They won't be making passes for some time yet. You'll find a couple of comics tucked into the seat."

"Good reading?" Bob asked me a few minutes later.

"Could be better."

"Quit reading and look below."

I followed his instructions and a wave of nausea swept over me. I called Bob. "I'm feeling nauseous. Any containers aboard?"

"You don't need a container. Just let 'er go between your feet."

I'd hardly gotten my earphones off before my breakfast and last night's supper went out the hatch between my legs. The updraft promptly swept them back into my face and all over my flying suit.

"That's great advice you gave me," I told Hemmons. The first fighter, making its pass at the drogue, drowned out his reply, but I could hear him laughing insanely.

We landed an hour later. Bob doubled over with laughter when he stuck his head into the rear cockpit. But that didn't stop him from ordering me to clean up the mess.

"Look who got drogue-sick," Holmsie greeted me cheerfully back at the hut. "Did he have you reading Little Orphan Annie or the Katzenjammer Kids?"

"You mean you can't get sick without the reading?"

"Reading's absolutely indispensable," said Brian. "Anyway, served you right. You Yanks, we've got to take you down a peg. Swaggering around so rich and arrogant. Disgusting."

Sometimes it didn't pay to be an American.

Two weeks before Wings Parade, in March, Bob Hemmons left on leave for his father's farm near Winona. He promised to be back at Dauphin in time to see Holmsie, Brian and me get our wings.

He didn't keep that promise. The morning of Parade we heard that Bob and two other instructors were dead.

While his fiancée waved goodbye Bob had lifted his Cessna from the farm's makeshift landing strip. He had misjudged the short field and failed to clear a line of trees at the edge. The plane crashed and flamed with no survivors.

After Parade we sat on our bunks and avoided each other's eyes till the avoiding became unbearable and we left the hut one by one for aimless solitary walks. That evening we had dinner in town with Brian's two goodlooking sisters, Rita and Joan, but the party broke up early.

We were scheduled to leave for overseas embarkation point in three days, no home leaves permitted. Meanwhile we had permission to relax with a little flying.

Holmsie and I went down to the flight line at eleven that morning and signed for two Cranes. Airborne, we did a little formation flying and then Holmsie motioned in the direction of Saskatoon. I gave him the thumbs up sign.

I knew what he had in mind: the bridge over the river. We arrived at Saskatoon and Holmsie pointed downward; I nodded.

The bridge loomed ahead. We approached to survey clearance and then pulled up and over. There was a lot of traffic on the bridge; a girl in a red coat waved gaily. We went around again, and this time I was in lead position. We let down to about ten feet above the water and started the run. Water flashed beneath, stone veered at me from ahead, and then I was under and through in a streak of dark. Holmsie followed. The danger had been more apparent than real; clearance at the top was about seventy feet and at the sides about sixty.

At Dauphin dispersal an MP jeep was waiting for us. Somebody had taken our tail numbers from the bridge.

Holmsie evidently planned to brazen it out. "Anything

wrong, Corporal?" he asked the MP in command as we were
marched to the Winco's office. The corporal was stolidly silent.

Wing Commander B.C. Andrews was an American, pleas-
ant-spoken and paternal with his boys. But not today.

"Airmen," he told us, "today you broke one of the most
serious regulations of this service. You jeopardized your lives,
the lives of others, and the King's property. Have you anything to say?"

I was just beginning to recognize the seriousness of the situation. Neither Holmsie nor I knew anything about air current
over water and under a bridge.

"Nothing, sir," I said.

"Under other circumstances, I would strip you of your
wings and bust you from the service. But I feel Bob Hemmons'
death had something to do with this. Sergeant Pilots, step forward and return to the rank of Leading Aircraftsmen."

With a razor blade Andrews neatly cut our sergeant's stripes
of a day from our tunics. We saluted and left. Outside Holmsie
cracked, "You and your American impetuosity," but I knew
he was as upset as I.

An anomaly again: an airman with wings but not the sergeant's rank that justified them.

That evening Holmsie and I got our overseas orders: departure from Halifax for England on March 26th with a two-
day stopover in Montreal. Brian Campbell was going on to
instructor's school.

I put through a call to Mother at home. Helen had prepared
her in advance with the truth, and written me she'd taken the
news well.

"*Josiçu*," Mother said over the bad connection, "you cannot
go to seminary in Canada?"

"No, *Mika*. Anyway, I'm in the RCAF now. Helen told
you."

"The RCAF, they have declared war against Hitler?"

"Yes, *Mika*."

There was a silence; distance crackled over the line. "*Josiçu*, you could join the American air force now that you know how to fly?"

"Yes, but I feel I owe the RCAF something after all the money they've spent on my training."

"The money you sent, you did not win it gambling?"

"No."

"They pay you little, Helen says. How then could you send money?"

"I'm a good boy, *Mika*."

"Not so much you stay good, as you stay alive. You promise me to stay alive?"

I promised.

At Halifax they put us into the shipping-out pool to await the next convoy. We spent the time counting the puzzled airmen who passed us wondering what could possibly account for two LAC's with wings.

We'd counted a dozen when an airman came up and asked for an explanation. Holmsie told him we were the first of a new suicide squad.

The second day they called us out in formation to witness the cashiering of a Pilot Officer who had failed to report for his sailing date and been charged with desertion in time of war. One by one his insignia of rank and buttons were cut away. He stood in the cold March wind, his loose coattails flapping, his eyes vacant of emotion. We heard later he was an American.

Next afternoon, in blacked-out Halifax harbor, we boarded our transport, a French ocean liner. In the slip beside her lay berthed a freighter with a torpedoed bow, the first war casualty I had as yet seen. The French ship was jammed with about three thousand men from every arm of the services.

Men were standing in little groups in the passageways, shooting the breeze. I noticed that a few were scratching.

With thumb and forefinger Holmsie removed from my col-

lar a well-nourished flea. Then he began to itch. Up and down
the passageway, men were moving under the lights to examine
each other's clothing.

News came that the bunks below were infested. Half an
hour later the port medical inspector came aboard, and not long
after that we got orders to evacuate the ship.

It was after midnight before we boarded another, a British
troop transport, but by 1 A.M. the tugs were pulling us out of
Halifax harbor.

I caught a few hours' sleep and went topside. We were in a
30-ship convoy, mostly troopships, formed up in lines astern
with two destroyers on the flanks for naval escort. Two Sun-
derland flying boats that would be leaving us soon roared
overhead.

"Sinister, ain't it?" somebody said at my elbow.

I turned. It was a little ferret-faced Canadian Army corporal. He was smiling.

"You know what can happen to us in the briny?" he asked
me, and then answered his own question "Torpedoes, mines,
surface raiders, bombs, storms, bad coal. The bad coal would
make us fall out of convoy and be soft touches for subs. We
could hit submerged icebergs, derelicts, or rocks near the
coast. That ship astern, it's wobbly, might crash into us in fog.
On this here particular tub we're in a very bad position, sailin'
second from the end. The wolf packs pick on stragglers."

"That so?" My blood was running cold. "How come you're
so well informed?"

"Got a brother in the merchant service. He's made twenty,
twenty-five trips. Got torpedoed twice."

Depressed, I excused myself and went below.

At dinner time that first night we had an alert. The convoy
speeded up and took evasive action, and the destroyers dropped
depth charges. When the all clear sounded I went topside with
Holmsie. Seconds later the corporal trapped us at the rail.

"Nice alert, exciting," he said with relish. "Watch for at

least half a dozen more. I figure the next one for tomorrow night, round six. The real thing, maybe. We might lose one ship, maybe two."

Holmsie stared at him for a moment, then swallowed. "I need some coffee," he said, and bolted.

"Nervous fellow," commented the corporal. "The nervous ones, they're first to get it."

The next three days, despite the corporal, passed without incident. On the morning of the fifth the destroyer escorts steamed south and began to drop depth charges. It was another false alarm, and the last.

The corporal was even wrong about our destination. He predicted Southampton, and it turned out to be Liverpool. We disembarked in a blackout, the men singing "We've a Lovely War to Win."

PART II

A LOVELY WAR TO WIN

CHAPTER

1

THE Liverpool fog was bad—or good—enough to make a blackout unnecessary, but a blackout was nonetheless in effect. They marched us through it to a second-class hotel and told us we'd be leaving next morning for Bournemouth. No chance to see what the city was most famous for, the statue of the liver bird atop the Royal Liver Building, still standing under the blitz. That night, along with the damp chill, a strange smell filtered through the window cracks, a smell compounded of rubble, war dust, and wartime coal.

At Bournemouth our billets were another second-class hotel, with no elevators, called the Marlborough. We were assigned rooms on the fifth floor. Holmsie and like-minded sybarites bribed the desk clerk to give them a relatively elegant first-floor suite, but I refused the deal on the grounds that since the hotel was empty the clerk should have offered us the suite gratis. "Stubborn," Holmsie said of me in disapproval. As a result I was the only man on the fifth floor, and when I came down to the lobby, puffing from the stairs, I got some odd looks. One long-nosed fellow from Ontario asked suspiciously what I was doing up there all by myself, flashing signals to the Germans? Holmsie told him I was reading some Cardinal named Newman. The fellow from Ontario was surprised; he hadn't known those Yank baseball players wrote books.

We were in Bournemouth for seven days, waiting for a physical check that took less than thirty minutes. The boardwalk, margining the steel-gray sea, was empty, shuttered and cold. There wasn't anything to do but go to the cinema and wait for tea and crumpets, served three times a day. Among the still ads for prams, beauty shops and trusses flashed on the screen in the intervals was a picture of a banana followed by the words, "This is a banana. Since it is wartime there are no bananas to be bought in England." The authorities wanted the children to know bananas existed.

We came back from the cinema one evening to an altercation in the Marlborough lobby. Standing at the desk, surrounded by a laughing group of RCAF men, was an angry young woman brandishing a pair of nylons. " 'is name is Woodbridge," she said, "and 'e comes from Toronto, and you can't tell me 'e ain't stayin' 'ere because I know 'e is. Now you tell 'im I'm 'ere and I want to see 'im."

The clerk protested that no Aircraftsman Woodbridge was registered at the hotel, but she wouldn't listen. "Stanley's 'ere all right, and 'e's going to get what for. Giving me one stocking one night and the other the next, and then when 'e didn't show up the following, I try them on and find they're a bloody size *twelve!*"

A roar of laughter drowned out the clerk's expostulations. The men swept off the angry young lady for a spot of tea or something stronger. She was still waving the offending nylons like a battle flag.

Holmsie turned to me aggrievedly. "You lout, why didn't you remind me to load up on stockings in Halifax? They were three dollars a dozen and over here you can't get a pair to save your life." He turned reflective. "Woodbridge, eh? We'll hear of that name again, mark my words. A V.C., a D.S.C. at least."

But we never did.

*   *   *

They broke us up in December. Holmsie went to a personnel pool waiting shipment and I was sent to Lang Newnton,
outside Leeds, for two weeks of operational flying in Oxford
twin-engines. P/O Ireland, the instructor, would point out the
airfields below for me to identify and I couldn't—they were
camouflaged too well. I knew German camouflage would be at
least as good.

For the first time I heard about combat—flak, bomb loads,
hostile fighters. We were to be especially alert to enemy fighters that might penetrate home base and lurk above the field as
we came in from ops. After a successful eight-hour mission,
they told us with typical British understatement, it was "rather
frustrating" to be shot down over your own field.

My closest friend at Lang Newnton was Lofty Williams, a
New Zealander. One night, after hours of directing runway
traffic, I suggested to him that we shoot some landings ourselves; no one had told us we couldn't. Minutes later we were
airborne in a couple of Oxfords, Lofty taking off first.

I shot landings for thirty minutes and then headed for Pundit
No. 1, the code beacon about four miles north near the traffic
landing pattern. By the time I'd passed it and made my turn,
Lofty's ship had long since disappeared. As I headed back the
fog suddenly settled in. Even worse, my gas was running low.

Making a square search of Lang Newnton, I tried to locate
the four Pundit towers that would give me a fix. Two were
unmanned and useless. I was lost. I realized my only hope, now
that my fuel was almost gone, was to make an emergency landing. Providentially a pattern of lights flickered into life below.
I went down to 800 feet and flashed an SOS, getting in reply a
green Aldis signal to land. Down I came through the heavy fog
to the landing strip. Both engines quit dead on the runway. I
had made it with seconds to spare.

"Where am I?" I asked the operations officer who hurried
up to the plane.

He mumbled a name I couldn't quite catch. "You're lucky,"

he told me. "Those runway lights would have been off in another five minutes. We were just closing down for the night."

The field was a good 60 miles from Lang Newnton. The telephone circuits were out of order; after an hour of trying I gave up and turned in on a cot. Next morning I gassed up and headed for home.

Lofty told me he hadn't been in the air for more than a few minutes; seeing the fog roll in, he'd made a right-hand pattern and then come in. As I turned away he added darkly, "Better see P/O Ireland, and quick. He thinks you deserted to the Hun."

I didn't see Ireland immediately, though later on I had to pay for that, too. My first stop was the chapel to offer thanksgiving. It wasn't too often that an apprentice pilot landed safely on his last drop of gas. I thought of my solo flight at Virden when the engine had conked out; maybe one man in thirty came out of either kind of crisis alive. Maybe I was going to be lucky in this war. Or was it likelier that I was using up my luck in training and would have that much less of it left for combat?

After a few days of cross-countries I got my next assignment: No. 22 Operational Training Unit at Wellesbourne, Mountford, Warwickshire, near Stratford-on-Avon. Accompanying my orders was a two-day pass into London over New Year's.

There was a huge Lancaster Bomber in Trafalgar Square with a pretty Wren stationed behind it taking pledges for the bond drive. Piccadilly Circus was all signs: GUINNESS IS GOOD FOR YOU . . . ODEAN BILE BEANS . . . WE'VE GOT TO KEEP ON SAVING . . . DRINK BOVRIL. In St. James's Park the winter trees were stripped and bare. There were sandbags around the elegant Regency façade of Carlton House Terrace and everywhere sandbagged walls and pillboxes, their black mouths menacingly slitted for the guns that would face the invader. Signs pointed to Anderson shelters and to refuge in the tubes, whose stations were lined with triple-decker bunks.

I had breakfast in a Lyons House in Clapham High Street that had boards instead of windows and no top floor; a buzz bomb had sheared it away. The waitress told me there'd been heavy damage in Clapham from frequent daytime raids. If I were in London overnight, she advised, stay in Westminster, where the shelters were more solid-like. I noticed that she jumped at street noises.

In Glover Square they were sweeping up glass, and the firemen had cordoned off a smoking building. I took a taxi to Mrs. Bennett's in Clapham Common, S.N., recommended to me by a flight sergeant at Lang Newnton who had stayed there on leaves. Mrs. Bennett had a clean house, he'd said, and cheap and quiet, if you didn't mind her pug dog, Bowser, always sniffing at the door. While Bowser chewed my laces the old lady, in her inevitable oatmeal cardigan, told me about her two sons and grandsons in service. She'd already lost one. I brought my kit up to the plain, severely furnished bed-sitting room, unpacked, and caught another taxi to Canada House near Trafalgar Square to meet Holmsie and Johnny Kelly, ex-Dauphin.

That night there was a bombing alert at 9 P.M. Kelly and I left the lounge to take a look outside while Holmsie stayed to romance his Wren at a canteen table. In the Westminster area the searchlights had coned a German bomber, and as the flak caught it the plane burst into flames. I watched the sky for a parachute but saw none, and I prayed for the pilot. As a fellow professional I could feel nothing for him but pity. The searchlights followed the mass of flaming debris to the ground.

The pavement shook from a nearby detonation and Kelly tugged at my sleeve. "Joe, what do you say we see what these shelters are like?" I followed him to the nearest tube. A mistake; the raids continued and the air raid warden wouldn't let us out. We spent the three hours to midnight watching adolescents necking in the shadows. "Happy New Year, Joe," Kelly said sadly as the hour struck. "I wonder if Holmsie's kissing his Wren."

At Canada House I'd heard the story of the Canadian who appeared there saying he wanted to join the RAF. The young man said he'd made an airplane with string, wax and parts of an old car, and flown it. A skeptical officer told him he would inquire. The Canadian's story was checked out and proved accurate; he had flown the sealing wax plane every weekend for a year. The young man was accepted into the RAF.

That had been in 1941. Now, two years later, there were still too few RCAF men in Britain to allow for all-Canadian units operating under RCAF command. This was not to change until May, 1943. Without a command of their own Canadians were inclined to be a bit defensive, and some of them blew off steam wth fancy boasting in the local pubs.

I hadn't been at Wellesbourne a week before a meeting was called at the officers' club for Canadian personnel at the station. Standing before the fireplace was Group Captain R.B. Jordan, D.F.C., and most of his ranking officers. Jordan had won his D.F.C. when he was over forty-five; in pre-war days he had starred for the RAF in hockey, cricket and rugby.

There was Group Captain R.B. "Tirpitz" Tait, triple D.C.S. and triple D.F.C., famous not only for leading the raid that sank the *Tirpitz*, but, in the socially conscious RAF, for the fact that he'd invited a Flight Sergeant who had successfully landed a crippled Wellington to drink beer from his own personal tankard in the officers' mess. There was Assistant Medical Officer Doc Williams, a granite-tough little Welshman, in peace time a well-known surgeon. There was Wing Commander P.M. Cooke, D.S.O., D.F.C., known as "P-p-press On Cooke"—he had a slight stammer—and my Flight Commander, Squadron Leader T.G. Moore, a fine footballer who had been on more than 70 raids. There was Chief Instructor Wing Commander Oldroyd, a Yorkshireman; Intelligence Officer Squadron Leader Bryant, D.S.O., Military Cross, and a hero of World War I, with his walrus moustache. Present also were the engineering staff, Senior Officer Wing Commander Starling, and his junior, Squadron Leader Sparrow. ("The Bird Men," they called them.)

Jordan was famous for the brevity of his speeches. It was said about him that he left "Morning" off his "Good." He said to us now, "Some of you are claiming that now you're here the war will be over in a hurry." He pointed to the wall where hung photos of Canada's great aces of World War I; Bishop, Barker and Collishaw. "You're wearing RAF wings," he went on, "wings worn by these men. If you can't add to what they stood for, don't detract from it. Any man who feels that what I've just said is unreasonable, chauvinist or pukka, had best step forward for the severing of his wings. Both he and the RAF would benefit."

No one took a step forward. Jordan grinned. "Gentlemen, certain philanthropists in Stratford have donated a large amount of beer for any purpose we choose to put it to. I'd say a party was in order. Eight o'clock here at the club; you are all invited."

It was the best possible introduction to the RAF way of doing things we could have had. There were others, including rugger. When a man wasn't flying he was expected to be out on the rugger field. The Canadian boys knew something about rugby, but as an American I found its rules difficult to follow. Though I'd played football in the States it was useless to me at Wellesbourne, and the ranking officers found my style so interesting that they made a point of stopping by the field to watch.

I barged opponents, propelled balls with my hands and arms, handled the ball in a loose scrum, and entered the scrum from our opponent's side. I tripped and barged on the line-out, ad-

vanced beyond a line ten yards behind the line of the touch,
fell on the ball and did not roll away. In three games opponents
scored six points on my penalty goals.

Finally Squadron Leader Geoffrey Moore, a fine player
himself, took me aside and in a single afternoon drilled the fun-
damentals into my head. Next day I scored three goals, one of
them the winning score, against the station champions. Moore
waved my thanks aside. "You silly clot," he told me, "you
don't think I did it for *your* sake, do you? Dear me, no. The
odds were seven to one against your team, and I had ten quid
that were burning a hole in my pocket."

Unlike the American system, an RAF pilot chose his own
crew. The rugger victory must have done something for my
standing at the field, for suddenly I had no trouble getting together a good crew, whereas previously likely candidates except for Johnny Kelly, had avoided me with shifty eyes and
transparent excuses. Gus Casorso, British Columbia, came in as
navigator; Don McEntee of Toronto as bomb-aimer; Will
Willmer, a Londoner, as wireless operator, and Johnny, Manitoba, as rear gunner.

My job was to learn to fly the heavy bomber aircraft, the
Wellington, and to weld the crew into an operational unit.
Affectionately known as the "Wimpy" from the name of the
hamburger-loving character, the Vickers Wellington was the
toughest of the older bombers. Wellingtons had returned from
raids with fuselages and wings practically stripped, apparently
unflyable. One Wellington, returning from Bremen, had
landed safely in England without flaps. In September 1939
Wellingtons took part in the first bombing attack by the RAF,
and in May 1942 in the first 1000-bomber raid on Cologne.
The reliable Wimpy had been the backbone of the early bombing campaign against Germany, and continued to be so until
the four-engined heavies gradually took over.

My first initiation into flak came after a month of dual cross-countries to various points in England and Scotland. Naval Command told Geoff Moore they were having trouble with blackouts at Sheerness and Chatham, and wanted somebody to do a night aerial survey to determine where the lights were showing. Geoff asked me if I wanted to come along for the ride and to get some experience in night flying.

The crew was from Geoff's D Flight, and he was pilot. We took off from Wellesbourne, making for the east coast and flying out into the North Sea. Then due south till we reached our current position off Dungeness Head. All went well; we were flying smoothly up the Thames Estuary, looking for blackout areas, when without warning the searchlights came on and heavy flak started thumping up around us, leaving big black puffs in the sky. Geoff cursed the Anglo-Saxons from King Alfred to Neville Chamberlin and took evasive action, tossing the plane about like a little single-engine fighter. But we were coned, and the flak was vicious. There was a sudden sound of ripping. Geoff put the nose down and dove, swinging hard from right to left. Then he pulled the stick sharply back and the Wimpy went up again, gaining altitude. The searchlights fell away.

A naval lieutenant had come along as observer, and Geoff grinned into his pea-green face. "Some of our batteries were obviously not advised of our experiment," he explained cheerfully. But at the field, after a night-flying supper of bacon and eggs and lashings of hot tea, nobody really felt worse for the "snowball" unless it was the naval lieutenant, who on landing discovered that a fragment of flak had hit within three inches of his head. That had been the ripping sound we'd heard.

On April 2, at 8:15 in the morning, the PA in the mess ordered Flight Lieutenant Lauro to report to A Flight immediately. Geoff told me we were doing an air test at nine and would take off on our first operation to Düsseldorf that night. He would be pilot, I copilot.

I collected the crew. At Dispersal we finished our cockpit

drill and took off on course over the English coast. Once there
Kelly tested his guns and McEntee dropped a few practice
bombs, Casorso checked his P-Box and Willmer his wireless
equipment.

Meanwhile Geoff and I were checking to see that the engines weren't overheating and the oil pressure was satisfactory.
We carefully tested the intercom and oxygen systems on this,
our last opportunity to determine if anything was wrong before penetrating deep into enemy territory. An hour and a half
later we landed back at Wellesbourne.

Geoff's orders were to take off for Düsseldorf at 1800 hours.
Gus went to the Intelligence Room to pore over maps of the
Ruhr area, paying particular attention to known flak and
searchlight concentrations and fighter airdromes. Kelly had a
last-minute swap-up in aircraft recognition. Briefing time
would be announced later.

Over lunch in the mess we discussed anything and everything but the impending raid. At 2:25 we reported to briefing.
Geoff Moore arrived a minute or two later, and at 2:30 sharp
Wing Commander Oldroyd came into the room accompanied
by Group Captain Jordan. The men rose. "Sit down, chaps,"
said Jordan, "and let's get on with it."

On the platform the curtains were open to reveal an over-
sized map of Germany. Routes were traced by thick pink-
colored lengths of wool string. We could see where the lines
went, to Happy Valley, the Ruhr. Our target, Jordan said, was
the Düsseldorf steel mills. Our route was Southwold to the
island of Shoen; and Shoen to Gelden, 20 miles from Düsseldorf, in hopes of misleading the Germans into thinking we
were headed for Essen. At Gelden we'd drop sharply south to
Düsseldorf. We would have an eight-minute run into target.
The moon would be good since Düsseldorf sat on the outside
of the loop on the River Rhine; we might well have visual
sight of the target and would be able to give it a good prang.
Take off was at 2030 hours.

Next was the armament officer, who came to the platform to brief the bomb-aimers on their loads. Some crews drew a mixed load of incendiaries and 500-pounders; others a load of 500's. Moore's crew drew a single 4000-pounder, as did one other.

Armament was followed by Navigation. Routes and various ETA's would be plotted with the navigators later on in the Navigation Room. Next was Intelligence, who pointed out the route. We shouldn't anticipate much trouble over Holland, but there was a big fighter base at Eindhoven, and no doubt these boys and those at Niemagen would be active in the area. We must remember the searchlight belt which ran more or less right up to the border of Germany on one side, and Luxembourg, Belgium and Holland on the other. It was 40 miles in extent and there was nothing for it but to fly on through.

Gelden, Intelligence went on, was a railroad center approximately 6 miles on the other side of the Maas River. Swinging sharply southwest, our route would take us between Duisburg and Kresau, straight down to the River Rhine. We would fly over the Rhine and then along its eastern side to Düsseldorf. Intelligence explained how important it was to knock out the Düsseldorf steel mills and shipyards.

Intelligence was followed by Signals, who spoke chiefly to the wireless operators, giving them their course signs and a list of enemy beacons with positions. After Signals came Gunnery, which reminded their boys to be watchful for fighters attacking from the dark side of the moon.

The Squadron bomb-aimer next had a few words concerning bomb loads, settings to be used on bombsights, and what to do in case of hang-ups.

Last was the "Met," or weather officer. Met told us there would be cloud over the North Sea which would gradually thin. Wind over the target was from the southeast. There should be no trouble on return; neither rain nor fog was predicted, nor any danger of icing.

Oldroyd read off our takeoff times, and captains were delegated to name one man of each crew to come forward to collect escape and ration kits. Oldroyd said he would see the crews
at night-flying supper at 6 P.M. Then Jordan ended the briefing. He said, "Go out and hit the bloody SOB's and hit them
hard. I want this squadron top of the ladder for bombing.
Drop your loads where it's going to hurt most and a good trip
to you all."

Geoff Moore and I went down to Flights to give the aircraft
a final going over. We checked the oxygen, the fuel supply,
the 4000-pound cookie on which the ground crew had chalked
some humorous obscenities to Hitler. Having satisfied ourselves
that all was "on the top line" with the Wimpy, we went to
Navigation, where Gus Casorso was poring over his maps with
protractors, slide rules and wind-velocity gauges. Gus gave us
estimated turning times for various points. Then Geoff and I
stopped off at Intelligence, where our route was marked for
flak areas, searchlight belts and night fighter airdromes.

Picking up the pointer, Geoff indicated my part in the op.
Since I had no experience with a "loaded" takeoff, he would
do the takeoff and show me how it differed from an ordinary
one. After we were on course and climbing, I'd take over and
fly to the Dutch coast. From then on to target Moore would
be at the controls and I'd keep an eye peeled for fighters in
the astrodome. Geoff would fly out from target and across the
searchlight belt, but coming across Holland I'd take over again.
If we were hit by flak Geoff would show me how to deal with
it. He would do the night landing. He slapped me on the back
and said he'd see me in the mess at six for night-flying supper.

I couldn't get much of the bacon and eggs down. Geoff kept
quoting from Shakespeare till I had a vision of dropping our
cookie on the Memorial Theatre in Stratford, with Falstaff,
Henry IV, Coriolanus and various supernumeraries blasted
skyward at a terrific rate. He finished his tea, stretched and
said he wanted the crew on Flight at 7:30 for our 8:30 takeoff.

We were to meet in his office in flying kit at a quarter to eight.

There he checked our escape documents and money and made sure there was nothing in our pockets which would be information of value to the enemy. Those of us wearing side arms had to give them up; there was nothing that would get us killed faster on the ground if the kite went down.

By a few minutes after eight the final aircraft check was complete. Geoff signed the "700," warranting that all was in order at takeoff. We climbed into the ship. Geoff gave orders for contact port and starboard, and the engines began their warm-up. Cockpit drill done, Geoff signaled to the ground crew to pull the chocks away and we taxied out to the taxi track.

It was a beautiful, starlit night. Red lights glimmered over the tops of hangars; the taxi track, with its blue lights, looked like an endless road. Our Wimpy, as one of the two carrying a 4000-pound load, was next to last to take off of the eight aircraft.

On our position short of the runway we swung into the wind, and Geoff, awaiting our turn, ran up the engines. The old Wimpies lumbered up for takeoff one after the other, and then we got the green.

Geoff knew he'd have to be well up in the 100 speeds before the heavy-laden crate would lift. In a steady climb at 125 m.p.h. he swung on to our first course to Southwold. Soon we were at 7000 feet. Crossing over the English coast, Geoff switched off the navigation lights and IFF (Identification Friend or Foe) and switched on the built-in radar-sonar device, which enabled our own aircraft to be distinguished from enemy planes. From now on, he said, we were liable to meet with trouble at any moment. Over the intercom he told Kelly to keep a sharp eye out for fighters, particularly down moon and from the dark side.

Our next pin point was the enemy coast, and he had to hit it right on the nose, on landfall. If we went too far north we'd run into Schidm and the Hague, and the flak over Rotterdam. If we got too far south we'd run into the heavy flak at Rousendall and Antwerp.

We kept climbing on course. At 17,000 feet, over the Dutch coast, Geoff gave me the controls. Settling in, I checked the fuel reading; we'd been flying for an hour and should have used a maximum of 90 gallons. Actually we'd used 85. Over the intercom Geoff told Willmer to be sure he'd wound in the trailing aerial after getting his last fix; he didn't want it hanging below in case he got in trouble and had to dive for the deck.

The stars looked close enough to touch. From the copilot's window on the starboard side Geoff was in a position to watch the star that mattered most on German raids—the North Star. If in a raid over Germany you got lost and your compass went west, all you had to do was find the North Star and keep it over your right shoulder on your starboard side, and from that you knew you were heading home. You might hit England anywhere between the north of Scotland and the south of England, but at least you'd get to the North Sea and know where you were from there.

We were still at 125 m.p.h. at an altitude of 13,500. In the astrodome Geoff was puffing on a cigarette. Smoking was forbidden but many captains allowed their crews to smoke as long as lit butts weren't dropped on the floor. Geoff returned to say it was a bright moonlit night and that we should have no trouble over the target. It was 20 minutes till our ETA over the enemy coast. The front gunner should be sighting the coast in six or seven minutes.

There was flak ahead to the south, rosettes of bursting flame in the sky. Geoff said it was probably from the Kraut batteries at Middleburg. If so we should be on course and in a matter of minutes see flak coming up at Rotterdam.

Three minutes later Geoff told me to look ahead to the left on the port side. It was Rotterdam, about ten miles away, and some poor devil had been coned by the German searchlights there. The colored flak climbed up lazily—light flak that went to around 10,000 feet. Geoff asked me in all seriousness if I didn't think it was pretty.

He told the bomb-aimer and gunners to keep their eyes peeled up and down and also on the ground. If they saw a flash below they were to yell "Flash!" immediately. That probably meant that batteries below were opening up and would give us the chance to stuff our nose down and lose altitude quickly. By the time the shell arrived we'd be 200 feet below it.

We were an hour to target, just south of Braden and Tilbert, when Geoff took over from me again. Seconds later Willmer yelled "Flash!" Geoff dove, pulling the nose first to left and then to right. There was a savage *c—rump* and a black puff of smoke blossomed off to the left. Geoff wove ten or eleven degrees right and left. More flak. Cheerfully he told me that the only kind of flak you had to worry about was the kind you didn't see or hear.

Off about two miles to the north a Wimpy, hit by flak, went down flaming. There was an enormous flash as its bomb load went up at about a thousand feet. Was it one of ours? I didn't ask Geoff and he volunteered no information.

Thirty minutes later we were over the searchlight belt. Geoff asked me conversationally what cone I fancied. The one slightly south? No, he didn't think so. He thought he'd rather try the one slightly to the north, because south was where the real mess was—Munchen, Gladbach and Reinhausen. He wanted to keep out of that lot. Admittedly Duisburg and Oberhausen, with their heavy flak concentrations, lay north on our route, but you couldn't have it both ways.

By now we were halfway through the searchlight belt. Off to the left about three miles away fighters were attacking a little silver dot caught in the beams. The dot dove and disappeared; immediately the Wimpy behind it flew transfixed in the searchlights' glare. We were almost through. So far our luck was good; we had been seriously menaced by neither flak nor fighters.

We were looking for the loop in the Rhine; on its eastern bank lay Düsseldorf. The name had an ominous ring; hadn't some pathological murderer committed some horrible crimes against children there? It occurred to me we were perhaps about to commit another. How many children would be among the casualties of tonight's raid? I told myself to try not to think in terms of absolutes but relatively; the other way lay madness.

We were over an area of heavy fires now and heading into the bomb run. On the I.P. Geoff turned the plane over to McEntee. McEntee began his easy corrections: "I've got the target now on sight, everything going along smoothly."

"Good show," Geoff told him, "let's try and make it on one run." And to the rest of us: "Keep your eyes peeled for fighters, because at bomb's away I'll give the signal to head for home."

McEntee said now over the intercom, "Steady now, approaching target." He sounded like a professional and I was proud of him. For fifteen seconds there was silence, and then Mac said, "Bombs away." The Wimpy lurched a little as the 4000-pounder dropped from its belly.

Geoff pushed the nose down to get a little more speed and made a diving turn away from target. There were bursts of flak all around us as Geoff took evasive action, heading for the outskirts of the city. Searchlights blinded us briefly. Then a sharp left turn and we were back on the route we'd come.

Half an hour later Geoff and I changed seats again. There was flak to the south as I turned slightly north on Gus's new course. Our ETA to the coast was an hour and twenty minutes. "Don't relax," Geoff told Kelly, "the Kraut fighters try to catch bombers coming home with their bloody guards down."

We caught the English coast well on landfall, joined the

circuit and requested permission to land. After the wheels touched down the camera was taken off quickly for film development.

Then we were off to debriefing. I was answering my third question when I knew I was going to be sick. The feeling passed, to hit me a short time later when we were going into the mess for night-flying supper. I stumbled off around the side of the mess hall and retched.

Someone put a hand on my shoulder. "Feel all right, Joe?" I looked into Geoff Moore's kindly, lined face and nodded. "O.K.," he said, "it's off to bed with you. Rugger at ten sharp tomorrow morning."

In early March, with a superior rating from Geoff Moore, I was assigned to No. 424 Squadron, based at Topcliffe, Yorks.

No. 424, the "Tiger" Squadron, had been formed in October, 1942. It was one of the eight Canadian squadrons called "Six Group" under the Canadian commander Air Vice Marshal G.E. Brookes. Before the end of the war "Six Group" was to grow to fourteen heavy bomber squadrons. It was part of the greatest air offensive in history, a concentrated year-long drive on Germany's industrial centers which lasted until D-Day and the softening of Nazi defenses and communications for the attack across the channel. Its battle record was "excelled by none and equalled by few."

Topcliffe was in the East Riding of Yorkshire, rolling, gentle country filled with aging, mellow towns: East Moore, Middleton, St. George, Croft, Leeming, Skipton. A peaceful countryside of great wide orchards, pastures, cornfields and woodland surrounded by the flat, gray English hills. Yet only fifty miles to the east the bitter North Sea roared against the coast, and from the East Riding pilots of the 6th took off for a major operation almost every time they left the ground.

The perils were many. Enemy intruders, as at Wellesbourne,

often waited for "Six Group" bombers above their own airfields when they came home at dawn. The Group's geograph-
ical situation was difficult: as the most northerly group in
Bomber Command, its flying time to targets averaged about
an hour more than that of southerly based groups. Yorkshire's
topographical features added hazards to operational flying.
Airfields were in close proximity to each other, increasing the
danger of over-flying the field orbits in climbing or descending. Industrial smoke from the Leeds-Bradford area came in
on the south wind, and on the north, smog from Middle-
borough. Because of these factors "Six Group" air crews flew
longer and under conditions of higher risk near home than
did others, and their ground crews worked longer hours under
greater pressure.

In March 1943 more than 10,000 tons of bombs were
dropped on German heavy industry targets in the Ruhr. The
attack of March 5 marked a turning point of the war in the
air. The main force of RAF bombers, made up of more than
400 Lancasters, Wellingtons, Halifaxes and Stirlings, dropped
more than 600,000 pounds of 4000-pound blockbusters and
incendiaries. When I and my crew arrived at Topcliffe on
the 12th the boys were still talking about the March 5th raid.

The violent explosions had hung a huge orange-colored
cloud in the sky and the sheets of flame which shot up to
heights of 6000 feet were so brilliant that they lighted the
dark cockpits of the aircraft. Men who flew near the rear of
the main bomber-stream saw clouds of smoke hanging 15,000
feet in the air as they left Happy Valley.

I flew my first sortie at Topcliffe the night of March 23, a
mining operation on the German shipping lanes off Heligo-
land in which I acted as copilot. Every squadron in the Group
was at Duisburg on the 26th, and two days later I was copilot
for the third time when the squadron bombed St.-Nazaire. On

April 2 I captained a Wellington with my regular crew for a raid on the sub pens at Lorient.

It was an easy do; on previous raids Lorient had been badly battered and flak was light. There was little above ground to catch fire. Yet one plane went down. After interrogation Don McEntee came to see me deep in the glooms.

"Skipper, the squadron was lucky today. Do you realize that on the average two or three kites in seventeen are lost on every raid?"

I said I realized it.

Don said dolefully, "It doesn't take a mathematician to figure a crew's chance of surviving a thirty-trip tour at this rate is about one in five."

"It's worse than that, Mac. I've lost my Sacred Heart medal."

He blanched. "Oh no! Can you borrow another?"

"None available at the station. I've got to write home for one."

Now he was positively white. "That might take weeks. My God, we'll be on five, ten trips before it arrives!" He lunged for his cap and started from the hutment, and I asked where he was going in such a rush.

"To town, to see what I can find at the jewelers."

I wrote to Father Lux in Chicago: "McEntee has figured the crew's chances mathematically and says our kite should be going down around mid-June, so pray for us. Please send me a Sacred Heart medal airmail—mine was lost and McEntee is frantic.

"We have a nice setup here at the station—mass and communion at 5:15 P.M. One can't be better prepared for combat nor be in a happier frame of mind when he hears mass and receives communion only a few hours before takeoff. To know that three of you in the kite have received earlier in the evening fills one with a kind of calm joy. I've named our Wimpy *Regina Coeli*, the Queen of Heaven."

I started another letter to Monsignor Gaffney at St. John's, but the words wouldn't come; it was as if I were on another planet with light years between us and no hope of communication. Had I, less than two years ago, walked the halls of St. John's in cassock and prayed in its silences? It seemed improbable. When a fellow officer came in and asked me to join him at the Officers' Mess I was glad of the interruption. He was going to teach me how to sing in close harmony, "Where Are the Lads of the Village Tonight" and "The Ball at Kirriemur."

We started a series of long missions to Frankfurt, Stuttgart and Mannheim. No. 3 to Frankfurt was one of the longest trips —over eight hours—and No. 4 to Stuttgart only a little less. Stuttgart was good weather with a "wizard" moon. Crossing the French coast two Junker 88 night-fighters settled on our tail. Odd bursts from Kelly's guns kept them at a distance and they broke off after twenty minutes without firing a shot. Kelly had been firing for so long that smoke had filled the cockpit nauseatingly; I had to open the side window to clear the fumes. Over the target we saw a fine fireworks display— sheets and sheets of orange 20 millimeter flak fired up to 10,000 feet. When we got back Gus Casorso told me that on bomb run another Junker 88 had passed overhead going in the opposite direction, so close that Gus had ducked his head beneath the astrodome. The Queen took seven big flak holes.

Mission No. 7 was again to Stuttgart. We crossed the French coast at Dieppe at around 10,000 feet and flew a route south of Mannheim. Looking over to Mannheim we could see some British planes caught in searchlights and flak; their navigators had gone off course and I was grateful for Gus's accurate plottings.

At Heidelberg we started our turn toward Stuttgart. Hitting the searchlights over the city I had to take evasive action, and the first bomb run was spoiled. On the next we came so close to another kite that I was forced to break off. I made the next run at 6000 feet, figuring that taking a chance on catching a bomb from another kite above was preferable to the risks of collision and flak at a higher altitude.

As we began the final bomb run McEntee intoned, "O.K., Skipper, I've got a pin point. Coming up on target. Air speed 140, altitude 6000. Now make a slight correction of three degrees left. Steady, Skipper, steady . . . Two degrees left, Skipper . . . Steady, hold her. Target coming up and bombs away . . . Photo-flash and a good strike."

Taking an immediate left-hand turn, I saw a sheet of light flak coming up beyond our altitude. I changed course with a hard right over the target. There was the sudden sound of bursting flak along the spars like bouncing ping-pong balls, and I felt a sharp, burning sensation down my left side. The kite was still in its steep turn. I pushed the nose down for speed, straightened her out and headed away from target. The crew was untouched, it developed; I was the only one hit. There was a hole in my flying suit at mid-waist and it was soaked with blood. I used my handkerchief as a bandage and took a whiff of pure oxygen as a pick-me-up.

Thirty minutes later, crossing the French coast, two JU 88's jumped us and for the next half-hour made continuous passes. It was harrowing. After Kelly had damaged one they broke off at the channel and we headed for home. I began saying the rosary with the stars as beads, thanking God for the narrow escape.

There were sixty flak and cannon holes in the Queen when we landed at base, more than enough to put her in for repairs. When the Doc probed me for flak fragments they dropped out easily; it had been a ricochet. Doc took three stitches.

Mac was waiting for me when I came out of hospital. "I hear there's a package for you at Admin from the States."

I knew he was hoping it was the Sacred Heart medal from Father Lux; he hadn't been able to find one in town. "O.K., let's go and see," I said, and started off. Then I stopped, aggrieved. "Aren't you going to ask how I am?"

"I figure you're all right, Skipper. You're walking."

It was the medal from Chicago. Mac asked me to start wearing it around my neck *now*.

In late April, preparing for takeoff on a mission to Duisberg in the Ruhr, I'd just gotten the green light when Johnny Kelly intercommed, "Skipper, can you pull off?" I asked him if something was wrong and he said no, he'd forgotten something. "Is it vital or can we go without it?" I asked, and he told me, "Skipper, I need it badly."

The Group Captain came over as Kelly got out of the plane. "What's up, Sergeant?" he wanted to know, and Kelly told him he'd forgotten something. Groupie made a face. "Must be pretty important to have your pilot pull off the runway when he's got the green light." Still, he asked no further questions and got Johnny a lorry to go back to his hut.

When Johnny returned I asked him what it was he'd forgotten. "My rosary," he said matter-of-factly. Only when we were underway did I remember that he was an Anglican and none too devout at that.

Duisberg was another hairy do. The sky seemed full of searchlights and flak and so much evasive action was necessary that I found it hard to keep steady for Mac's bomb run. On return strong winds and more evasive action took us off course; Casorso finally fixed our position over Amsterdam. At the Zuider Zee an Me-109 angled in for the kill and broke off after a long burst from Kelly's guns.

When we got back the Squadron Leader was waiting for me on the runway. I knew from his expression that something bad had happened. The news had come over the Operations wire an hour ago. My mother had died of a heart attack.

"You better pack a bag and take a week off," Squad told me. "The funeral's set for day after tomorrow."

Numbly I went back to barracks and started packing. All

I could think of was that Mother, more than anything else, had wanted her son *Josiçu* to offer, as Father Lauro, her funeral mass. Midway through I stopped and went to Ops. I didn't want to go home for the funeral, I told them. My mother's sister had died in one of Hitler's Yugoslavian ovens and her nephew, a Partisan, put up against a wall and shot. I wanted to go up tomorrow night again with my crew.

Squad said, "Sure you won't change your mind?"

"No, sir."

"Well, you're due for a change of scene anyway. You'll hear about it tomorrow."

Next day they told us Squadron 424 was moving to Dalton, Yorks, to be equipped for operations in North Africa. There we'd be part of an all-RCAF bomber wing, No. 331, under Group Captain Dunlap, together with the 420th ("Snowy Owl") and the 425th ("Alouette"), both French-Canadian.

I had been promoted to Flying Officer.

I went over to Wellesbourne to say goodbye to Geoff Moore.

"North Africa's all sand, sweat and flies, Joe," he told me, "but an easier do than Six Group. Less fighters, searchlights and flak, and then of course there's the Italians. Something like moving down from your major leagues to—what do you call 'em?"

"The minors."

"Quite. Yet they're developing rugger players out there, men like Crawford and Milner and Jones. Don't forget when you're in the scrum that Wellesbourne sends out only *top line players*. Now let me diagram for you a couple of new plays I've come up with. . . ."

CHAPTER
2

ON May 21 Sq. 424 left Dalton for Port Reath on the coast, our English departure point for flying to North Africa by way of Gibraltar. Since our radio loop needed fixing, the Queen left a day later than the rest of the squadron.

It was a rough 12-hour trip. Two German fighters jumped us over the Bay of Biscay but we finally lost them in heavy cloud. Crossing the Spanish coast, Franco's ack-ack batteries tried to knock us down. Landing on the postage-stamp runway at Gibraltar, we almost overshot it into the sea, and once we were on the ground what Gus confessed left me weak and trembling. His radio bearing from stations in France had been inaccurate. If he hadn't spotted from the astrodome Cape St. Vincent, Portugal, our first turning point, his ETA would have been fifteen minutes and probably fifteen miles off. Which meant that we would have run out of petrol miles before reaching the Big Rock and had to ditch in the sea.

That night we loaded up on oranges in town. I hadn't seen an orange since Saskatchewan.

Next afternoon, still a day behind the squadron, we left for Raz-El-Ma, Morocco. Fez was a short trip away by truck and we wandered around the dirty, unsanitary streets aimlessly. Willmer kept saying, "I was never farther from London than

Birmingham, and now they've put me down in the middle of the bloody A-rabs, by God." We went to an Arab coffee house for dinner. I was paying the check when an RAF type with a handlebar moustache stopped at the table. Taking the money out of my hand he returned half of it and dropped the rest on the waiter's tray. "Bloody overcharging wogs," he said to the waiter's retiring back. "Can't trust a ruddy one of 'em. Bound for the desert, are you?"

We nodded.

"Well, watch out for Arab saboteurs in German pay. Last week they planted a bomb at British HQ in Rabat. It wasn't pleasant. Cheerio." He moved away.

McEntee paled. "What did he mean, Skipper?"

"Odds are going up, Mac. One in six now, maybe. Lots of Arabs don't like the British here."

"But I'm a *Canadian*, damnit!" howled Mac, to laughter.

We caught up with the rest of the squadron at Talergma, Algeria, and had a two-week wait there till our base was ready at Pavillier, Tunisia, in the Sousse area. Squadrons 420 and 425 were based elsewhere within a radius of 40 miles. There wasn't much to do except read, sleep and go into Constantine and Monaster for swimming, shopping and rubbernecking. One day in the marketplace I found a Mohammedan *ulema* selling rosaries. I bought two and gave the man 500 francs. When he handed me change I waved it away and asked him to say some prayers for us. A look of horror came over his face and he pressed the money on me saying, "No, *Effendi*, a thousand times no! For this much money I would have to pray for *five years!*"

On June 22, in a driving rainstorm, we arrived at Pavillier. Our tents still weren't pitched and we had to sleep in the kite. M.T. trucks were filled to capacity with sleeping airmen and officers.

Next day the rain stopped, and after spending another night in the same way everybody felt dirty, wet and miserable. Our only food was bread and soup. Then the mud began to dry and we started putting up the wooden frame tents.

It was nice to get rid of the mud, but that meant that we had to cope with the sand and the dust. Sand and dust were everywhere; in the engines, in your eyes, your hair and even your food except when it rained, when everything turned back into mud. Sand was in the water and on the surface of everything that had a surface.

The grittiness became synonymous with the heat; grit on your face and body was the same as being hot. You had the idea that if you could only wash all the grittiness off and get into some clean clothes you'd be cool, despite the high temperature and humidity. Once a week, when the water bowzer pulled into the base, we had a half-minute shower.

And if it wasn't the dust and the black beetles that swarmed into the tents it was the sweat and the flies, and the wet nights and the cold mornings. If you could get rid of the flies, you thought, you wouldn't sweat so much. And if you didn't sweat so much you wouldn't feel so hot. Soon we were going around bare-chested, having shucked our RCAF issue shirts and suspenders. The only trouble with this was that the RCAF hadn't provided belts.

Then there was the food, which was poor. There were only service rations available in the mess, which was another tent, and we supplemented this sludge with eggs, when we could buy them from the Arabs, figs, tea and the potent native wine. Over stoves improvised from cast-off equipment and empty shell cases we brewed our tea, which somehow always tasted like glycerine. It was a big day when we could go into town for a French or native meal, pork with spice-flavored beans, or *kush-kush*, ground pork.

Often you heard from the tents voices raised in song:

> Behind every silver lining
> A dark cloud is hiding,
> And only troubles lie ahead.
> Cheer up, Old Man, you'll soon be dead.

Squadron 424 began operations on the night of June 27, Corpus Christi Sunday, with an attack on San Giovanni, on the Italian mainland across from Messina. Mass was celebrated at 7 A.M. near the mess overlooking the runways that were nothing more than bulldozer-packed sand with a few landing lights strung along them. Two of our ground crew were at the service, and as we walked to breakfast they told me everything with the Queen was on the top line. Yet they nonetheless went through a final general inspection that lasted two hours. By the time they finished the temperature had reached 132° in the shade. Inside the Wimpy it was 152°.

After a light lunch we had a siesta till four, but the flies and the heat made sleep impossible. At four thirty we heard we were on that night. When the sun had vanished below the hills the kites were brought into line for takeoff.

The Queen was number four of eight aircraft. "All set for takeoff?" I called and in quick succession got affirmative replies from the crew. After a final cockpit check I slowly advanced the throttles. The engines roared louder as the throttles opened wide. Quickly the Queen's speed built up although the heavy 4000-lb. bomb held her to the ground. The red lights marking the end of the runway came into view as the speedometer reached the 100 m.p.h. mark and I began to lift her for takeoff.

Suddenly the kite shuddered and runway dust filled the cockpit. Shaking violently, the plane leaped into the air. I pressed down on the brakes to stop the spinning wheels. Keeping throttles advanced, I tried to build up airspeed and get some height. We circled the drome and at 1000 feet the Wimpy felt normal.

A red flare went up at the end of the runway: trouble on the ground. For the first time since takeoff I broke silence and told the crew there must be something wrong below. I knew they were worried about the peculiar takeoff but I couldn't afford to show I was worried too; they'd all get the jitters.

"What's the course, navigator?" I asked, and Gus answered, "0-9-1 degrees, Skipper. You can climb to operational height."

I asked Mac to check the bomb bay. He looked through the peephole and intercommed, "Skipper, our cookie's gone. The nuts must have been oversize and the bomb vibrated off on takeoff."

At least, I thought, it hadn't exploded. With weather and visibility good I decided to go on to target and drop our 500-pounders. It was preferable to pulling an abort on our first North African mission. And in any case the field hadn't signaled us in.

On our approach flak was light and inaccurate. With "Bomb's Away" there were answering bursts, seconds later, below in the San Giovanni freight yards.

Flak exploded near the tail and Kelly yelled, "Let's get out of here!"

Back at Pavillier the erks were grimly apologetic. We'd lost our cookie when the kite was only three feet off the ground. Had we been any lower the bomb would have cata-pulted the plane, and had we been any higher the 4000-pounder would have exploded. Another Wimpy had crashed into the unexploded bomb, wrecking completely but with no loss of life. Still another aircraft had taken off over the wreck before the ground crew had discovered anything amiss and sent up its flares.

The ribbing I took for flying to target with a cookieless bomb bay lasted a week. At least three officers, knowing I was a devout Catholic and assisted Father Laplante, the chap-

lain of Alouette Squadron, asked me with straight faces if
I'd drop a 4000-pounder on Rome. "Rome's an open city," I
told them evasively. Garbled versions of the bomb episode
were still alive at RAF bases in Tunisia a year later, and it was
immortalized in the RCAF combat manual.

For the next three months Bomber Wing 331 was active in
an all-out bombing campaign which softened the Axis defenses in Sicily and Italy in preparation for the Allied invasions. Airfields, railroad centers and lines of communication
were attacked again and again and thousands of leaflets scattered over Italian cities advising civilians to evacuate. Raids
were carried out almost every night for as many as five without
a break. The total for August was no less than twenty-five.

The consolation for all this work lay in the weakness of the
opposition. Time after time I wrote in my crew report "enemy defenses weak or negligible." Except for one or two key
points, such as Messina and Naples, anti-aircraft guns were
few and inaccurate, searchlights likewise few and night-
fighters rarely encountered. Nothing could have been in
sharper contrast to the terrific opposition from flak, searchlight cones and enemy fighters 424 had run into against German targets in the Ruhr. As a result our Wimpies were able
to bomb their objectives from much lower altitudes than had
been possible over the Reich, and losses on the whole were
extremely light.

Yet men died. On July 6 aircraft were standing by ready for
takeoff when one Wimpy, loaded with 5000 lbs. of high explo-
sives, caught fire and blew up. At the time I was waiting in
line for mess, and like everybody else I jumped for the nearest
slit trench. Seconds later another Wimpy with full bomb and
gas loads exploded, sending smoke and shrapnel 500 feet into
the air, the flaming petrol and debris starting several grass
fires. Several airmen in the vicinity were hit by flying shrapnel;
three were killed and a dozen wounded or burned. I saw one

man aflame, running in a circle until he collapsed to the ground; it was too late for the blankets others were rushing to him.

There was no doubt that saboteurs were responsible, and I thought of the RAF-type's warning in Fez. A round-the-clock guard was put on all planes in the squadron and base security stiffened.

All those who had been involved in the fire-fighting were given a 24-hour leave in Monaster, a small town ten miles from Sousse on the coast. Gus and I missed the truck but got a ride in on an A Flight car. We had no bathing trunks; at the beach Gus went in the water in his underwear shorts and I wore my khakis. Just as we were coming out a group of French girls sat down on the beach to chatter.

"I'll bring you your pants," I told Gus and left the water. But all I did was lie down on the sand. Everytime Gus yelled for his pants I raised my hand with one finger pointing to the sky in timeless insult. It was an hour before the girls went home, and Gus emerged from the water as wrinkled as a newborn infant.

On July 9 Allied invasion forces set off across the narrow strip of sea to Sicily. Over them, laying down an aerial barrage to cover the landings, flew medium and heavy bombers of the North-West African Air Forces while the Navy shelled the mainland with heavy artillery. Meanwhile other Wimpies patrolling over the sea and the Sicilian coast reported seeing large numbers of barges and ships of all descriptions converging on the landing beaches.

The Queen was to be part of the sea patrol but we were canceled. All we could do was stand by a fig tree eating half-green figs and watching the American planes from nearby 9th Air Force bases rallying overhead. From this operation Pilot Officer Leddy did not return, but we found out later he had crash-landed near Sousse. Leddy and crew were back at the base next day.

We were briefed again for an op over Sicily but an hour before takeoff Sergeant Trefenenko's Wimpy exploded just as it left the ground. The Sergeant and his four-man crew were killed. That afternoon we were part of the burial party at Kairowan Cemetery, outside Tunis. Coming back in the truck, Gus lit a cigarette with shaking fingers. "This sabotage is beginning to get on my nerves," he said, speaking for all of us.

"The Queen's a lucky ship," said Willmer, who spoke seldom. "Everybody says so. Why else would Dunlap want to borrow it? Everybody says nothing'll ever happen to the Queen." He sounded hopeful.

"Trefenenko won twenty thousand francs at poker," said Kelly thoughtfully. "He was going to send it home to his wife. He borrowed a stamp from me, but he hadn't mailed the letter. Somebody'll have to see that letter gets mailed."

My logbook for the next few days read:

"Sunday, July 11. Briefed for Augusta in Sicily but Allied advance so fast our target changed to Montecorvina, an airdrome southeast of Naples. Drome easily spotted; light flak; forty planes destroyed on the ground. On way home saw paratroopers being dropped on west coast of Sicily. A beautiful sight, like white gardenia petals floating to the ground. But behind a battle royal raging—naval and flak guns firing, invasion barges approaching the beach. One plane, probably U.S., exploded in mid-air.

"Tuesday, July 13. Target Messina; objective to bomb last ferry and docks in operation. Almost a full moon and you could see Mount Etna 20 miles away. On the way back 20 mm. flak swept up in our direction and I quit breathing and said a prayer and heard Father Lux asking: 'What are you saving yourself for, Joe?' and I answered him, 'This, I guess.'

I started to laugh and Gus wanted to know if I'd gone crazy. But the flak quit and there was no further trouble. On this trip two planes shot down, one from Sq. 429. Ron Mang, Davidson, Jack Garland and Vanderbeck did not return. Jack Garland was so handsome that even the Arab girls turned to look at him in the street. The lines of Laurence Binyon's beautiful poem kept going through my head: 'They shall grow not old as we that are left grow old;/ Age shall not weary them nor the years condemn./ At the going down of the sun and in the morning/ We will remember them.'

"Wednesday, July 14. Full moon with good visibility. Arrived at target area early and circled a few miles west of Capri to waste a little time. Could see Vesuvius spouting flames. Into target at 11,000 feet but the searchlights and flak drove us back over the bay. Made three more runs but couldn't get in. Headed for secondary target, Naples docks. While holding steady for the picture a heavy flakburst underneath the Queen and another off to the side. 'Let's get the hell out of here, Skipper!' yelled Kelly and I went into a dive giving the ship all she'd take. Eight flak holes on landing; McEntee examined them very carefully.

On July 22nd our destination was Salerno to drop leaflets. Fifteen miles coming back from target near Ustica Island, north of Sicily, the kite suddenly dropped its left wing and began to slip and spin to the left. I kicked right rudder hard and with all my strength pulled the steering column to the right in a vain effort to lift the left wing. Slowly the Queen began to come out of the slip and partial spin, but I was still fighting the controls.

The altimeter showed we'd lost fifteen hundred feet. I put my full weight against the steering column and yelled into the intercom, "Put on chutes and prepare to abandon aircraft on my command."

McEntee, white, handed me my chute. "What's wrong, Skip?"

"Aileron controls are jammed," I told him. "Don't know whether I can hold her up or not. Give me a hand."

With Mac's weight on the controls I was relieved of some of the strain and could try to fasten my chute. But with the chute in the way I could less effectively handle the controls, and pushing it aside with a sickening feeling, I asked Willmer to send a top priority message back to base requesting permission to abandon aircraft, if necessary, in the Mediterranean. Permission was granted.

We were at 1500 feet now, very little altitude in which to clear the crew and struggled into my chute. If I lost control of the kite the Queen would flip over on her back and crash into the sea.

Gus came in on the intercom: "Skipper, don't you think we better ditch than abandon the kite by chute?"

"We're going to try and make base," I told him. "Kelly can't swim. Better pray we don't run into any fighters and that the controls don't give way."

It took three hours to get to the mainland, every man in the crew spelling Mac and me at the controls. Over the Mediterranean a German or Italian cruiser took some pot shots at us and when I saw a Red Cross ship below I was going to give the order to ditch when I made out its German markings. At the drome I circled widely to prevent the wing from dropping. Slowly we lost height and came in for a landing with the crash trucks and ambulance waiting. We had a long approach to make and as I was about to touch wheels to runway a crosswind pushed us away. I opened throttle and gave it another try. This time, with allowance for crosswind drift, we approached the runway, but again the drift carried us away. To counteract it I opened up the outside engine to bring the aircraft back in line and we landed.

The erks told me that during one of my steep turns our

astro compass box had rolled back and jammed the aileron controls. Gus should have kept the box tied down properly, and I told him so.

Poker-faced, he handed me an orange. I laughed and began to peel it. I was bonesore and weary and so was every man in the crew, but it was too hot to stay in a flap.

My log book ran: "After such a shaky do Squadron Leader Klassen thought we should go out again so as not to lose our nerve. A fairly easy trip to San Giovanni till we reached the N.E. point of Sicily where the searchlights were plentiful and there was moderate flak. We made three runs over the target to drop our bombs—I still insisted on accuracy to save innocent lives and the crew was willing to go along—and then we proceeded to another point to drop leaflets. One shell burst fairly close to the tail. Kelly yelled, 'Skipper, what are we waiting for, the end of the war?' and I cleared out for home. On the way one of the classy new Italian fighters came in close, did some fancy stunting, and then sheared off as Kelly gave him a burst. Gus commented sourly over the intercom, 'These Eyeties got no guts.'

"July 24. 48 to Monaster to swim, eat, sleep and haggle with the merchants. Our favorite an Arab called, for no apparent reason, Geef Knife. Geef Knife sells melons. We bargain with the fellow for a long time and try to skin the last franc from his price.

" 'Your melons are green, Geef Knife.' "

" '*Non, non! Rouge, rouge!*' "

" 'No *rouge*, no pay, Geef Knife.' "

" '*Pas de vert! Rouge!*' "

" 'Green, damn it. One franc.' "

" 'Two franc.' "

" 'One franc, Geef Knife, thou great thief of the bazaar.' "

" 'Two franc. *Rouge!*' "

" '*Vert*. One.' "

"Sadly. 'One franc, messieurs. *Thees* melon. But two francs for the *rouge*.' "

"Tonight wrote Father Lux: 'I still keep your words before me: "What are you saving yourself for when the Lord lost Himself so that we might be saved?" The crew has heard me use the phrase often and associate it with my insistence, at whatever risk, of hitting the military objective only and avoiding scattered bombing. On the way back I ask McEntee, the bomb-aimer, several times, "How did we do?" and he must answer we were right on target or else I cannot rid myself of thoughts of the innocent killed or injured because of our inefficiency. Father, you can't help but make an act of contrition for those you might have killed, and you fall asleep thumbing your rosary for the innocent. One can't rid oneself of the afterthoughts and prayer is the only outlet.'

"July 25. Mussolini resigned. A lull in the bombing while Badoglio's new administration takes over.

"Tonight tried to make a phone call. The exchanges have code names and it went like this:

"Hello, Masterful, I want to call Nevertheless. What's that, I get Nevertheless by going through Lemonade to Hardtack? Thanks. Give me Lemonade, please. Hello, Lemonade, give me Hardtack . . . What's that, I get Hardtack by going through Biscuit to Contretemps? Give me Biscuit, then. The line is busy? No, Lemonade, I am *not* through . . . Give me Mountbatten and I'll go through Hades. You say the line to Mountbatten's out? Yes, I'm calling from Royal, I mean Sherwood. Then can I get—Oh, forget it. Can't remember who I wanted to call . . ."

"Wed. July 28. Phil Heden's Wimpy blew up on takeoff. His last mission; he and crew were due to return home tomorrow. Taylor, Souche and Barnes also killed instantly but Bjornsen, the rear gunner, lived for a while. Since we were next in line for takeoff I was able to get to the kite in time to help pull him from the turret. Dangerous work; bullets from

the machine gun clips exploding in the fire. Next day, operations canceled. Mac, Gus and I represented the crew in the
guard of honor that followed the boys' remains to Kairowan
Cemetery. There were graves of Africa Korps dead here,
wooden Iron Crosses above their heads; many of them no
more than sixteen or seventeen. At the base Doc Lindsay
asked me to write Phil's wife and sort out his personal things
for shipment home. Tunisian guards arrived to stop the sabotage and relieve ground crew losing sleep on guard detail; an
elaborate password system has been instituted. Anybody
approaching the aircraft must have a good reason.

"Sat. Aug. 1. Target Foggia. Coming back decided to fly
over Dalmatia to take a look at my father's birthplace near
the coast. No sooner were we over the island than Kelly
yelled, 'Fighter!' It was an Me-109 on our tail. He came
close but never opened fire, and I figured he could only be
unarmed and in training. When we landed Gus came up and
said, 'Flight Sergeant Casorso requests that you kindly save
your sightseeing for North Africa.' "

"From behind the dunes the wild dogs howl: these are the
animals abandoned by the soldiers of both armies who were
killed or captured. They roam the desert in packs in search
of food and so desperate and savage are they that we shoot
them on sight. Now from one of the tents a shot rings out.

"Monday, Aug. 3. Target Paoli in Southern Italy. Should
have turned back because rear turret out of commission but
Kelly and the rest of the crew being willing we carried on.
Target, freight yards, small and hard to find. Moderate flak.
Made five dummy runs before Mac dropped his bombs. Kelly
a bit resentful: 'Skipper, couldn't you have compromised on
four?'

"In pitch-black darkness, coming back to the tents from
the op, we were challenged by the Tunisian guard. 'Who
goes there?' asked the guard in French, and with a sinking
feeling I realized that all I remembered of tonight's password
was that it had something to do with world statesmen. Loudly,

but not too confidently, I called out, 'Roosevelt!' There was a pause and the guard repeated his question. 'Churchill!' said Gus, and then as the guard pulled back the bolt on his rifle, the click terrifyingly loud in the night, I told the boys softly, 'Hit the dirt when I call out Stalin.' 'Stalin!' I said, and the five of us threw ourselves to the ground. *'Passé,'* replied the guard, but we were slow to get up from the sand. McEntee brushed sand from his mouth and said, 'I could have sworn you were going to say Hitler.' "

The pause in the bombing was short-lived. By the first week in August, Wing No. 331 was active again, going out night after night without a break. Our objectives were to smash the Axis harbors and railroad yards, blast the last shreds of Axis resistance in Sicily, and harass the retreating Nazis.

The Queen was beginning to be talked about as a preternaturally "lucky" kite. Not only had there been our two narrow escapes with the lost bomb and the jammed aileron, but our kite damage from flak was about half that of other Wimpies in the squadron. When, for various reasons, other pilots took the Queen up they had remarkably easy trips with much the same minimum of damage.

This led to some curious developments. Pilots appeared at my tent to ask when my crew was getting its next forty-eight so they could put in a request to fly the Queen. I was offered as much as two thousand francs for any valuable advance information. People knew I attended mass and communion regularly, and attendance at Catholic religious services zoomed, several Protestant boys hedging their bets to appear as observers. Then my rosary was gypped.

I tacked a notice to the bulletin board saying, "Please note that the rosary borrowed from Flying Officer Lauro's quarters was not a Catholic but an Islamic rosary. Its return will be appreciated."

Next day there was an answer: "Sorry, chum, but taking no chances."

Three officers and four crewmen dropped into my tent to

talk religion. I referred them to Father La Plante, the Alouette squadron chaplain. Father told me an officer and three
crewmen had asked to take instruction.

Gus, a good Catholic, was disturbed by all this. "Suppose
we go for a Burton," he said. "I mean I think the Lord's with
us, He must be, but what if He changes his mind?" He shook
his head ominously. "It won't do the Church any good."

With a dozen missions to go they gave us a 48 and another
crew took up *Regina Coeli* while we were off the base. The
plane went down from flak over Italy but all five crew members parachuted to safety without a scratch and were taken
prisoner. Everybody said the Queen had been a lucky ship
even in her death.

They gave us another Wimpy and tension, already building, became close to intolerable. When, on August 16 and 17
we had to turn back with engine trouble, the crew took it
hard. But the trips thereafter were so easy, with one exception,
that we couldn't have asked for a smoother ride. The exception was a trip to Taranto in late August when we ran into
heavy flak and landed on one engine. A tire blew when we
hit the runway and the Queen II nosed into a ditch, pitching
my head against the plexiglass. Doc Lindsay, the Medical Officer, could find no injury but the next day a blinding headache
set in that lasted for hours. The Doc had only aspirin to give
me, and a shot, and they didn't work. Then suddenly the
headache improved although a throbbing persisted. I found
that pure oxygen at high altitudes helped when the pain got
severe.

Gus Casorso came down with yellow jaundice on our next
to the last trip and we had to get another navigator for the
last two. When the Queen's wheels touched down Wing
Commander Roy was waiting to salute every man in the crew.
Their commissions had come through and they were now the
only all-commissioned crew in the squadron, and for all I
knew, in North Africa. When I'd asked Roy to put in for

commissions for all four men he'd told me the chances were one in five thousand. Of course I was delighted for the boys but my headache was so bad that I had to go back to quarters to lie down.

I woke to see the crew standing by my cot. Somehow they'd gotten Gus out of hospital. Mac stepped forward and presented me with a fragment of shell casing that had the names of the crew engraved upon it. "We won't stay long, Skipper," he said. "We just wanted to say thanks for everything."

Before I could answer they'd left. I sat looking at the shell casing for a long time.

September 8 we got news of Italy's surrender. I dropped in on Winco Roy to check on my transfer to Mosquitoes, the fast, plywood planes that dropped pathfinding flares for the bomber crews.

Word had come that morning and it was in the negative. "Sorry, Joe," Roy told me. "You've got to take the usual nine months' standdown after the end of your tour and then instruct."

"Did Doc Lindsay rat on me?"

"What?"

I saw he hadn't. "Groupy," I said, "I want to fly Mosquitoes."

"These regulations make sense. You never know when combat fatigue's going to hit you."

I'd joined the RCAF to fly. If they wouldn't let me fly any more and the priesthood was still closed to me, then there was only the alternative of flying with the Army Air Corps. I went back to my tent and wrote the Corps in London requesting a transfer and not mentioning the headaches. Now all I had to do was persuade Doc Lindsay to keep mum when they checked my medical history.

Within the week we were cleared from the station to return to the U.K.

CHAPTER
3

MY Army Air Corps transfer came through in early November while I was at Wellesbourne flying unofficial missions with Geoff Moore. From one of these missions we almost failed to return when flak knocked out the starboard engine and two Me-109's attacked over the channel. By December 8 I was home with a week's leave before reporting to Hendricks Field, Sebring, Florida, for conversion to B-17 Flying Forts. Two days later Dwight Eisenhower was notified of his appointment as Supreme Commander, Allied Expeditionary Force. I wondered if I'd be back in Europe in time for the invasion.

I saw Father Lux and gave him two cartons of North African cigarettes. Passing Assumption Church, I caught a glimpse of Father Stukel at the rectory window. I ran into Father Bob Degnan and Vince Schuster, with whom I'd gone to pre-seminary school at Quigley Prep. Bob was long since ordained and serving as a missionary in Colombia. Vince had given up his plans to be a priest and was married and working in the city. One thing that Vince and I had in common was that neither of us had been ordained; with Bob the fact that he was now a priest set us apart as much as did my uniform with its embroidered RCAF wings on one side of my tunic and the silver Air Corps wings on the other. We talked with constraint, and watching Bob's black suit and Roman collar disappear down the street was painful. During mass at St. Theodore's I found it hard to concentrate.

My roommate at Hendricks Field was an ambitious, guardhouse lawyer type who made my life miserable when he figured out that my Air Corps rank equivalent to Flying Officer was Captain, not First Lieutenant.

"For God's sake," he badgered me, "are you going to let them get away with it?"

"Yes," I told him. "It doesn't matter all that much."

"Maybe not to you," he said bitterly, "but to me," and he beat his breast and gnashed his teeth, "it's torture."

From time to time I caught him watching me intently when my headaches were bad, and once he asked if the Air Corps knew about them. "The Corps knows everything," I said, and was afraid for a while that out of his guardhouse lawyer perfectionism he'd turn me in.

By February I was night flying on the big 4-engine Forts. Once my instructor told me to do some shallow, half-needle turns. When I did he grabbed the controls and said, his voice shaking, "Are you crazy, man? Do you call that a shallow turn? You want this plane to spin in on you?"

"Maybe my turn was a little steep," I admitted, "but it seemed to me that at 150 m.p.h. I had good airspeed."

"Just make those turns shallow," he snapped.

When we were on the ground he bugged me again about the steepness of my turns. Getting a little hot under the collar, I told him, "If this airplane can't do more than a full needle-width turn, it's not going to stay in the air against the Germans."

He looked amused. "And how would you know?"

Another instructor standing nearby knew about my RCAF record. "Lauro's had a couple of years' night flying with the British," he said.

My instructor reddened. "I'm sorry."

"Don't be," I told him. "I'm here to learn what you have to teach me."

The other instructor guffawed, and mine, muttering something, walked away. For the rest of the course he was decidedly cool. He couldn't believe I'd meant exactly what I said and I couldn't persuade him I hadn't been putting him down. The fruits of another anomalous situation.

At the end of training the Colonel asked me to stay on at Hendricks and instruct on B-17's. A man with my combat experience would be invaluable to the instruction program.

"Sorry, Colonel," I told him. "I want to go back to combat."

"Fellow, they won't *let* you go back. All returnees from overseas have got to stay stateside nine months to a year."

"Colonel, those are Air Corps regulations," I reminded him. "I transferred from the RCAF."

"That's just a technicality, Lauro, I can't ship you out. Your records say you're a returnee."

I was an anomaly again. I asked the Colonel if he'd let me try to clear up things with 2nd Air Force HQ in Fort Worth, and he said O.K. Two days later I was on a flight to Texas.

Two generals interviewed me, a one-star and a two. "We've got the word on you," the brigadier said ominously. "You want to go back to combat."

"That's right, sir."

"We need men like you as instructors," the major general said. "You've done your stint. Relax."

"Sir, are you grounding me?" I asked him.

The major general picked up a paper from my file. "Air Corps regulations state that a returnee must serve stateside for nine months to a year."

I sighed. "Sir, I was in the *RCAF*. Is Air Corps jurisdiction retroactive to another service?"

The brigadier said, "Are you going to hold us to a technicality? I think you want to kill yourself."

"Maybe the lieutenant could profit from some talks with a psychiatrist," said the major general.

"I'm asking you," I said, "not as officer to officer, but as one man to another. I want to fly in combat with an American crew. The best crew maintenance is in combat. Lately I've heard of a lot of fatalities among instructors. Will you do me a favor, General? . . . General?"

They finally gave in. Back at Hendricks I got orders to go to Casper, Wyoming, to crew up. My roommate was glad we were parting company; the strain had been too much for him.

"Promise me one thing," he begged, "that when you crew up you'll put in for Captain."

I said I'd think about it.

On the flight line at Casper were not the B-17's I'd transition-trained on at Hendricks but B-24 Liberators. I didn't know how to fly B-24's and told Administration so. Administration said it was impossible that I'd been trained on B-17's. If I'd been trained on B-17's, I wouldn't be at Casper.

"But I'm here," I reminded them.

They checked with Hendricks. Hendricks suggested that Casper send me back. I asked if there wasn't somebody at Casper who could give me some instruction on B-24's. That hadn't occurred to them. They assigned Captain Brasher to me on the understanding that if I hadn't learned how to fly a Liberator in a week they'd have to send me back to Hendricks for reassignment elsewhere.

I mastered the B-24 in three days; the only difference I could find between it and a Flying Fort was that the Liberator was more sluggish and took off like a boxcar. But it was a worthy sister ship to the Fortress—lean, graceful, suggesting the airliner of the future with its narrow fuselage, tricycle landing gear, and unique airfoil wing design.

Now I could pick a crew. I'd met Lt. Harry Fisher, a young Southerner from New Orleans who was working in the tower.

An ex-B-25 twin-engine pilot, Harry was scheduled to go overseas soon and wanted to sign on as a copilot. Though I sensed he was a frustrated fighter jockey, otherwise Harry looked like a good man. He said he'd keep his eyes open for a navigator and bombardier.

Next morning he showed up at my hutment all excited. Last night, he said, a crew had crashed on a practice bombing flight in the mountains. The pilot and copilot had been killed but the rest of the crew was intact. All good men. Did I want to talk to them?

I was dubious. "Go easy, Harry," I told him. "These fellows are going to be jumpy for a while. You don't know what you're taking on with a crash crew. Let me see what the medics say and I'll check with operations."

But if I was reluctant the men were not; there weren't that many pilots at Casper with experience. One by one they dropped by for a talk, and within twenty-four hours I had a ten-man crew.

There was myself, captain, and Lt. Harry Fisher, copilot. Lt. John Ball, of Michigan, was bombardier; Lt. Frank Trumpeter, Pennsylvania, navigator; S/Sgt. Gene Litchfield, Texas, engineer; S/Sgt. Charley Halder, Illinois, waist-gunner; Sgt. Trilba Davis, Tennessee, tail-gunner; S/Sgt. Clark Boyer, Oklahoma, waist-gunner; S/Sgt. Art Valois, Massachusetts, ball-turret gunner; T/Sgt. Lloyd Burton, Kentucky, radioman and substitute waist-gunner, a career airman who had been in the service for some time. Next to me, Burton, at twenty-four, was the second oldest man of the crew. The others were all kids of nineteen or twenty, except for Harry Fisher, who was twenty-three and a married man.

I talked with Burton a bit longer than the others.

He said, "I like the experience you've had and I'd like to be on your crew, but I don't know if I'd fit. Most of the guys are clean-cut, religious; I mean they go to church and all."

"You don't go to church?"

"Hell no, that stuff's garbage. I depend on myself. That's how I got out of that crash alive."

I could believe he depended on himself; he was powerfully built, he moved well and he had the skeptical eye of the professional. Yet there was something sensitive about Lloyd, too. I told him about the Queen of Heaven in the RCAF and our close shaves and he grinned at me. "You buy that, Lieutenant? That God spared you because you prayed and lived clean?"

"I can't prove He didn't."

He hunched his shoulders. "Well, I've got to be honest with you about the religion. I don't want you getting sore because I don't go to church like the others and I have some fun in town."

"So far as I'm concerned, if you get enough sleep going to town's your own affair. So is church. I just want a job done."

"I do a job, Lieutenant," he said, and we shook on it.

On our first B-24 practice mission we dropped 15 bombs at 15,000 feet with good results. But the crew was jumpy; they all wore chutes and on takeoff, when I fed No. 2 engine with an over-rich mixture of gas, they thought it had caught fire. Not that I blamed them. I could understand the tremendous psychological strain of going up again after a crash, and the plane we were flying was an old crate that should have been on the scrap heap.

In the next weeks they simmered down quickly. It usually took three months for a crew, welded together by practice flights in bombing, high altitude formation flying and gunnery, to become a unit; it took us a little over a month. About my only problems were a slight antagonism between Burton and Litchfield, due to their close quarters in the plane, and the late hours Burton was keeping.

"Yawning's one thing," I told him. "Falling asleep at your set's another."

He grinned at me sleepily. "You satisfied with my work?"

"When you're awake it's first-class."

"Skipper, calm down. When we're in action they won't allow me to go to town."

I let it go at that.

On May 18 we left Casper for McCook, Nebraska, a dusty, windblown town with a population of 6000. It had one theater and a YMCA. "You brought me to this one-horse burg on purpose," Burton accused me.

We were here for practice flying. One day we went up in an old war-weary B-24 that barely got off the ground. At 6000 feet two engines conked out and I SOSed the tower I was coming in for an emergency landing. The tower told me to wait; landings were being shot on the field. I shut them off in mid-sentence; you couldn't fly a plane and argue with the tower at the same time. When I landed there was a jeep at the runway to take me to the tower for an explanation. Gene Litchfield came along for the ride.

The major on duty had pulled a tour in the Pacific and wore his authority unlightly; he gave me a hard time. Why had I shut off the tower? This was an emergency, I told him; I'd been faced with the alternatives of landing immediately or crashing. Where had I gotten the experience to make such a judgment, he wanted to know. I was too browned off to do more than stare at him, but Gene asked to see the major privately for a moment. When they came back he was more cordial.

"Lieutenant," he said, "I think you're crazy to go back to combat after a European tour. The odds are too steep. Next time don't cut off the tower."

On the 6th we heard of the Allied invasion. After the most intense bombardment in military history, our assault forces had landed along the French coast from Le Havre to St. Vaast-la-Hougue. It was the beginning of the end, at least in the ETO. Gene Litchfield asked me if this meant we'd be going overseas; the rumors were that Hitler would surrender in a matter of days. I reminded him there was still the Pacific.

One day I was checking the gas caps on the wing when Frank Trumpeter came out of the plane and said, "See you later, guys. Got a heavy date in town." I told him to give us a hand on the checkup; we had a lot of work to do before we shipped out from McCook. "My work's all in my briefcase," Frank said, and kept on going. I jumped off the wing to the ground and went after him.

Seconds later I felt a sharp pain in my left ankle and pulled up short. I limped back to the plane, followed by a resigned Frank, who was muttering, "You should see her, Joe. I mean they don't grow many like that in cornhusker country."

Later, at the Officers' Club, Harry Fisher glanced at his watch and suggested going to chow. I got up, but couldn't walk. Fifteen minutes after that I was in the hospital. The X-rays showed bone chips on my ankle from an old football injury; the condition had been aggravated when I'd jumped off the plane. The doctor prescribed heat lamp treatment and rest.

That was Friday. On Saturday I told the Doc I intended to go to mass the next day. He said no. I said I had a $10 bet with a buddy that I'd never miss mass in the Air Corps. He gave me a look but capitulated.

Sunday afternoon Harry dropped by the hospital with a worried frown. The crew had heard rumors they were going to get another pilot because I was due to be in hospital for "at least a month." Our plane was scheduled to leave McCook by the middle of next week. The boys were beginning to feel they were jinxed—first the crash at Casper and now this.

Next morning I told the Doc I wanted to be released. "Are you crazy?" he asked me. "You can't even walk to the can."

I got up from the bed and limped around the room. Then I explained the situation. The Doc said, "You think you can fly a plane?"

"I can, with a copilot."

He was doubtful. "Well, the best I can do is give my O.K. to a test flight. I'll call Operations."

The major who ran the test flights came by that afternoon. He turned me down on flying with Harry Fisher; regulations were that I had to fly alone.

I called Ops. The CO was on the long-distance phone, and I said I'd hold on. The switchboard cut me off. I called back. I'd just identified myself to the CO when the board cut me off again. When I finally got the CO he asked me why in hell I'd hung up on him and said I'd have to take the major's word. I said if I took the major's word my crew might never get to England alive. Anyway, a B-24 was flown by two men, not one. There was a terrible pause. Then he said he'd check with the area commander and call me back.

He didn't. Harry came back that night, grim. The word was they'd about chosen my replacement; also that I had a serious infectious disease. "That true, Skipper?" he said, inching his chair away from bedside.

The CO called back next morning. The area commander had checked with Washington and Washington had checked with its legal man. I was right; a B-24 was flown by two pilots, not one. He'd be glad when I was off the base.

"All right," I briefed Harry, "a B-24 has dual controls. I can only use my right foot, so you'll have to worry about the left rudder pedal. Once you feel a little pressure, push, and I'll counteract with right pedal."

"You think it's worth it, Skipper? This is a delicate operation. We could crash."

"You think it's worth it, Harry?" I asked him. He hesitated, then grinned.

Next day we passed the test. By June 12 we were in Topeka to pick up a B-24 to fly to England. Painted on the side of the plane was a flamboyant nude with the scripted legend, "Vera the Virgin." The B-24's last pilot asked me for $75 for the painting.

"This plane isn't mine," I objected. "We'll be losing it in Scotland."

"Beautiful, isn't she?" the pilot asked wistfully. "My crew'll hate to lose her. How about sixty-five bucks?"

I shook my head. "Even if I was keeping the plane I wouldn't want the picture."

He was dumbfounded. "What do you go for, 'September Morn'?" he said, and walked away.

Half an hour later Frank Trumpeter came up and said, "Skipper, that's some beautiful blonde. Or don't you like the type?"

"Frank, has that guy been bending your ear about that picture?"

He grinned, and I told him, "Whether you like her or not isn't the point. We're losing the plane in Scotland."

"You don't think fifty bucks is worth having the picture till we *get* to Scotland? If we chipped in it would only cost us about five bucks apiece. Five bucks isn't much for a good morale booster. Not when you're flying on the 13th."

"I think you can get him down to forty," I said. "The guy's desperate."

Frank got him down to forty-five. On June 13 we flew Vera from Topeka to Maine, and from Maine across the ocean to Labrador, and from Labrador to Iceland, and from Iceland to Scotland, where we lost her for the B-17 we flew from Scotland to London, and from London to 567th Squadron, 389th Bomb Group, at Hethel, south of Wellesbourne. Vera flew high and clean, like a real lady. My ankle trouble had cleared up.

I had something in common with the veterans of the 389th —we had both served in the desert. Constituted in 1942, the 389th had moved to England the summer of 1943 and been assigned to the Eighth Air Force. Almost immediately it was sent to Libya, where it began operations in July. The Group flew missions to Crete, Sicily, Italy, Austria and Rumania, and received a Presidential citation for its participation in the famous low-level attack on Ploesti in August, 1943. The Group returned to England in August and flew several missions against airfields in France and Holland. Operating temporarily from Tunisia in September and October, 1943, the 389th supported Allied operations at Salerno and hit targets in Corsica, Italy and Austria. It resumed operations from England in the same year, concentrating on strategic objectives in France, the Low Countries and Germany. In the Normandy invasion it had flown support and interdictory missions, bombing gun batteries and airfields.

Since all American airdromes in England were built to a uniform plan of specification required by the Air Ministry, Hethel looked much like Wellesbourne or Topcliffe. Dispersal was favored; buildings and facilities were spread out over the station in all directions, and bicycles and jeeps were essential for transportation.

The four squadrons of the group were assigned areas or sites on different sides of the field. Each site was composed of a group of Nissen huts where the men lived, and a few additional buildings which housed the squadron orderly room, supply and showers.

About 500 men were billeted in each area. There was a consolidated mess for the enlisted men, a combat crew mess, and an officers' mess. The officers' mess was run in conjunction with the officers' club, another large adjoining building. There was a lounge with chairs and tables, a ping-pong table, and a bar. The headquarters area of the base included the officers' club, Group HQ, Group operations and intelligence, and a small chapel.

Colonel Bob Miller, commanding officer of the 389th, was a West Pointer but you wouldn't have known it from his easy, avuncular ways. When I told him I was anxious to get the crew's feet wet he laughed and said, "What have you got against the Germans?"

I filled him in on the crew's bad experience at Casper. Action, I felt, would settle them down. The Colonel said he'd schedule us for some formation flying, after which we'd go on to our first op without delay.

That afternoon my crew joined three others that had arrived at the squadron the day before for a new crew briefing with Colonel Miller, the three base chaplains, the operations officers and medics. Finally Father Gerald Beck, the Franciscan chaplain from Cincinnati, took the Catholic boys of the *Regina Coeli II* aside—Halder, Boyer, Valois and me.

A nickname for him came easily to mind: "White Flak." Not very tall, heavily built, with short-cropped, prematurely gray hair, Father Beck was a formidable personality. Outspoken, direct, no nonsense about him. Step out of line and he'd shoot you down.

He warned us about the Iron Crosses for VD that decorated some of the Squadron HQ's at Hethel, and other AAF bases around the world. There were a lot of kids in the Air Force, eighteen and twenty years old, who were away from home for the first time. It was easy for them to get into trouble.

I'd never known Charley Halder had a sense of humor until he said, "Father, it's funny, but I heard a story last night about the best damn gunner the 389th ever had. He wasn't mad at the Germans—he was just mad because on the only forty-eight-hour pass he ever had he went to town and caught syphilis. It sort of made him feel better to go up there and shoot at somebody."

The Father beetled his brows and said, "Now hear this. He might have gotten rid of his anger that way, but he sure as hell didn't get rid of the syphilis."

Father Beck was already a legend, and I'd heard of him in North Africa. He had entered the service in 1941 and, as part

of an SOS unit, gone overseas to Persia. On the Russian Life
Line, a supply line of over 900 miles between Persia and the
Soviet, he had, for seven months, served Catholic and non-
Catholic troops alike, sleeping and eating outdoors in summer
heat and winter cold. In June 1943 he was transferred to the
Middle East and later sent to Benghazi, North Africa, to assist
Father Bronssard, head chaplain of the 9th Air Force.

When the 389th left England for North Africa to support
the Sicilian and Italian invasions, Father Beck transferred to it
from Benghazi headquarters.

Because he lived with them in sand, sweat and misery, the
men of the 389th came to call Father Beck "The Desert Rat."
He flew with them on so many missions, against regulations,
that the Air Force finally gave up on grounding him. It
started one day when he was distributing communion in the
equipment room and learned that three Catholic members of
a crew had gone out to the plane without the sacraments. The
ship was getting ready to take off when White Flak came
rushing out in his jeep, *Hellzapoppin'*. He knocked on the
hatch, entered the plane and began to give communion. The
plane started off down the runway with Father Beck aboard
and he completed his first mission.

Another time, over target with the flak intense, his deep
voice came over the intercom, "All right, Smith, I know
you're not praying!" Smith called back, "You're wrong,
Father. I'm praying for you because I know you're praying
for us." Father growled, "Listen, Smith, don't pray for me.
I'm praying for me and I'm not getting through so good. You
pray for *yourself*."

He was close to the enlisted men, whose hutments he shared
often. Once a sergeant asked him for some altar wine to use at
a party. The Father hesitated, then said, "Well, I'd rather you
were drinking altar wine with only 10 percent alcohol than
the stronger stuff you get around here for a fortune. Just
leave me enough for mass tomorrow."

Though he held the Air Medal, given to flying personnel only, Father Beck didn't wear the decoration but kept it in his pocket. The medal kept turning up regularly at Lost and Found. Father drove *Hellzapoppin'* around the base at such a clip that the medal was always falling out on the runway. At least four sets of B-24 tires had passed over and rolled it flat.

The Father knew of my North African tour. When the others had left he snapped at me, "Lauro, you've got God in your eyes. How come you're in uniform?"

I didn't want to discuss my reasons; I was tired of being an anomaly. "I could ask the same of you," I said, and his lined face broke into a wintry smile. Never again during my tour of duty at Hethel did he try to sound me out, although I was in his company almost every moment I could spare from the crew.

We had a few days' formation flying with the Squadron Leader, Major Emery Ward. The countryside, with its hedgerows, its meadows crossed by cold, clear streams and dotted with fat cattle, its endless fields of Brussels sprouts, was achingly familiar.

I was being introduced to some of the differences between day formation flying and the individual night flying methods of the RAF. With the latter, once you'd taken off you were on your own. In no case did you follow another plane. If you saw his flaming exhaust and tail-light, it was up to you to turn away to avoid being taken for a hostile aircraft. The only lights you kept on over England were your navigational and tail-lights, and once over the North Sea you made sure all your lights were out.

In the RAF each plane did its own bombing over target. The Air Force bombing method was by saturation, with from 40 to 48 planes following a lead crew. All ships bombed on signal of the lead plane's bombardier.

The chief hazards of the British method, aside from flak

and attack by fighters, were in taking off in bad weather and
returning in early morning fog. In formation flying the problems lay in turns and in stalling, and in the powerful propwash of preceding planes. Also the sun, reflecting off the
wings of daylight bombers, was blinding even with sun-
glasses. Still another difficulty lay in rallying in the air with
three or more squadrons. The lead crew fired flares to form
on, and if the signal was red-red the glare would sometimes
blur it out, especially at a distance. If it was time to set course
you'd be too late to join your own squadron and would have
to tie in with another going to the same target. This was a dis-
advantage both to the odd plane, which became a straggler,
and to its original formation; four flights of twelve planes
each, closely flown, gave maximum protection against fighters.

In the early days of the AAF, before 1943, American
bombers had suffered heavy casualties because American
fighters with the range to escort to target were lacking; moreover, the Luftwaffe had the cream of German fighters in the
air. With the advent of the P-38, with a radius of action of
520 miles in October, 1943, American bombers became less
vulnerable. By early 1944 long-range fighters equipped with
wing tanks were able to provide escort for B-17's and B-24's
as far as Berlin.

On July 18 we were posted for operations the following
day. When I went to barracks to tell the crew they had a
barrage of questions: where, what kind of target, what kind
of bomb load. All we knew, I told them, was the date; details
would have to wait till briefing at 2 A.M tomorrow. "Details,
the man calls them details," Gene Litchfield said, sobbing.

By 8 P.M., after checking with some of the veteran crews,
the boys had at least six targets, including Hamm, Essen and
Fluery, France. One waist-gunner with ten missions behind
him said it had to be France; they wouldn't send a green
crew to Germany on its first trip. A tail-gunner said we'd
have an easy one to Pau, France. A radioman said he'd dreamt

last night that the high brass had decided to concentrate for a while on Stuttgart, Mannheim and other heavily defended targets. A turret gunner felt in his bones the weather would be so bad tomorrow we'd be scrubbed. He had enough confidence in his hunch to give odds on it.

"All of which," I told them, "means you know absolutely nothing more than you knew this morning. That's just as well—it's better not to know everything at once. You worry."

Chuck Halder made a face. "Skipper, I'm *worried now*." I noticed that a corner of Burton's lip was raw from biting.

"We worry about them all," I told them. "You never get used to combat. I was just as afraid on my last RCAF mission as I was on the first."

We went to bed early. At 1:30 Harry Fisher, John Ball, Frank Trumpeter and I were awakened in our corner of the Nissen officers' barracks by the operations clerk shining his flashlight in our faces. The other eight men in the hut, officers of other crews, slept on.

I swung my feet to the chilly floor and glanced balefully at the squat English stove that had gone out hours before. The small coal scuttle that stood beside it was partly filled with coal, and over the black lumps lay a sprinkling of cigarette butts and burned out matches.

The place needed a cleaning, I thought, putting on my heavy wool socks. The map of the U.S. on one wall with signatures of fliers scrawled over home states lay under a film of dust. So did the Varga and Petty pinups. The muslin blackout curtains had grime at their edges and the blankets an unwashed smell. Back issues of *Yank* and *Stars and Stripes* had fallen from the table to the floor.

I put on my fresh, long G.I. winter underwear, fresh to absorb pre-takeoff moisture before the climb to North Pole temperatures, and got into my fleece-lined trousers and jacket. Then I slid my feet into the pair of heavy-duty, broad-toed G.I. enlisted men's shoes, necessary to protect the ankles against the shock of landing by parachute. Moreover, without heavy-duty shoes you were likely to pull up lame after negotiating a few miles of rough country on your escape route.

I checked my face for smoothness. Smooth enough; I'd shaved the night before. Nothing chafed whiskers as much as a tight oxygen mask.

Next I checked the contents of my B-4. All present and accounted for—parachute harness and chest pack, Mae West and throat microphone, furlined gloves and chart-board with clips on which maps and other mission data were mounted. The Mae West had to be double-checked to insure that the inflation cartridge was unpunctured, and also the chest pack, to make sure the ripcord mechanism was unbroken.

I'd finished my double check when I saw the faces at the door. All of them were sleep-fogged; the pilots they belonged to must have been peremptorily awakened by an alarm clock at this unholy hour. These same four or five men had dropped by the hutment last night before bedtime. For some unaccountable reason, then as now, they had seemed interested in my corner of the hut.

"Something I can do for you, gentlemen?" I asked them.

They left hastily. I wasn't to find out the reason for their visits until the mission was over.

Now on to combat breakfast. Ball and Trumpeter had been kidding Harry Fisher, a great steak man, that the squadron served steak on mission breakfasts. When we got our toast and powdered eggs at the steam tables, Harry said he didn't see any steak.

"You've got to ask for it inside," I told him, and Harry disappeared into the kitchen. There was a roar of laughter from the cooks and he came out again, red-faced and muttering, "I'll get even with you for this."

Briefing was at 2:15, after prayers in the chapel with its little red flickering vigil light. In the small theater-like briefing room next to operations the older crews were dozing off, the newer ones staring intently at the curtained wall maps as if they could pierce through the muslin to what lay behind.

I felt as if I'd been here before. If that was true, what in the devil was I doing here now? I wondered.

Briefing began with the weather officer. Weather reports received the night before from the RAF, the underground and our own air reconnaissance, indicated an overcast over target six to eight-tenths; we would be bombing on flares. Ops said Colonel Miller would be lead pilot of 40 planes, and drew the curtain to show us Saarbrucken, Germany. There was an audible sigh. It could have been worse, that sigh said; on the one hand Saarbrucken with its marshalling yards wasn't too far from the French border and thus no deep penetration was indicated. But on the other hand, it was near the heavily defended areas of Stuttgart, Frankfurt and Mannheim, and that meant fighters and moderate to heavy flak. What we had to be especially careful of, said Ops, was flak over Strasbourg and Nancy, France, both on our route.

Navigation then gave us rallying point and altitude courses to turning points and I.P., after which the briefing was turned over to Colonel Miller. We'd form at 18,000 feet, he told us, at a signal of red and green flares. Bomb run would be at 26,000 feet. There would be P-51 and P-40 fighter cover from the French coast into Germany, and on return from French coast to base, but not over target area. Let us be wary of the Hun.

Despite my excitement I felt suddenly depressed; Saarbrucken was a heavily populated area.

We went to the equipment room to put on the lightweight, electrically heated flying equipment. Over the PA system came Father Beck's call, "High right squadron—high right!", a signal that he was entering now with the Blessed Sacrament for holy communion. There were 40 planes on the mission. This meant that 400 men would be flying and normally 120 to 130 of them were Catholic.

The Protestant and Jewish boys stood to one side as we received Our Lord—their chaplains would be through a little later. Was I mistaken, or was there an extra tenderness in the way Father Beck blessed Halder, Boyer, Valois and me? He knew this was our first mission. When he said to others, low left and high, "I'll be praying for you and waiting for you," would the same immense concern be apparent beneath the familiar words, familiar at least to him? A question whose answer only the future could supply, assuming we returned from Germany today to get it.

We heard the Father's "Low left—low left!" from the next equipment room as we piled into the light little British weapons carrier, swiped from the RAF, that would take us to our dispersal point. As they approached their own points pilots yelled out the identifying tail letter of the B-24 they were flying that day. Coming to our area, I called out "O-Bar!" and the crew jumped off. O-Bar would be the next Queen of Heaven if they let us keep her, and I hoped they did because she handled well.

At the fog-shrouded hardstand the ground crew and armament boys were loading 500-lb. bombs into the bay. They had been up for hours, checking and rechecking. Now the crew began their various last-minute checks inside and outside the plane. They seemed too busy for a case of nerves to develop at this point but Chuck Halder was pale and Lloyd Burton's sallow complexion muddier than usual.

I checked the bomb bays with the armament boys and asked John Ball to go over the bomb bay safety devices, and Harry Fisher to check the tires, gas caps and locking devices on the ailerons and flight instruments. Meanwhile the gunners were checking their turrets, guns, ammunition belts and oxygen lines. Ball had already rolled out the colored maps and charts on his desk. With the senior ground crew chief I made a final visual check of the entire plane, starting with the four engines.

Minutes later the tower signaled "start engines" with a

green flare. I kicked over our four 1200-horsepower Pratt-Whitneys. As each one caught, spluttered, then churned the moist air, the ship wrenched and shook. While the engines idled I checked the oil pressure on each, then the oxygen and intercom systems.

We awaited the taxiing signal. Colonel Miller's lead crew ship was already in position. Of the 40 planes scheduled to take off within ten minutes we were number 10.

There were a lot of ways you could get killed in a Liberator, it occurred to me. A man's oxygen mask could freeze up and he'd pass out; unnoticed by the rest of the crew he could be dead in ten minutes. He could get hit by fragments of flak or 20 mm. shells ranging in size from a tennis ball to gravel. He could sustain a hit by a rocket projectile or a bomb from a plane above him. He could crash head-on with a German fighter with a dead pilot in the cockpit—or with one of his own planes going down. Any one of his four engines or several gas tanks could stop an explosive slug and seconds later his ship could be a flaming inferno. A couple of his engines could go out, he could lag behind his formation, and be cut to pieces by enemy fighters at their leisure.

I thought of Father Lux, and his "What are you saving yourself for, Joe?" but I didn't laugh.

The green taxiing signal flashed from the tower. I put on the brakes, revved up the throttle half-open, then idled the engines as I released the brakes. The Liberator slowly followed L-bar plane into take off position. Down the runway and into the crisping morning air. At 110 I gradually lifted her off the ground and we were airborne and climbing on full throttle to 800 feet.

Over the intercom Gene Litchfield said, "Two minutes, Skipper; left-hand turn to ninety degrees." I started the next two-minute leg on crosswind; then a six-minute down-leg with a steady climb of about 200 feet per minute. I made a box pattern, flying two minutes on the short leg, six minutes on the long, the pattern set so that no two planes would collide.

The sky was overcast to 10,000 feet. I was flying on instruments in a thick pea-soup fog. Yet once we had broken through to sunlight at 12,000 there was an instant feeling of liberation; no longer were we flying blind.

We took position in formation, high right, circling interminably at 22,000 till all planes were in order on the lead crew. Each plane was in formation to avoid propwash, and about a hundred feet below the higher echelon. Our wing snuggled into the plane ahead of us at about a distance of ten feet. I was constantly on the throttle to avoid collision.

Colonel Miller set course for the initial turning point over the North Sea. As we crossed the French coast I told the crew we were now within range of enemy fighters. Their reactions so far had been good; making allowances for the stresses of a first mission, I no longer had a jumpy crew.

The course was Strasbourg, in a feint to confuse enemy radar. As we passed south of Nancy and over the Maginot Line, approaching the Siegfried, Miller reminded us we'd take evasive action over the latter, where we could expect to run into flak. Once there we turned 15 degrees to the left and 30 degrees to the right as flak came up lazily off to starboard.

South of Strasbourg, about two hours later, Miller intercommed that we were approaching our due north turning point. When we hit it, to throw off the listening Jerries, he would give not our direction but say the code words, "turning toward target directly." "We're well boxed in, boys," he told us. "Hold your positions because we can expect fighters: if they see any daylight they'll fly right through."

Somebody tapped my shoulder. Burton. He asked to borrow my flak suit, and since I wasn't using it I told him to go ahead.

It was time now for a final check of all equipment. Art Valois, in his lower ball turret, intercommed that his hydraulic

system was O.K. Curved fetus-like in a small ball in his haz-
ardous and uncomfortable position, he dangled 25,000 feet
over the earth. He could revolve and turn to track down
enemy fighters with his twin fifties, but if the hydraulic system should fail he'd be trapped and a sitting duck.

In his cramped radio compartment Burton was maintaining
constant contact with other bombers in the formation. John
Ball, seated before his battery of switches, dials, calibrations
and lights, made setting on his intervalometer. The rest of the
crew was a little tight now that we were approaching target.

As we approached Saarbrucken the flak started coming up.
Lloyd Burton was standing beneath the top turret where Gene
Litchfield operated, looking up at the bursting flak, and I
could see that under his oxygen mask his eyes were bulging
with fear.

Yet he was well protected. My flak suit lay on the floor
under his feet, he was wearing his own flak suit, and he had
his helmet on his head.

"Don't worry about the flak puffs, Burton," I told him over
the intercom. "They've spent themselves. The ones you worry
about are the ones you don't see, which means there's no use
worrying in the first place." It suddenly occurred to me I was
talking with a slight English accent—the influence of Geoff
Moore.

But there was a rattle of flak fragments against the fuselage
and Burton kept rooted to the spot. As much to distract him
as anything else, I told him to check the bomb bay doors and
see to it they were open and didn't creep shut.

Word came from the lead bombardier that we were approaching target and Harry Fisher began monitoring with
command; from this point onward, until the first turning command after the bomb run, only the pilots would be in communication with command. The rest of the crew would have
only inter-crew communication in case of trouble aboard the
ship.

I kept the ship socked in and steady, trying to forget about the flak. The lead bombardier started his countdown and seconds crawled as he called, "Bomb doors open . . . On target . . . Bombs away." We could see the clusters of bombs descending simultaneously in streams of 1000- and 500-pounders. I knew they were landing below in patterns of 100–1500 feet but I couldn't see them; visibility was only fair.

At turning point we ran into more light flak. Off to the left one B-24's engine caught fire from a direct hit and it dropped out of formation. The plane behind moved up quickly to take its place.

I'd answered command's question about hangups in the negative when the P-47's and P-51's came up and wagged their wings. We could hear the fighter command over the fighter band that Harry Fisher was monitoring: "Come on, Big Friend, let's get out of here. You're safe now, thanks to us. Do I hear any expressions of gratitude?"

It was about then, when we were at lower altitude and off oxygen, with bomb bay doors closed and the plane slightly warmer, that the odor set in. First insidious, sniffable; then full-strength and overpowering, the stink of frozen urine, thawing.

Gene Litchfield started laughing maniacally over the intercom: "My God—I took a leak in my helmet and Burton—he put it on when the flak started coming up—he's got it all over him!"

I glanced back. Burton was shaking his fist furiously at Gene and about to clamber up into his upper turret compartment.

I intercommed: "Knock it off, Lloyd. It's not Gene's fault you put on his helmet. Back to your station."

Quarantining him didn't do much good. The odor by now had penetrated the entire plane, and complaints poured in over the intercom. Halder requested permission to throw Burton overboard. Boyer demanded he be stripped. Trumpeter would have been content with strangling him. John Ball groaned and groaned. I compromised by ordering the bomb bay doors open and trying not to breathe.

The men and bombers headed for home, dodging flak alleys, keeping on the alert for enemy fighters. Chuck Halder threw the switch on his interphone and began to sing a mildly obscene version of a popular Air Force song. Now that we'd made our first mission it seemed like no time at all till we were circling Hethel to land.

I touched the wheels down on the asphalt landing strip and the ship heaved and lunged down the runway. Minutes later we were loading ourselves and our equipment on a six-by-six pulled up in front of the hardstand. Burton still stank.

We didn't have anything to say but we were grinning. Bob Miller had been right about the trip; it hadn't been so bad after all.

I wasn't back at the hutment five minutes when the same group of men who had poked their heads in that morning reappeared in the doorway. They were looking at me; on their faces was a common expression of fascinated disbelief.

"All right," I said. "This is the third time you've been here, peering at me, by damn." (I never swore harder than that.) "I deserve my privacy and I'm not a freak. What's the story?"

One of them, a goodlooking boy with black hair, stepped forward. "No offense, Gloro. Don't you know you've been sacking out in a jinxed bed?"

"Jinxed bed?"

"The last four pilots who slept in that bed went down on their first mission." There was a murmur of corroboration behind him.

He turned to file out with his friends. Over his shoulder he added, "Don't worry, we won't be back."

Wasn't I entitled to congratulations? I felt a little hurt.

CHAPTER
4

DURING the spring of 1944 the air assault on *Festung* Europe had increased in intensity, building up to invasion. In May it reached high point when the Eighth and Ninth USAAF combined with the RAF to drop more bomb tonnage than in any earlier period. After D-Day there was no slackening in tempo and the 389th was as busy as any other bomb group in the air. During my first two weeks at Hethel we flew ten missions with only four days' rest in between.

Mission No. 5 was as rough as any I'd experienced in the RCAF. My log book entry read:

"Take off: 0645

"Landing: 1200

"Mission: accomplishment of unaccomplished Mission #4 (poor visibility over target): to bomb German troops and supplies a few hundred yards north of St.-Lo battle line. Not far from Lisieux, birthplace of St. Theresa, but saw no shrines. Purpose to allow Allied thrust northward. Flak intense and accurate at target area. Two planes out of the six in our squadron flying this mission high right shot down in flames and damage to others. Our navigator dome pierced and John Ball's desk chewed up by a cannon shell, leaving him untouched. Trilba Davis in his tail-gunner's slot had harrowing

144

time with an F-W 190 going better than 400 m.p.h. that
zoomed up on our tail and kept on coming. The Jerry was
within 100 yards and closing fast. Trilba literally shoved the
F-W back with a long burst of lead. When he eased off on
his guns the German started coming in again. Trilba didn't
have much ammo left; he swung his guns on the F-W's right
wing and simply sawed it off. The Jerry went down.

"Krauts had expected us back and gave us a pasting. Being
in the first wing over the target, 567th was most heavily hit.
27,000 100-lb. bombs dropped by the AF in an area 1 mile by
4½ miles upon enemy troops stationed 1500 yards away. Col.
Miller was on the ground sending up a screen of fire as a
marker. We bombed only on one side of it. Coming back over
the coast could see invasion barges and shipping bottled up
below."

Mission #5 had at least one effect I hadn't anticipated.
After interrogation the Protestant chaplain took me aside and
said, "Lloyd Burton dropped by. He was all shook up there
today."

I told him all of us were and he shook his head and grinned.
"Can't believe you were, Joe. Heard you didn't take your
Scotch." He was referring to the post-mission glass of Scotch
all of us were entitled to; today I'd donated mine to Harry
Fisher.

"Never do, Padre," I told him. "Took the pledge."

"Lloyd asked me for the pre-mission prayer schedule," the
chaplain went on. "Said he wanted to pray with me a few
minutes before every trip, but that if I told the crew there'd
be hell to pay." He laughed. "Can you figure out why a man
should be ashamed he's made his peace with God?"

"Maybe he hasn't made his peace yet," I said, turning away,
"but I'm glad Lloyd's sitting down at the conference table."
I was annoyed he'd told me about Lloyd's request when Lloyd
had wanted the padre to keep the matter quiet. A man who
made a concession was entitled to the conditions that went

along with it. Or maybe what was really bothering me was the pounding pain at the top of my skull; coming back from St.-Lo the headache had set in for the first time since I'd returned to England, and it was still with me, and I was worried. I couldn't bear the thought of being grounded, especially since I knew Harry Fisher, although one of the best copilots in the squadron, was temperamentally unsuited to captaining the plane.

That night the boys threw a party to celebrate Trilba's first downed Hun. Harry Fisher had somehow scrounged a bottle of 15-year-old Scotch. Father Beck came over to me, looked around to see if anybody was listening, then whispered, "Joe, you promised anybody here your share of the Scotch?"

"Father," I said, "I didn't know you drank."

He scowled at me. "I don't, damn it. It's for Trilba. The bottle's almost empty and the poor boy's had exactly one slug."

On July 27 General H.H. Arnold commended the entire Eighth Air Force: "The continued all-out efforts by your heavies day after day is most gratifying. It shows to all of us that your combat and maintenance crews are true teams. Please convey my appreciation to all concerned for their untiring efforts and my congratulations for the splendid results obtained."

"Splendid results" maybe for somebody else; for me the last four missions had been disasters. Because of poor visibility we'd bombed on P.P.F. Even in perfect weather it was impossible to bomb with perfect accuracy—with a flight of 40 planes or more you had only to be one degree off, one mile an hour faster than the lead bombardier had set his sights, and you'd miss the target. How many had my bombs slaughtered as a result? These thoughts kept me up nights and made the headaches worse. Though I kept my misery from the crew and it helped to write home of it to Father Lux, White Flak sensed something was wrong and cornered me for a talk.

"What's the problem, Joe?" he asked me bluntly. "Need a rest?"

"No, Father."

"Nonsense. Something's bothering you. I know you don't want to talk about it or you think talk won't help. You're probably right. I'm going to get you some leave."

I reminded him I wasn't due leave till completion of mission #10.

"Hell, you've flown eight. Colonel Miller won't quibble over two. He does I'll tell him I'm sick of sitting on my butt while the crews're up there having fun in the wild blue yonder."

That was the way White Flak got his way, by threatening to smuggle himself aboard a Liberator. Then I remembered that if I went on leave the crew would be assigned another pilot, and opened my mouth to say so.

Father Beck held up his hand. "Don't worry about the crew; they could stand a rest, too. I don't like the way Harry Fisher keeps hunching that left shoulder, and Frank Trumpeter's developing a twitch in his right eye. John Ball's been stuttering a bit, too."

I stared at him; the boys had seemed all right to me. But checking up later, I found he was right. Harry did have a hunch and Frank a slight twitch. But it was interesting that John Ball hadn't begun hesitating over his words—yet.

On the day the Third Army broke out of the Normandy peninsula at Avranches, they sent us to a Tudor manor house about fifteen miles from Hethel. It had a tennis court, croquet lawn, boxwood hedges and flower gardens, now mostly producing vegetables for Britain's impoverished larder. There was even an old gardener in corduroys and collar stud, with his gardener's basket.

"Oh my," groaned Frank Trumpeter, "what a romantic spot to court a girl in, and all I'll have for five days' company is you three hairy guys."

"Plus some other hairy guys," Harry Fisher said, indicating three other Ninth Air Force officers who were investigating the grounds.

"Maybe there's a beautiful heiress of a daughter around," John Ball said hopefully, pointing to the high mullioned windows along the terrace. "Imagine being the son-in-law of a lord—Rolls-Royces, a seat in Parliament and the shooting season."

"You forgot Ascot," said Harry Fisher moodily.

Inside the damp barnlike stone hall there was a fire burning in the intricately carved Jacobean fireplace. Tall-backed, heavily carved chairs sat stiffly around. A carved stairway at one end led gloomily upward. Harry looked uncomfortable. "I've seen at least five horror movies that could have been set in this place. You think it's got ghosts?"

John Ball, the realist, laughed. "I sure as hell don't see any young heiresses."

A uniformed housemaid told us tea would be served in the drawing room by the mistress of the house, Lady Harcourt-Williams, at four thirty sharp, and a houseman took our bags and showed us up to our rooms.

The bedrooms were high-ceilinged and dark-paneled with windows facing on the garden. The closet door groaned when I opened it but the closet itself was as clean as a Gestapo HQ and the featherbed soft as an Air Force colonel's cheek. I wondered if the walls had secret panels.

At tea the old lady of the manor, in her cardigan, tweed skirt and brogues, told us she had two grandsons in the RAF and one in the Navy. She lived alone in the place. She believed in spirits and the occult; Aleister Crowley, the occultist and diabolist, had once investigated the house and testified to spirits who inhabited it; more, these spirits visited her occasionally and she knew them by name.

"That so, Ma'am?" Harry said politely, buttering an already buttered scone. "Who are they, if I may ask?"

"Well, there's a girl named Mary, very pretty, who murdered her husband around 1780, and a young man, Percy, who strangled his wife during Queen Victoria's Diamond Jubilee. And an old maid, Dolly, who used to cook here in my dead husband's father's time. She didn't kill anybody; she was just very devoted to the place."

"That's nice," commented Frank Trumpeter, putting down his teacup. The silence that followed was broken only by the arrival of the other American airmen staying at the house who were late for tea. Our hostess, moving slowly down the vast halls with the help of a cane, showed us some of the other rooms—the library, filled with leather-bound sets of Surtees, Fielding and Scott; the music room, with a harpsichord under a duster and an ancient phonograph in one corner; the billiard room, gun room, still room and larder. Then we went out for a round of croquet in the fading light.

After dinner that evening Harry, twisting restlessly in his hard chair, suggested we go into the village, about three miles away, for a couple of ales.

I rang up the local taxi but couldn't seem to get them—a doctor and two frightened women answered before I finally gave up. Then Harry tried and got the constable, who wanted to know why a young man like him wasn't in the army, fighting for his country.

John Ball got the bright idea of finding some bicycles and wandered away, returning to say that the other airmen had gotten to them first. He was limping; he'd turned his ankle in the dark, making his way by cigarette lighter to the gardener's cottage.

"Some poker, gentlemen?" Harry said desperately, and our spirits lifted, only to plummet again when we realized we'd forgotten to bring cards. By now it was too late to wake the old lady, who had retired right after dinner.

We went up to bed, Frank Trumpeter carrying with him a copy of *Jorrick's Jaunts*. Going by candlelight to the lavatory, about the equivalent of a city block down the hall, I stubbed my toe against a refectory table. I was just getting to sleep when there came a knock on the door. It was Harry Fisher, a candle held unsteadily in his hand.

"Skipper," he said. "There's strange noises in my room."

"Could it be your own breathing, Harry?"

"Skipper, I don't like this place. Can we go back to base tomorrow?"

I yawned. "We're here for five days, Harry. No more, no less."

"I could use a drink. You think it would be all right if I went downstairs and tried to find one?"

"The old lady doesn't drink, Harry. She didn't even offer us sherry."

"Yeah, you're right. Goodnight, Skipper."

"Goodnight, Harry."

I'm a good sleeper but I was so used to a hard Air Corps cot that it was an hour before I drifted off again. I heard no noises.

Three days later we were ready to join the Luftwaffe to see some action. Croquet, tennis, billiards, even successful poker with the 9th Air Force men had palled. The village was as charming as its gleaming pub, but some American warriors had recently done some local girls wrong and the atmosphere was cool, if not hostile. If a brace of young women entered the place while we were there a watchful silence immediately descended. We'd have a couple of ales, throw a couple of darts, and then mount our bikes for the ride back to the manor house.

Frank and John agreed that it was disgraceful how the Air Corps maintained no liaison whatsoever with the English in respect to the social lives of American officers at British rest homes.

"You think they'd at least send over a few nice-looking girls for dances," Ball complained. "That main hall would make a great dance floor."

"Why not a couple of Wrens to keep us company?" asked Trumpeter wistfully. "Better than ghosts. Lady Harcourt could act as chaperone."

"Harcourt-*Williams*," Harry Fisher corrected, sealing a V-mail letter. "Anyway, you're dreaming." Harry was the envy of us all because he had an attractive young wife to write home to and because, furthermore, it was clear that the Air Corps, in collaboration with the Limeys, and for all we knew even with the Krauts, had mounted a conspiracy to keep the healthy, red-blooded men of the 567th from meeting English girls.

Harry wrote home every day; since we'd been here he was constantly en route to or from the village post office. In fact he'd had words with one of the 9th men over monopolizing the house bikes.

Our last night of leave dragged its way toward us on leaden feet. The men of the 9th had already departed. We regretted there had been no real sign of Lady Harcourt-Williams' ghosts; it would have helped. Harry kept on insisting they'd visited his room. Various articles of his had fallen off shelves to the floor, and his shoes had moved from one closet to another. Then there was the white glow or nimbus he'd seen at the end of the hall one night, going to the lav. It had moaned.

John Ball wouldn't buy this. "You moved the shoes yourself," he said, "and that white glow was from those five Guinnesses you had in the village."

"How come it moaned?"

"It didn't moan. *You* moaned. You know what Guinness does to your gut."

That night we went to bed before eleven; transport back to Hethel was picking us up early tomorrow morning, and besides, there was nothing better to do.

When the music woke me I groped for my luminous-dialed watch—it was a few minutes after one. I swung my feet to the floor and then the significance of the music, light and tinkling, occasionally fading to near-inaudibility, hit me. This was harpsichord music, the intricate variations of a baroque sonata or concerto.

My blood ran cold. There was a harpsichord in the music room. Who could be playing it with such authority? Who *would* be playing it at this hour of the night?

I lit a candle and went to the door. I jumped at sight of the white figure across the hall; then I realized it was Harry Fisher, whose room was opposite mine, standing in his doorway.

"My God, Joe," Harry whispered, "what is this? That music—"

"I don't know. Let's investigate."

"It's the ghosts. It *must* be the ghosts. *You* investigate."

I went down the stairs slowly, leaving Harry behind. In the flickering candlelight the shadows were huge, menacing, but I told myself they were only shadows. The worn carpet under my bare feet was harsh, a needed touch of reality.

The music room was near the bottom of the stairway. As I approached it the harpsichord music grew louder. Scarlatti, I thought; or Vivaldi, the Master. I pushed open the door and moved inside.

Near the windows, through which pale moonlight came, the harpsichord bulked under its duster, unplayed by human hands.

The music seemed to be coming from a corner of the room. As I stood there, candle in hand, it hesitated, wailed, then ground to a stop. I went over to the ancient Gramophone. There was a record on the mouldy baize turntable. A Corelli sonata.

It was then I realized I was stark, buck naked. In summertime I slept without pajamas.

I left the music room and moved to the bottom of the stairs. In a sudden draft the candle puffed out. From above there was the sound of muffled but uncontrollable laughter.

Somebody poked their head over the railing. "Martin?" Lady Harcourt-Williams asked. Martin was the butler.

"No, Ma'am," I answered, moving out of visual range. "It's Lieutenant Lauro."

"What are you doing down there at this hour, Lieutenant?"

I asked her if she'd heard the music. She said no. I said I'd explain tomorrow and asked her to leave her candle at the top of the stairs. Lady H. withdrew.

Trumpeter, Ball and Fisher were waiting for me in my room. Frank lay on the floor, shoulders heaving. Ball sat on the side of the bed, holding his stomach, tears rolling down his cheeks. Harry Fisher perched on the window seat, smiling faintly. He was still pale.

Then I started laughing. Finally I closed the door so Lady Harcourt-Williams wouldn't hear.

August, 1944 marked the high tide of Allied fortunes in the West. Penned for weeks in the Cherbourg peninsula, the Allied armies broke out and overflowed into Northern France. At first it was a trickle into Brittany; then a stream toward Paris; finally a flood that swept away the German armies and carried all the way to the borders of the Reich. Paris fell and almost all of France was liberated; the German armies in the North were encircled and destroyed.

My log book reflected the part that American air power played in these successes:

"Mission #11, August 4. Target airfield and supply depot, Schwerin, Germany. Flak intense at target; moderate en route. A dozen holes in the Queen of Heaven. Burton, at the waist guns, shot down an Me-109 that attacked from the wrong angle. Our squadron not being in correction position to bomb the target, proceeded to nearby Lubeck, industrial center on the Baltic Sea. Dropped bombs there with good results.

"Later dropped in on Chuck Halder and found him depressed. Asked if he was low because Lloyd had happened to take over his guns when the Me drilled in. Shook his head and told me a good friend of his in his hutment, name of Kamaroski, had gone down with Johnny Noble's crew. It had been Kamaroski's final mission, his 35th. At least the third time I've heard this story.

"Mission #12, August 6. Target oil refinery storage dump at Harburg, Germany. Flak intense at target but not too accurate; still, a fruitcake from home that Gene Litchfield had aboard sustained a direct hit two feet from his station. Excellent job of bombing by waves of 8th Air Force Liberators; we seem to be getting stronger every day. Great fires were raging and black smoke rose to thousands of feet. On way home attacked by flight of F-W's that bored in with unusual desperation and with far from the usual Luftwaffe insistence on careful approach. Squadron shot down three with no losses.

"Mission #15, August 13. Flak none. Target eight 88 mm. cannon located on small island about a mile off the coast of St.-Malo, France. Battery prevented advancement of Allied forces. Island completely wiped out with 96 1-ton blockbusters dropped by our group. Returning, F-W bored in, firing fast, when Clark Boyer at top turret got him dead to rights. Kraut's guns stopped firing but he kept coming head-on. This took only about four seconds but it was enough time for me to freeze. Then I remembered this had happened to me before over the Mediterranean and I snapped out of it, rammed the controls forward and down we went. The F-W passed right over us, missing the plane by less than six feet.

"This mission being on the 13th, Gene Litchfield had put a sign on the plane door reading, 'Is This Trip Really Necessary?' "

That evening Bob Miller called me in with a proposition—did I want to take lead crew?

"It's an honor, Joe," he told me. "It means a promotion for you and you'll fly only every three or four weeks. Besides, you've got the luckiest ship in the group."

I told him I'd take it up with the crew. They realized the honor involved—there were only three or four lead crews to a squadron—and they wanted the promotion for me. But definite disadvantages existed: the lead crew spot was dangerous, and flying every month or so, it would take a year to finish our tour. There was also the possibility that Bob might find one or two crew members not up to snuff and replace them. We wanted to stay together; staying together was one good reason why we were still alive.

I gave them the night to think it over but they were definite in their reaction: no. Burton groaned, "I'll bet this means we don't get our forty-eight to London."

I went back to Bob and reported. He sighed, "Everybody wants to go home. I'd hoped you felt you were flying such a lucky ship you could fly lead in a breeze." Then he picked up the phone and authorized our 48.

It wasn't much fun in London. The enemy V1 raids made the nights sleepless. The balloon barrage, we heard, was proving ineffective with the buzz bombs, and Fighter Command was now trying to deal with them directly. At night, from 20 miles out and at 5000 feet, Fighter Command would sight a V1's exhaust and, diving on it at 800 feet, get one wing under the infernal machine, tip it, and upset the gyro. Many bombs spun into the ground and into the fields. To prevent them from turning into the attacking planes required great flying skill. Some pilots had as many as 25 V1's to their credit.

It looked as though the Germans were a bit late with their secret weapon. Had they used it in 1942, when British morale was low and the island defenders less confident of victory, it might have been a different story. Now the V1's were considered little worse than a bloody nuisance.

During the day in London there was only the Red Cross Club and movies and reading the papers whose headlines blared that the Third Army had reached Argentan. Harry Fisher narrowly avoided a fight with some RAFers when he said the 8th Air Force was the best damn air force in the world. Lloyd Burton was stood up by a Wren at the elegant Hotel Connaught. Chuck Halder got the runs from fish and chips, and Frank Trumpeter lost a pound and two shillings in a phone booth, trying to figure out the British system. Gene Litchfield got stood up by a Red Crossette at Claridge's.

Worst of all, Bob Miller called me at the Red Cross to say that *Regina Coeli II* was no more. Another pilot named McGowen, known for his cockiness, had flown it in our absence and, returning from his mission, had overshot the runway. Putting on his brakes, he'd ploughed through a barbed-wire fence and into a field. The ship had been completely demolished but nobody was hurt. "It's a miracle," Bob said.

When I was silent he added, "I'm saving the best damn ship in the squadron for you, Joe."

"Bob, the *Regina II* was the best ship. I don't see why you had to give it to Gorgeous McGowan." I hung up. Then, thinking better of my manners, I called him back to apologize, but the operator told me it would be half an hour till I could get through.

The boys took the news as hard as I had. "I don't like to say it," Trilba Davis said grimly, "but I think this is where our luck bails out." Harry insisted I buy a couple of new religious medals before we went back to base; anything would—could —might—help. Chuck Halder thought of some Carmelite nuns he knew of in Michigan and cabled them to pray for us. On the way to Hethel the crew tried to think of what they could do to Gorgeous McGowen but short of murder nobody came up with anything better than taking clippers to his beautiful curls.

When Gorgeous McGowen moved into the hutment next door I found a way to get back at him for wrecking *Regina Coeli II*.

During our 48 in London the crew had pooled its resources

and bought a spring-wound phonograph. It came complete with 50 popular records and other people were borrowing it constantly. "Elmer's Tune" and "Moonlight Cocktail" were almost worn out, and "Chattanooga Choo-Choo" scratched; "Don't Sit Under the Apple Tree" had unaccountably warped. Then Gorgeous borrowed it for a party in the snack bar to which none of the crew were invited and broke three records, among them "Stardust," one of my favorites. Gorgeous taught all the British girls to jitterbug; he was a great dancer. He didn't offer to replace the broken records.

Gorgeous must have drunk too much at the party and came down with a stomach bug. He was confined to quarters for a day in bed, and since our mission had been scrubbed that day, I saw my chance. I picked up a copy of *Stars and Stripes* and started playing the collection's only semiclassical record, Richard Crooks singing "Little Star of Bethlehem" and "The Holy City," over and over again.

McGowen came in about twenty minutes later. "Hey, Lauro, can you knock it off? I'm trying to sleep." He didn't look so good; even his perfect hair (it was rumored he had it set in the village) was tousled.

"Sorry, McGowen," I told him. "I like this stuff."

"I hate it. I always thought you were a Holy Joe; you make it sound like Sunday." He left. I turned up the volume a notch. It had started to rain and I wanted him to hear the music over the drumming on the roof.

He was back in ten minutes. "Look," he said, and there was desperation in his voice, "One of them isn't so bad but I can't stand the flip side. It's giving me the willies."

"That's 'Holy City.' It's a great number. Calms me down. Doesn't it calm you down, McGowen?"

He stared at me from the doorway, light dawning. "You paying me back, Lauro? By God, I bet you're getting even."

I said conversationally: "You know, McGowen, no two planes are exactly alike. They're like women, about whom

you're such an expert. And some of them, the planes I mean,
are duds. *Regina II* was a great plane. She saved our lives a
couple of times. She even saved yours. The ship we got to
replace her was a lemon—cowl flaps one day, turbo the next;
then the juice for our heated suits fizzled out, McGowen. We
had two aborts before the ground crew fixed her up, and we'd
never had an abort before. We don't like aborts—do you,
McGowen?"

"Star of Bethlehem" was over; I flipped it and put on "Holy
City." Then I picked up *Stars and Stripes* again. When I
looked up he was gone.

I played the records for another three hours. By that time
they were getting on my own nerves. McGowen didn't come
back. I heard later that he'd gotten dressed and gone to the
infirmary. It was raining harder and he caught a cold.

Three days later McGowen went up with his crew and was
reported missing. I felt awful till I heard he'd landed safely in
Sweden. A few weeks later he was back, cocky as ever. He'd
had his usual luck with the Swedish women.

I wrote Father Lux: "Yesterday we completed our 22nd
mission and that brings my total to 80 in both services, thanks
to Our Lady's protection and Our Lord's guidance. I cannot
believe that we don't have that protection and guidance, given
the luck that is being talked about in the 567th much as it was
in Squadron 424. More happens to us than it does with other
crews and we get through particularly tough spots without a
scratch when all around us other planes are catching it.

"For instance, on our last mission both Liberators on our
wing tips were shot down by a box barrage of accurate flak
over target that by every rule in the book should have gotten
us, too. Yet we had only four holes on landing. This despite
the fact that after the 18th or 20th mission the odds against
staying alive go up sharply, the loss of *Regina Coeli II* and the
crew's feeling that our luck had finally run out. It's gotten so

that crewmen from other ships are approaching me for 'future vacancies' and I found out the other day that a tail-gunner and bombardier had asked to see, respectively, Davis's and Ball's health records at the hospital. If Trilba and John were grounded they wanted to be first on line to step in. Other pilots, Protestant and Jewish, are wearing religious medals. One came up to me the other day and asked, 'What do you think of St. Jude?'

"Of course I know the Lord's eye is not on me alone. But I can't escape the feeling that even my headaches, which have been quite bad recently, serve a purpose; despite the pain, I'm better able to concentrate in the air on my job, perhaps because I'm working on getting rid of the pain and therefore react to crises in a looser, more relaxed way. Still, when the headaches get really severe there's the danger of over-controlling the plane and getting into trouble. Now please don't write me again to report these to the Doc. I know there's absolutely nothing he can do; they simply don't respond to medication and if I go to hospital too often they'll say I'm coming down with combat fatigue. I just know that if I'm grounded the crew will go up with another pilot for the last time."

I spoke too soon, or maybe it was the odds finally catching up with us, or Our Lord's sense of humor. My complete log book entry for Mission #24 ran:

"Mission: Hamm, Germany

"Take off: 1130

"Landing: 1700

"Target: One of Germany's largest and most important railroad marshalling yards east of Ruhr Valley. Through here come industrial materials for Berlin and the Eastern front. Handles 10,000 carloads of freight daily; important transportation nerve center of the Reich.

"Load: 6-1000 G.P. bombs.

"Altitude: 23,000 feet for bombing and 25,000 feet en route.

"Flak: moderate and inaccurate

"Plane: *Regina Coeli III*

"Enemy fighters in our vicinity but didn't attack; fighter escort scared them off and gave pursuit. Flew high right. Engine trouble on #2 engine on return at 25,000 feet over North Sea. Oil leak started spraying oil and prop wouldn't feather, started to windmill. Normally this meant a fire or a runaway prop that would cut Harry and me to pieces where we sat as well as the plane. Told Harry to push his seat back to be out of the path of a runaway and he said the hell with that, no preferential treatment. Suddenly the prop froze stiff, much to our relief, but at lower altitude, with the plane flying slower on three engines, we were a sitting goose for any prowling Jerry fighters. Ordered crew to throw overboard any loose equipment such as waist guns, flak suits and sent out an SOS for sea rescue in the event of ditching. All of us knew the North Sea was so bitter cold at this time of year that it would be a matter of 5 or 10 minutes before we froze to death in the water.

"Then another engine ran rough, but managed to cut back power to conserve it. Landed on two engines. Discovered only then that Burton had thrown overboard our 100-pound, $1000 camera."

Because of the camera I was in no mood for what came later. Col. Ramsey Potts, who had replaced Bob Miller, called back to Washington the week before, asked me in for a talk after Interrogation.

I paled when I saw the medical reports on his desk, and tried to look unconcerned.

"Joe," he said, "these medical reports bother me. You say there's nothing wrong with you but you keep asking for stronger and stronger analgesics and barbiturates. They've checked everything from your toenails to your eyes but can't find anything wrong. What's the story?"

"Nerves, I guess, Colonel."

He wasn't smiling. "I think it's the beginning of combat fatigue. These two tours of yours are catching up with you.

Luck like yours can't last indefinitely. Did you know Charlie Baker of the 560th?" I said I hadn't. "Well, last night he won five consecutive games at Bingo. You know the odds against that. Today he went down over Bremen."

I couldn't think of anything to say.

"I think I should scratch you and put you on Operations. Your experience of German targets in the RAF could make you invaluable."

"Colonel, you can't do that," I said. "I owe it to the crew to finish with the boys and send them home safely. When I finish the tour it'll be time to consider Operations."

What saved me was the shavetail who came in and put the Interrogation reports on Potts's desk. Mine happened to be on top. He glanced through it. "Well, you had a rough time up there today—we'll talk about it later. Get some rest, Joe."

"Later"—I wasn't off the hook yet. I felt so low that I went back to the hutment and played the Richard Crooks record for a solid hour.

> Central Chancery of the Orders of
> Knighthood
> St. James's Palace, S.W. 1
> 12 October 1944

CONFIDENTIAL

Sir,

The King will hold an Investiture at Buckingham Palace on Tuesday, the 24th October, 1944, at which your attendance is requested.

It is requested that you should be at the Palace not later 10:15 A.M.

DRESS—Service Dress, Morning Dress, Civil Defence Uniform or Dark Lounge Suit.

This letter should be produced on entering the Palace, as no further card of admission will be issued.

Two tickets for relations or friends to witness the Investiture may be obtained on application to this office.

I am, Sir,
Your obedient Servant,
M.H. Stockley, Major,
Secretary

Lieutenant Joseph M. Lauro
D.F.C., USAAF

I didn't know what "Investiture" meant and for a while thought either the RAF was arresting me for damaging the King's property while in its employ, or that this was an invitation to a formal cocktail party at Buckingham Palace through auspices of the Red Cross. It was only when, on rereading, my eye caught "D.F.C., USAAF" in the lower left-hand corner that I realized the British had awarded me a Distinguished Flying Cross for my RCAF service.

When the word got around at Hethel everybody wanted a pass. Gene Litchfield said it was one of his ambitions to see King George in the flesh; hadn't I known he was a great Anglophile? Harry Fisher was curious about the inside of Buckingham Palace. Pilots from the 564th and 560th offered me a hundred bucks and "the hottest pair of dice since Lana Turner." I told them the award was two weeks away and I had a couple of missions to return from first. Anyway, I thought my two passes should by rights go to my Group and Squadron commanders.

The Queen returned from Düsseldorf, Cologne and Mainz. It almost didn't come back from Mainz. In one of these disasters so classic they write them up in the combat manuals, a squadron only three minutes in front of us lost 29 planes out of 40 when one of the other squadrons was two minutes late in moving up to its slot and twenty Me-109's peeled off out of the sun and came in individually on a single pass. It was a matter of our fighters, up ahead, being two minutes and six miles late in getting to the stragglers.

On the 24th Ramsey, Emery Ward and I presented ourselves at Buckingham Palace.

We were ushered into a big room where about a hundred
RAF, Navy and Army personnel waited. These were the men
to be decorated. Ramsey told me that once a month decorations were awarded by the King to never more than a hundred
men of the combined services. I seemed to be the only American officer present.

A spit and polish major of the Royal Marines completed our
inspection, and after another half hour we were led into the
adjoining, high-ceilinged throne room whose oil paintings,
chandeliers, mirrors, chimney pieces and clocks recapitulated
nearly every period of British history. From the walls Kitch-
ener at Omdurman, Gordon at Khartoum, Raglan at Bala-
clava, and Haig at the Somme stared down.

Here, standing in an enclosure roped off from the 200-odd
guests, we awaited the high-ranking officers who would escort
us, individually, to the King seated on his blue-carpeted dais
under a gold-finished canopy. King George was flanked by an
Army general, a Navy admiral and a Royal Air Force Marshal.
Each held a sheet of paper with information on the awardees
of his branch of service.

After fifteen minutes they called my name. I joined my RAF
escorts at the door; then we walked smartly in step down the
red carpet, made a sharp left turn, and stopped three feet in
front of the King.

Our simultaneous salute was returned by King George and
the officers. The Air Marshal handed the King my decoration
and read my citation out loud. I was commanded to take three
steps forward and the King pinned the D.F.C. on my tunic and
said, "I'm happy to be giving you this decoration. I see you're
back in service again with our American friends. We're very
grateful to you and the other Americans who flew with our
forces in the early days of the war. According to our records,
you're of Croatian descent."

"Yes, your Majesty."

"You'll be meeting King Peter of Yugoslavia tomorrow," he added, smiling, and shook my hand.

The King had spoken with a slight speech hesitation, and I remembered having read that he stammered. Returning to my place, I thought of what an ordeal these long public ceremonies must be for him. But what was this about King Peter of Yugoslavia?

Other names were called. The last, an RAF Pilot Officer, was the most impressive. Across his face hung a black veil. As he moved down the red carpet his escorts guided him by an elbow. The Air Marshal read his citation: he had entered a crashed and burning plane and extracted three comrades at the cost of his eyesight, both hands and a disfigured face. I knew I'd never forget the way he rubbed the stump of his right hand across the D.F.C. after the King had pinned it to his tunic. Or the way the King said nothing, because there was nothing to say.

Later an aide told me King Peter would receive me tomorrow morning at eleven at his suite at the Savoy. My audience with the young monarch was pleasant and lasted for about an hour. The King remarked on my RAF uniform and wings with its U.S.A. shoulder patch and asked me why I had joined the Royal Air Force. I told him that any man who valued freedom had good reason to fight for a people who had the courage to withstand Dunkirk, the Luftwaffe bombings and the buzz bombs. Speaking in Croatian, the King asked me about my parents and family. I told him how my father and mother had come to America at the turn of the century and raised eight children there. I mentioned my relatives now in German concentration camps. My family, I told him, must face the possibility that their relations in the old country would not survive; if they did not, and one day I was ordained as a priest, I hoped to say a mass for them in Croatian. Then the King's aide entered with a message, and with exquisite courtesy King Peter saw me to the elevator.

Back at the base the crew presented me with a set of hair-brushes. On their backs were gold plates engraved with the words, "In memory of meeting two kings in two days, by damn." While I was admiring them, Gene Litchfield suddenly grabbed one of the brushes from me, squinted at the engraving and moaned, "Skipper, they forgot to capitalize 'king'!" He was miserable till we found a dictionary that spelled king with a small *k*.

I had seen the signs of combat fatigue coming on with Lloyd Burton since Mission #20—depression, withdrawal, irritability. Yet it hadn't been so bad I'd had to speak to Ramsey Potts about grounding him; we were close to the end of the tour and I didn't want to take any chances with crew morale by substituting another man. So far we hadn't had a single replacement, and I knew the boys felt superstitiously that this was one reason for the Queen's luck.

Nor had we had a single abort, turning back after takeoff due to plane trouble or crew problems. So when on Mission #28 to Munster, Burton handed me a note at 9000 feet that he had pains in his side. I radioed the tower to have a meat wagon waiting on the runway and another radio operator on deck with whom we could complete the mission.

When I landed the meat wagon was there to take Lloyd to hospital, but no radio operator. I radioed the tower and asked where my replacement was. "Go to Dispersal," I was ordered. "Mission scrubbed."

"No need to scrub," I told the tower. "We can climb on course. Get me another radio man."

"Joe," the voice said. "This is Colonel Potts. Go to Dispersal. You're too late to take off."

I didn't want an abort but it was the Colonel talking. At the hospital Lloyd told me he'd had enough. "I'm no good for you any more, Skipper. Everytime I go up I'll get sick and you'll have to abort."

"What's the Doc say?"

"That I'm O.K."

This particular M.O. was an anti-Freudian who was hell on what he called "illusory complaints." Sure enough, when I asked him about Burton he said there was nothing wrong with him and that he could fly tomorrow.

"He can't," I said. "He's got combat fatigue."

The M.O. shot me an annoyed look. "I say there's nothing wrong with him. You want to make sissies of your men?"

"You take care of the medical side," I said with some heat. "I'll take care of my plane and the men who fly it. Some men can get to thirty-five missions, some can't. I don't fly that man again; he'll go berserk. You transfer him to another crew and I'll buck you."

"You've got too many opinions, Lieutenant," the doctor said coldly. "I'll see the Colonel about this."

Potts called me in that afternoon. "What's this I hear about your run-in with the Doc?"

I explained. "This boy had enough at twenty missions. Now he's gone seven more. He's the kind who wants to finish but knows he can't."

"The Doc's a good man," Ramsey said doubtfully.

"So is Burton. Do you want to send him back to the States as a mental case? I brought him over and I want to get him home in one piece. I'm not complaining about our medics. But one thing I remember about the RAF—the medics had the right to send any man on a twenty-four-hour pass or a seven-day leave just by looking at him. If they thought a man needed it you couldn't buck them and the Group Captain had to go along."

"You think I ought to ground him?"

"Do me that favor, Skipper."

"Well, I'll take your word. You've been in this game longer than any of us. Anything else?"

"Yes, I'd like to put Burton in for a D.F.C."

Potts laughed. "Joe, they don't hand out D.F.C.'s after twenty-seven missions."

"Colonel, Burton's worked hard. Not that he's expecting it, but if you send him home with nothing he'll feel he's failed the crew and failed himself. He may never get over it." I tried to grin. "You want that on your conscience?"

Lloyd was grounded. A month later, at Dress Parade, he got his D.F.C. The bit of metal hanging from a ribbon made a lot of difference; he looked like a new man, although you don't get over combat fatigue that easily.

"Skipper," he told me later, "this medal belongs to you."

"I've got one already," I told him.

"There's two things this calls for," he went on. "One's to offer thanksgiving and the other's to throw a helluva bash. You game on both?"

I felt this was quite a compliment from a man who had once told me he could do without God. So I prayed with Lloyd in the Protestant chapel and went to his party at the enlisted men's club. Somebody spiked my Coke and I ended up doing the Lindy with one of the Red Cross girls.

On November 9, the day before our last mission, I checked into the hospital with so bad a headache that it was agony to move. They gave me something new in sedatives and it helped. When Chuck Halder and Clark Boyer dropped by I could see they were upset. They didn't like the idea of having Harry Fisher as first pilot for their last trip.

"Harry tells us he'll bring us through," Chuck said, "but we know he's nervous as a cat. He's used to you in the captain's seat."

I asked them to tell Harry to come in for a talk. Harry admitted he was worried he'd let the crew down. At the same time he didn't want to chicken out on his last mission. "Why couldn't I make fighters?" he groaned.

I told him I'd try to get another first pilot, and asked Ramsey Potts to assign the best man he could find. It wasn't so easy. Two men were reluctant because on its final mission a "lucky" ship was all too likely to run out of luck. But the third man he approached, a pre-med student and rationalist named McNary, had no objections, and the crew flew to Hanau under Lieutenant McNary and came back without a scratch.

When I came out of hospital I asked Ramsey about the transfer to RAF Mosquitoes on detached service he'd promised me after our 15th mission.

He shook his head. "The plan's phasing out. I want you in Operations."

That was medium bad news; I'd hoped to be flying with Geoff Moore again.

"Colonel," I said, "I'm not the Operations type. Ship me back home fast and I'll get a new crew for the Pacific."

"The Pacific! If I had my way I'd ground you for the duration. Now hear this. I'm determined to keep you alive even if you hate me for it. Forget about Ops but you're going to be here for as long as I can keep you. Instructing, preferably till the Japs surrender. Thank God for Leyte."

"What happened at Leyte?" I said, although I knew perfectly well that last month at Leyte Gulf, in the biggest naval action ever fought, the U.S. Navy had destroyed Japanese naval power.

He picked up a paperweight. "Kindly get out of here. I'm busy."

That afternoon Ramsey pinned to my tunic the D.F.C. and a sixth oak-leaf cluster to my Air Medal. Then he put me back into hospital for a few more days for "tests." Then he gave me a week's leave in London. Then he assigned me to training C-47 pilots on four-engine planes, but orders were delayed and I spent an interim week helping Father Beck repaint the chapel. It was December 20 before the crew and I caught a C-54 for the trip home.

Gene Litchfield had four duffel bags full of fleece-lined fly-

ing jackets he'd collected from missing crewmen on the understanding that if they went down he'd get their jackets, and
if he went down they'd get his. I'd warned him they'd be
taken away from him before we left the U.K., but Gene said
he had faith in human nature. Not only did he have to give up
the flying jackets, but he had to pay a stiff fine for his own G.I.
clothing he'd given away to make room for the jackets.

When I discouraged him from complaining to Major Ward,
he looked at me darkly. "Ward? Are you crazy? I'm going
to take this up with Hap Arnold."

Twenty minutes before the plane took off a cable arrived
for me from Chicago. It was signed by Father Lux and read:

> ARRANGEMENTS MADE FOR YOU THROUGH CARDINAL STRITCH,
> BISHOPS O'BRIEN, MORRIS AND FLETCHER TO RETURN TO ST.
> JOHN SEMINARY AS SOON AS DISCHARGED. YOUR WAY TO
> ORDINATION DEFINITELY CLEARED.

I HAD a week's leave in Chicago over Christmas. Father Lux's jet black hair had grayed; it was hell, he said, dealing with writers and printers. "It took a Cardinal and three Bishops and your war record," he told me, "but you're back in seminary to stay. Father Stukel finally admitted you weren't a member of his parish in 1925, and since you had a fine recommendation from Father Kern, the brass decided they could waive Stukel's lack of recommendation. Your appealing the matter to the Apostolic Delegate put a little crimp in things —sometimes it doesn't pay to go to the top, which you've no doubt learned in the service. Can you start at St. John's next month?"

I laughed. "Do you know of any way to get me out of this uniform? I'm in for the duration plus six months, though I bet I've got as many points toward discharge as anybody in the Air Force."

"I'm going to check with the authorities. Any man deserves to get out after two tours of duty."

"Jesuitical reasoning," I told him.

Chicago was talking about Bastogne; the rescue of the besieged American troops had been a fine Christmas present for the nation. Both the Germans and the Japanese had lost all the major battles of the year, and in the Pacific Mindoro had been invaded to bring the war that much closer to Tokyo. Still, the Japanese were fanatical survivors with a talent for rearguard action, and the Pacific war wasn't over yet.

My orders were to instruct at Liberal Field, Kansas, for about a month but first I was supposed to proceed to Santa Barbara, California, for a few weeks' rest cure. "Why," I asked Area Command, "do I have to take a rest cure in California when I've been reassigned to Kansas? Doesn't the AF have a rest home closer to Kansas?" The AF didn't want to talk about it, so I took a train for California.

A pregnant girl, on her way to meet her husband in service, got on at Denver, and we rode together for the rest of the way. The train was so crowded it took an hour to get to the men's room and back, and you gave up trying to get to the diner for meals. The girl wanted ice cream at 2 A.M. and sweet pickles at 4, and once she said she just had to have a watercress sandwich. That was too much for the chef. "Boss," he shouted at me, "dere's a war on! I got to feed five times as many people as I used to befo' them Japs bombed Pearl Harbor! A man gits his wife in a fambly way with a war goin' on, he admits he made a mistake an' he don' ask other people to help him out with watahcress sandwiches!"

The rest home in Santa Barbara was an ex-hotel in the Spanish Mediterranean style on the oceanfront. When I checked in at the desk the girl asked me about my wife and, when I shook my head, seemed puzzled. In the dining room at lunch I was the only man to be sitting at a table by himself; everybody else had a date. I thought to myself, These boys aren't wasting any time.

At breakfast the next morning the same girls were sitting with the same men. Things sure had changed in the States since the war. I went out to the beach for some sunbathing. I was the only man on the beach without a girl, and got some funny looks. A fellow came up to me and said sympathetically, "She run out on you? Trust 'em as far as you can throw 'em, I always say." He moved away before I could answer.

That afternoon I stopped at the desk. The girl said, "Did she get here yet?"

"Who get here? I'm not waiting for anybody."

"Well, where's your wife?"

I told her I wasn't married, and she frowned. "You're supposed to be married to be here. This place is for married personnel. I'll call the Major in charge."

"They tell me I'm supposed to be married," I told the Major. "I'm not."

"Who posted you here without a wife, damn it?" the Major demanded angrily. "Nobody gets posted here without a wife. We've got a perfect record."

"Sorry to spoil it."

"Somebody goofed, and it wasn't us," he said unhappily. "I'll get orders for you from Santa Barbara Airbase."

"Can't I stay on?" I asked him. "I need the rest. I came here all the way from Chicago."

"Not without a wife," said the Major, and went to call the Airbase.

They booted me out that afternoon. I spent the next two weeks at Santa Barbara Airbase, writing letters and reading. One letter was to Father Lux: "I've applied to train a new crew for combat in the South Pacific. I know you won't see it my way, Father, but I keep thinking of your 'What are you saving yourself for?' and just can't see myself in the Air Force nursing a headache when American boys are still dying in the air and on the ground. I can't help but feel that if the Lord had wanted me at the seminary during the war He would have left me there."

They shipped me to Liberal for a month of instructing and in late March I reported to March Field, California, for assignment to a new B-24 radar ship. My application for a new combat crew had been shelved. I never found out why; maybe the headaches had something to do with it.

The radar ship was one of the only two in the country, the other being on the East Coast, and had a million dollars' worth of radar equipment aboard. It was severely restricted; officers up to and including the rank of colonel weren't allowed on board without a pass.

The plane flew at 1000 feet at constant altitude and speed, and could plot radar installations within half a city block. We practiced on sites from the tip of Southern California to Northern Canada. Aside from me, the officers of the crew were all Yale men and all expert mathematicians, an indication of the ship's special status.

Lt. Helen Wilhelm, one of the nurses at March Field, came to me with a problem. She was to be godmother to a new baby born to a nurse friend in Portland, and badly wanted to attend the infant's baptism. Was I by any chance flying to Portland? It so happened we were leaving tomorrow for Canada to plot sites along the way, and Portland wasn't far off our route. I told Helen I'd speak to the boys. My copilot, Bill Walthour, was against smuggling unauthorized persons aboard. "You know what'll happen if we get caught. Besides, this plane has more security than Barbara Hutton."

"All we've got to do is develop engine trouble between San Francisco and Portland," I argued.

Jim Poulson, one of the radar operators, was an Eric Ambler fan and liked intrigue. He had, he said, use of a staff car. He could bring Helen and a nurse friend she'd since invited along out to the plane while I got the MP guards away from it. Our departure time was 3:30 A.M. It would be dark then, which would help.

"All right," Bill gave in reluctantly. "But I have a feeling something terrible's going to happen."

Next morning I got the MP's away from the plane for a while by telling them I'd seen prowlers outside the guard fence. Poulson's staff car pulled up on the nose with the two nurses in battle dress, and we got off the ground without any trouble.

Near Portland I requested permission to land for engine trouble. The tower told me Hamilton was closer, but I ignored them and came in. A staff car was waiting for us near the strip with a colonel in it. "You were ordered to land at Hamilton," he told me.

"Was I?"

"All right, I'll give you a lift in. Our crew chief's on his way to look over your engines." He licked his lips. "Radar, eh? Can I take a look?"

"Sorry, Colonel," I told him. "Top secret . . . No need for your crew chief, by the way; I've got two topflight mechanics. But you can run me and a couple of people I've aboard in to the base."

I told the mechanics to tell the crew chief when he arrived that the engines had already been fixed and that they were waiting for return of the Captain. Then we went in to Portland base.

The nurses were back on time, Helen with snapshots of her godchild, but accompanying them were two Navy men and a Wave who would be AWOL if they didn't get back to San Diego Naval Base tonight.

Jim Poulson shook his head ominously. "I knew there'd be trouble. It'll be breaking regulations to take them aboard." But the Wave was very pretty and I told them to get in the plane.

We didn't get off the ground for another two hours because the field crew chief had insisted on fussing with the engines and put one on the blink. Meanwhile March Field was calling frantically to find out if there was anything seriously wrong. When we landed at March we discovered the sailors had made off with Poulson's and my flying jackets.

"Well, Skipper," Jim asked me, "you sorry for your good deed?"

"At least you got a date with that Wave," I said sourly.

He blinked. "I didn't. I asked, but she said she'd already made one with you."

I'd heard about the base psychiatrist, Major X, from Father Flaherty, March Field's Catholic chaplain. Several WAAF's at the base who had gone to Major X to discuss their anxieties about fiancés and boyfriends in action overseas, had emerged from his office in tears. It seemed he'd advised them to ease their tensions by starting affairs with men on the base. The nurses the girls had complained to were incensed; these were kids, eighteen-year-old small-town girls who were homesick and out of their depth. Father Flaherty had told the nurses he could do nothing if the girls were afraid to speak up against a medical officer.

I had been to see the senior medical officer, a lieutenant colonel, about my headaches, but his pills had done no good. The colonel suggested I see the psychiatrist, Major X, "a wonderful guy—no nonsense about him."

I made an appointment, more to meet the major than in hopes he could do anything for me. My headaches came from a war injury, not from any unresolved childhood conflicts.

As luck had it, while I was sitting in the major's waiting room, an air corps nurse, known for her unbuttoned lip, passed by. "Joe, what are you doing here?" she asked me. "Picking up one of my crew members," I told her. But she knew something was fishy, and I was sure that in no time it would be all over the base that Joe Lauro was going to the psychiatrist.

Major X kept me waiting more than half an hour. I was impressed neither by his office nor by the man who occupied it. The bars on the windows made the room look like a padded cell. The major, sitting behind a cluttered desk, was a small man with a pencil moustache, pouched eyes and a nervousness I found hard to reconcile with his profession. He drummed the fingers of one hand on the desk as he leafed through my medical report with the other, tapped his toe, smoothed his forehead with a nicotine-stained finger.

"Mauro, I understand you have headaches," the major said, biting his lip.

"That's right, sir."

The major smoothed his forehead. "You married?"

"No."

He lit a cigarette. "You have any relationship with a girl?"

"No."

"That's your trouble," the major said. "Get a girl." He tapped his newly lit cigarette in the overflowing ashtray.

I got to my feet. The major looked at me in alarm. "Where are you going?"

"Out," I said.

"You can't. You're my patient."

"That's what you say. I wouldn't be your patient if I thought I was Benito Mussolini. First of all, you didn't even bother to get my name right. Secondly, I'm a Catholic. Two of our commandments have to do with sexual morality. I've been in combat for four years, depending on God to survive. Now I don't intend to insult Him by turning promiscuous to get rid of a headache I got because of an air accident."

"That's what *you* think!" said the major eagerly. "Now sit down and I'll tell you all about it."

But I was already out the door.

One of the young girls the major had counseled to have an affair disappeared from the base and was found in a nearby hotel comatose from an overdose of barbiturates. This was enough for a call to Washington, and within a few days the major had left March Field. He was replaced by a fifty-year-old colonel who told all the girls that before they married they'd better fall in love with an older man to get over their attachments to their fathers.

I wasn't at March Field long enough to find out if he was right.

Father Flaherty, who came from Brooklyn, had no contempt for the good life. He liked his before-dinner drink in the company of attractive women. At his table in the Officers' Club you were always sure to find the prettiest Catholic nurses on the base. This made him very popular with the officers at March, and it was hard to get a seat at Father Flaherty's table. But Father was impressed by the fact that I'd never missed a 5:30 mass unless I was flying, and he sat me on his right-hand side.

One evening he said to me, "What's the matter, Joe? I've introduced you to at least a dozen goodlooking nurses. Countless times I've left the table to give you a chance to make a pitch. The other boys are getting jealous."

"Maybe I'm married," I said, and told him the story of my brief rest cure at Santa Barbara.

Father Flaherty answered shrewdly, "I know you're not married. I looked up your record."

I said he didn't know if I was engaged.

"I doubt it. Come on now, why don't you take one of these girls out?"

"Maybe I'm tight with a buck."

"Don't give me that, you're getting flying pay."

"Maybe I don't want to make some nice girl a widow."

When Father wouldn't buy that I had to break down and tell him I was going back to seminary. Thereafter he was careful not to invite the nurses to sit at his table when I was there. This led to hurt feelings. I overheard one nurse saying to another, "Joe Lauro turned Father against the nurses and the word is he got rid of Major X. I wouldn't trust him if I were you."

*   *   *

Father Flaherty said he was going to buy drinks for the house on the day the Japs surrendered, but Hiroshima and Nagasaki changed his mind and they put a crimp in my celebratory mood, too. We stayed in Father's quarters listening to the madhouse outside and trying not to think of the 200,000 dead, maimed and dying.

"Truman must have known what he was doing, eh, Joe?" said Father.

"I guess so. We're not a nation of killers." Somebody shot off what sounded like a cannon. "He saved American lives. We've got to look at it that way." Father fidgeted in his chair. "Look, Joe, you feel like celebrating, don't let me keep you."

"I'm happy, Father," I told him. "I'd just as soon stay here with you." I'd joined the crew at the Officers' Club for a while and listened to endless choruses of the "Whiffenpoof Song," a glass of ginger ale in my hand, till it occurred to me I was putting a damper on things and that Father Flaherty could use some company.

We jumped as a string of firecrackers went off beneath the window. There was a howl of drunken triumph, then a more distant shattering of glass. "I hear you'll be about first at the Field to be discharged," Father Flaherty said.

"Father Lux's letter to the Air Corps helped, and anyway I've got so many points they're calling me the Porcupine."

"What must have been a French Seventy-Five went off in the direction of the mess hall, and the hutment walls shook. The Father's crucifix fell to the floor. I rushed to put it back, and Father smiled.

I was discharged December 30, 1945. By mid-January I was back at St. John's in Little Rock. It felt more strange to be out of uniform than to be wearing a cassock again.

PART III

FATHER
LAURO

CHAPTER

1

ON May 17, 1949, at St. Andrew's Cathedral, Little Rock, I was ordained a priest by Bishop Albert Fletcher. I was the first American ex-service man of World War II to join the holy priesthood. The average priest achieves ordination at the age of twenty-four. At thirty-eight, with five years out for the RCAF and USAAF, it had taken me fourteen years. I was probably the oldest ordinand in the history of St. John's Seminary and possibly the oldest in the history of the state.

Forty people had come down from Chicago for the ceremony. They included John Boyle, now State's Attorney; Dr. Vince Maurovich; Walt Maurovich, now on the Chicago police force; Tony Gates, now an attorney; Ray Mathys; Mr. and Mrs. Angelo Salerno, and my family. Father Lux was ill and unable to make the trip. He'd wired me: "Now I know what you've been saving yourself for. Be warned however of the curate's difficult life."

During the eight-day retreat that precedes ordination, when an ordinand may, without prejudice, step down from the priesthood and return to lay life, I had sought God's blessing in my calling to the priesthood. The self-questions were persistent: "Is this my vocation? Am I worthy of it? Will I be a good priest, or is the lay state my calling?" I had prayed and found joy in the conviction that my sense of vocation was strong, although I feared that should I fail God would demand His justice.

So much was expected of a priest. Not only the demands of celibacy, of obedience, the renunciation of the fatherhood of the flesh. As Bishop Fulton Sheen has written so eloquently, a priest must grow in Christ; Christ must take the place of his personality. In the confessional, when the priest absolved, it was Christ who absolved; in the mass, offering the Body, it was Christ who offered His body to the Father. And as in the sacraments, so in all the other acts of the *alter Christus*, who must atone for the sinful, speak for the dumb, plead for the Judases. Nothing that happened to others could be alien to him. Not their grief, their poverty, their despair; their hope or their joy. A priest must grow in Christ in love beyond all human love. I was weak, I was often ill, I had in me a streak of stubborn rebelliousness against intermediate authority at odds with a perhaps too passive acceptance of ultimate authority that must be mortified before, in emulation of Him, I could "bow to the stroke" and make myself a Victim in the prolongation of His Incarnation.

At the seminary there had been similar retreats, and the need for a similar decision, during the sub-deaconate, at the end of my third year of theology, and the deaconate in November when I had begun my last semester at St. John's.

Now I and my six fellow ordinands stood at the doorway of the Cathedral. We were vested in white albs and carried red chasubles on our left arms. As the choir burst into the "Ecce Sacerdos Magnus," we moved slowly down the center aisle toward the sanctuary. Passing my seated family, I caught a glimpse of my sister Helen's blue dress.

I took my place in the sanctuary, standing before the marble altar as Bishop Fletcher descended the steps and took his seat on the small chair before the altar.

"*Adsum*," I answered as the roll of ordinands was called.

The Bishop's hands on my head communicated to me the priesthood of Christ. The sacred oil moistened the palms of my hands, consecrating them forever. At the Consecration I spoke for the first time the sacramental words: "This is My Body ... This is the chalice of My Blood. . . ."

Towards the end of the mass the priests rose and knelt once more before the Bishop. Readying us for the long hours we would spend in the confessional, he lowered the chasuble of each to its full length and declared: "Whose sins you shall forgive, they are forgiven them; whose sins you shall retain, they are retained." Then came the question: "Do you promise me and my successors reverence and obedience?" To which we, prostrate on the floor, answered, "I will."

After mass we new priests went to Bishop Fletcher and gave him our first priestly blessing; then we stood at the communion rail to bless our relatives and friends as each knelt before us. I was an *alter Christus*, another Christ to offer sacrifices and to call down God from heaven and to take the people's prayers to Him. I spoke the words *"Benedictio Dei Omnipotentes,"* raising my hands in the circular motion until the fingers touched; continued, *"Patris et Filii, et Spiritus Sancti,"* tracing with my right hand the sign of the Cross, then concluded with *"Descendat super te et maneat, semper. Amen,"* placing both hands on the blessed one's head.

It was over. I felt a kind of calm joy that would be incomplete until I had said my first private mass at the seminary tomorrow.

A romantic, perhaps sentimental part of my nature had led me to assume that, with my return to St. John's after my discharge from the AAF my problems were over and I was anomalous no longer. Nothing could have been further from the truth.

At thirty-five I had been sixteen years older than the average seminary student in my class. Seminarians came to me with gripes that I, as a kind of auxiliary father figure, was expected to adjudicate with Monsignor O'Connell, the rector. People in Little Rock thought I was a faculty member and greeted me as "Father" on the street.

It wasn't that I had any difficulty, as an ex-G.I., settling down to seminary life; seminary discipline was no problem because it was so similar to that of the military. The problem lay exclusively in the Latin required for Father John Feeney's course in Moral Theology. Both the class texts and the examinations were in Latin and I'd had only two years of high school Latin and this many years ago. The endless hours I had to devote to Latin brought on the headaches and in my first half year they were so bad that Monsignor O'Connell insisted on a complete medical checkup at Mayo Clinic. The doctors there recommended a year off for a complete rest but couldn't guarantee a cure, and I talked Monsignor O'Connell into letting me stay on. Somehow I muddled through Father Feeney's course. Once when he called on me to translate I was at a complete loss and silent. A minute passed, then two, while I struggled hopelessly with the text. Finally Father urged me mildly, "Faster." The class exploded into laughter I found more amusing in retrospect than at the time itself.

At Christmas, 1948, Bishop O'Brien had written me to ask if I wanted to say my first mass at Assumption Church where I had been baptized and served as acolyte. Father Stukel had retired earlier that year, he went on; there'd be no embarrassment involved. I wrote back saying that for various reasons I'd prefer Monsignor Kern's St. Theodore's Church, if the Bishop could arrange it. Revenge had no appeal to me. Monsignor Kerns replied that he'd be delighted.

For my first public mass later in May St. Theodore's was packed with a crowd of more than 800. Several Little Rock Fathers had come up for the noon service, and a number of my classmates at Quigley Preparatory, long since ordained, were there, along with schoolmates from St. Raphael's grade school and De Paul, and many people from the neighborhood. Bishop O'Brien was absent for the reason that if he attended one first mass he would have to attend all of them. He had sent a set of breviaries as an ordination gift. Father Lux preached the sermon, titled, *For What Are You Saving Yourself?*

Later there was a reception and dinner at the South Shore Country Club for about five hundred people, lay and clerical, and the family. All left gifts of money; these, together with my $5000 savings from the Air Corps, totaled about $9000.

"You're a rich priest," Father Lux told me, deadpan. "Watch out you don't take to expensive tobacco, like me." He glanced at my ill-fitting clericals. "Get yourself some decent clothes, will you? You know what St. Augustine said about the necessity for a certain amount of worldly goods. Remind me to give you the name of my tailor."

"They don't ask you to dress well in the Arkansas Missions," I told him. "Most hill country people are dirt poor."

"And they hate the Catholics, eh? You're going into quite a situation."

It wasn't quite that bad, I told him. The war had helped bring many of the insular, fiercely independent hill country people into the modern world. Yet he had a point; it wouldn't be easy. My first assignment was to Harrison, Arkansas, in the Valley of Crooked Creek, to assist Father Chinery at Harrison's Mother of God Church. The story they told about Harrison was that as recently as the 1930's, if a Negro, Jew or Catholic happened to be on the streets after sundown, he was told to get out of town.

Father Lux rubbed his well-barbered cheek. "Well, I can promise you one thing—they're not going to like your Chicago accent." He looked around. "Where's that waiter? I didn't want to ask while the Sisters were around, but I could use a drink."

*   *   *

Driving his mission car, Father Harry Chinery came down
from Harrison to pick me up at the seminary. He was a goodlooking young Philadelphian who had been ordained seven
years ago in '42. I followed him back to Harrison in the
secondhand '39 Chevvy I'd bought in Chicago with part of
my G.I. savings. Coming through the mountains at Conway,
Arkansas, skirting canyons 500 to 600 feet deep, my lights
failed and I had to tail the Father's tail-lights for an exhausting
90 miles through the heavy mists. Then, when we arrived in
Harrison, Father Chinery pulled up in succession at several
substantial houses, each of which he identified as the rectory.
The rectory turned out to be a five-room old frame house in
need of a paint job. It was considerably bigger than the
church, which was little more than a wooden hut.

Father Chinery announced we had no housekeeper and
would share the cooking. He opened the kitchen cabinets to
show me his stock of groceries. They were filled with half-
gallon Mason jars of preserved string beans.

"I get these from the parishioners," Father said. "I've been
saving them for three years."

"You must like string beans."

"Not especially. It's just that I like the jars. They have so
many uses."

"But if you don't eat the beans," I asked, "how can you use
the jars?"

"Oh, now that you're here we'll be eating the beans," he
said confidently. It occurred to me he hadn't asked if I liked
string beans. I didn't.

He explained my duties next morning. The mission covered
five counties. Arkansas was mission country because there
were only 45,000 Catholics in the state, less than 2 percent of
the population; in the Ozarks the figure was half of one
percent. I'd be responsible for masses in Eureka Springs, about
50 miles from Harrison. Father Chinery would take the Sunday masses in nearby Mountain Home, and at Harrison's little

wooden church. Since Eureka's St. Elizabeth's Church was so dilapidated as to be unfit for use, masses in Eureka would be held for the present at the Crescent Hotel. Weekdays I would drive to Eureka Springs to work on the reconstruction of St. Elizabeth's.

"Reconstruction?" I said. "That's news to me."

Father Chinery nodded. "I forgot to tell you. St. Elizabeth's is in very bad shape. Your predecessor—he's in a rest home in Kansas now, slight breakdown—had to hear confessions under an umbrella, and a couple of people got hurt when the staircase to the choir loft collapsed."

I asked how much money Home Missions had set aside for the restoration, and Father told me I could have a thousand dollars. How many parishioners would I have in Eureka, I asked him, and thirty was the answer. Thirty! How could I be expected to rebuild a church with so few parishioners to contribute to a building fund? Did the Bishop expect miracles?

Father didn't deny it; the diocese was both poor and small in population. As with any other priest, it was up to me to solicit help from my friends back home. Anyway, he'd heard I'd had experience in construction work. I thought of Father Lux's warning about a curate's hard road and changed the subject.

It was only when I was at the Harrison Garage getting the lights on my Chevvy fixed that it came to me: Father Chinery's parish route covered 56 miles, mine, 100. I'd have to find a Eureka Springs parishioner who could put me up during the week . . . I just hoped it wasn't string beans tonight for supper.

It was string beans and stew that night and for the next two nights, too. Father observed cheerfully that we were making a good dent in the first gallon jar. Fortunately, before the end of the week the Lee Morgans of Eureka invited me to move in with them till living quarters were ready at the church. Lee managed the electric company in Eureka and his wife Katy was a fine cook. Besides, I was getting a little discouraged by my reception in Harrison. The tradesmen were fine and never overcharged, but very few people I smiled at in the street or said hello to smiled back.

Father Chinery asked if I'd gotten the cold shoulder near or around the Boone County Courthouse, and I told him yes. "Well, that's probably the explanation," he said. "You can't expect people coming out of a courthouse to be so all-fired pleased with the world." He thought a moment. "Or maybe it's that people in Harrison think one Catholic priest in town's enough. They don't really hate us, Joe. You see, the Klan wears robes and we wear cassocks, and some folks get a little confused."

Eureka Springs was the western seat of Carroll County, but its principal business was providing services for the old and the health-seekers who had come to its mineral springs for more than fifty years. Over sixty springs existed within the city limits, and could be tapped from faucets set into rock every few yards along the single through street that wound between the valley walls. Limestone caves, deep and mysterious, summoning up memories of Huck Finn, also abounded, some of them opening directly off the main street.

Since it clung to valley slopes so steep that there were few level spots in town, you puffed going up streets and went down them skidding. Eureka Springs was full of architectural curiosities. You could reach all seven floors of the cavernous Basin Park Hotel on Spring Street without taking the elevator or climbing the stairs: the position of the building against the mountain side made every floor a ground floor. In a similar way, the parishioners of St. Elizabeth's Church on Crescent Drive could walk directly into the second-floor auditorium. I had already heard avid boosters claiming that the church was the only church in the world that could be entered through its bell-tower, but this was an exaggeration, of course.

St. Elizabeth's had been built by Richard Kerns, an immigrant Irishman whose family had settled in Iowa. After the Civil War Kerns had gone to Fort Smith, Arkansas, and his first business venture there was trucking and transportation with mules purchased from the government as surplus war supplies. His transportation interests expanded from Fort Smith to Fayetteville and the Missouri state line, and together with General Powell Clayton, a governor of Arkansas, Kerns built the St. Louis and North Arkansas Railroad. He planned a railroad to start at Kansas City and pass through Eureka Springs, and on to New Orleans. Eureka Springs was to be his repair shop, but he ran afoul of labor trouble and the railroad never went through. It was Eureka's first major disappointment, and not her last.

In 1903 Kerns was staying at the Crescent Hotel with his beloved old mother. As he was setting out for a trip in a horse-drawn cart, Mrs. Kerns, walking down from the hill, stopped on the stairway to wave to her son. When Kerns returned from his trip his mother was dead and he decided to build a church on the spot where he had seen her last; this was the reason for the church's unusual construction. First the dome was built as a chapel for such immigrant railwaymen as worked in the town; then Bishop Morris suggested building a church for Catholics of the town who at the time had only a little wooden building like that in Harrison.

Eureka Springs had at least one celebrity. Carry Nation had lived for a while in the Arkansas Ozarks and made her last temperance speech in Eureka. The reformer's followers had built Hatchet Hall, a frame building on Steel Street to house an academy for the training of young prohibitionists. On Carry's death the project was abandoned, but Hatchet Hall still stood, barnlike and forbidding.

Many of the older homes in town had been turned into boarding houses and were occupied by ailing pensioners on

Social Security, struggling to get by on $80 a month. Nearly all the old retired people had to take odd jobs, most of them working in the gift shops and at the Crescent Hotel, overlooking St. Elizabeth's, for as little as $100 a month. Eureka Springs had no hospital or ambulance. The nearest hospital was at Rogers, 35 miles away.

At St. Elizabeth's things were going discouragingly slow. If my first introduction to the church was any indication, I had a long way to go. The last three rotten basement steps gave way as I went down them and I flew across the floor and into three feet of cinders, banging my head against a broken stone angel. My good trousers were torn and I'd scraped my knee to the raw. Upstairs a wasp zeroed in and stung me on the wrist, and as I fled to regroup my forces, a tile falling from the rotting roof glanced off my shoulder.

Conditions in the church itself were so bad that I wondered how Bishop Fletcher had considered the building, built in 1904, salvageable. Old age and a leaking roof had contributed as much to its deterioration as neglect. Great patches of plaster had fallen off the walls to reveal the lathing beneath. The pews needed a complete restripping and revarnishing. Cardboard served for windowpanes. Part of the roof had fallen in and was covered by canvas. The sacristy was completely plasterless and the electric switchboard hung on its cables. The stairway to the choir loft was rotted through and a new floor, steel-beam supported, would have to be put in. Vandals had entered the church and filthied it up further, if that was possible. The Morgans and their houseman, "Nigger" Rich, had tried to clean up but the wasps in the bell-tower had driven them away.

First I'd have to smoke out the wasps. The roof would come first, the walls second; then a new terrazzo floor, and finally a complete paint job. My salary was $25 a week from the parish. There was $1006 in the parish bank account. The reconstruction would cost a minimum $12,000. I had around

$9000 in G.I. savings and ordination gifts. It was a start; the Lord would provide the rest, I decided. He *had* to.

The first thing I did was throw out, to the horror of some parishioners, the old wooden confessionals. One lady appeared at the Morgans' to protest. She wouldn't, she said, feel comfortable confessing her sins in a new box; the old ones, roofless though they were, had made her feel at home. Later I heard she'd appeared at the city dump to rescue one of the confessionals and had installed it in her bedroom. Eureka Springs was a town of eccentricities.

A local estimate to strip and revarnish the pews came to $350; too much money. I asked the ladies if they couldn't take over. Lee Morgan donated the basement of the electric company, another parishioner his pick-up truck to carry the pews to the basement, and the ladies set to work. They were making good progress when one afternoon Katy Morgan drove up, brakes screeching, with a problem. One of the working ladies was in tears. When they had broken for lunch to go out to the cafe, a passerby had called her a drunk and demanded to know if she intended to destroy herself and her family.

"Why?" I asked. "Was she drinking?"

"Oh no, Father Joe," said Katy. "You see, the fumes from the varnish remover make us all pretty tipsy, and when we come into the fresh air, some of us don't walk so straight."

I asked Katy to put the ladies on shifts, two hours on, two off. That way they'd keep their reputations.

I had hired three professional workmen at $8 a day each to tear out the plaster, but every time it rained they took off and went downtown to drink beer. I fired them and asked the men parishioners to help. One of my most willing workers was Boss Hawley, a seventy-year-old convert. Annie, Boss's wife, objected to his working at the church because of his age and senility, so he kept his overalls in the basement and told her every morning he was just going down to St. Elizabeth's to watch. One day, a few weeks before Christmas, a chunk of plaster fell on Boss's head and knocked him cold. I drove him to the hospital at Rogers where they examined and discharged him. His wife came to the church to thank me. "Father," she said, "Boss is sure perkier since his accident. You figure you can arrange another knock on the head?"

Removing the plaster meant taking out and replacing the rotten lathing, and twenty parishioners were busy night and day. I heard rumors that the neighbors were saying we must be expecting a visit from the Pope. Working myself from eight in the morning till midnight, I made an interesting discovery: at this breakneck pace the headaches didn't bother me, but if I overdid by just a hair, they'd put me to bed for a couple of days.

During one of these times Katy knocked on my door to tell me there was a lady parishioner downstairs with a complaint that couldn't wait. I went down to the parlor. My visitor came straight to the point. She'd heard I'd hired a Nazi butcher to play the xylophone at Christmas Eve mass. This was a desecration. She understood I'd fought with the Australian army during the war; how could I countenance such an unpatriotic act? If I persisted in my plan she'd have to write the Bishop.

I told her, "First of all, it's not a xylophone Mr. Kukler's playing, it's a zither. He's no Nazi butcher but a Viennese woodcarver, a refugee from Hitler. Nor did I hire him—he's donated his services because we can't afford an organ. Finally, the zither's mentioned in the Old Testament as one of the instruments permitted in church services. Now if you want to write the Bishop, I'll give you his address."

She couldn't find a word to say in answer and left. My headache felt so much better that over Katy's protests I went down to the church. Boss Hawley had insisted on mixing the plaster and gotten into an argument with the plasterer, who didn't like his work, but otherwise things were going well.

Mr. Kukler played Bach on his zither as accompaniment to Katy's singing for midnight mass on Christmas Eve. It was a great success even though the pews still weren't ready and everybody sat on folding chairs. The Christmas trees Lee and I had cut down in the woods to hide the worst spots of the chancel and sanctuary walls were admired. Several Protestant visitors, touched by Mr. Kukler's performance and by the decorated cardboards the children had made for the paneless windows, gave donations. Only one embarrassing thing happened. During the Consecration the ladder to the choir loft toppled over with a crash.

One afternoon after the New Year I came back to St. Elizabeth's after my catechism class in Berryville to find that one of the Christmas baskets I'd delivered to the hill people had been returned to the church.

"You should have seen their car," one of my parishioners told me. "From the Year One. They had trouble getting up the hill, and the backfires brought all the neighbors out."

The Christmas basket, with its canned and other goods, had been untouched, and I felt bad about it. But the parishioner laughed. "You've got it wrong, Father. Them people didn't return the basket because they couldn't use the stuff. They thought you'd made a mistake leaving it with their kids. They kept telling me, 'We're not Catholics.' I told them that didn't make any difference to you, but they wouldn't believe me."

I asked the parishioner if he knew their name, but he shook his head. "Real towheads, man and wife, with four towheaded kids. That's all I can tell you."

I thought back to the forty or fifty families in the hills Lee and I had left baskets with, and remembered one shack beyond the ridge where the parents hadn't been home and two of the yellowest towheads I'd ever seen had shown me into the place so I could leave the basket on the kitchen table. Of course in the Ozarks there were many towheaded families, and

not a few albinos. When the great tide of immigration had
swept westward to the Pacific, passing by the backhill sections
of the mountains, the hillsman had "kinned-up" with his "first
cousins" and "last cousins." For more than half a century
there had been little marriage with outsiders, resulting in a
remarkable purity of the Anglo-Saxon types that had settled
in the area.

Next afternoon, with the Christmas basket in the back seat
of the Chevvy, I drove out beyond the ridge. It had rained
the night before and the dirt roads were muddy. I got stuck
more than once, and lost twice. Finally an old granny in a
poke bonnet, dipping snuff, directed me to a decaying shack
near a choked-up creek. She said the people I was looking for
were named Southworth.

It was the right place all right; an old fenderless Ford
roadster from the 20's stood in the yard under a tattered tar-
paulin, a headless doll near its right front tire.

I knocked on the door. There was no answer and I knocked
again. Inside I heard stirrings.

"Who you be?" a man asked, and I identified myself.

"You sure you ain't the sheriff?"

"I just told you who I was. Do I sound like the sheriff?"

"What you want with we-uns? We ain't Kath-a-licks."

I told him I'd explain if he'd let me in. The door swung
open. I'd been inside hill country houses and their poverty had
ceased to shock me; this one was like most if a shade better;
any hillman who had a car or truck, of whatever antique vin-
tage, was considered fairly well off. Only a few of the windowpanes were broken out and there was a clean quilt on the
brass bedstead. The old cook stove looked in good shape and
the table had all four legs.

The little towheaded girl clutching the hand of her lank,
washed-out mother pointed a corn cob at me. "Mama, this is
the man was hyar to leave the groceries."

"That's right," I told the woman's husband, a spavined

wreck in bib overalls with burned-out eyes. "You brought them back to the church. Well, here they are again."

"We ain't Kath-a-licks," the man said, and his angular wife nodded.

I told them they didn't have to be.

"We ain't a-goin' to jine yo church," the man said. "We're good Baptists."

"You stay Baptists. But there's no reason why you can't accept something you need and that's freely given." I had to be tactful. The Ozarkian had pride. He wanted to earn, and wouldn't accept anything you just gave him.

The woman smiled slightly, "Mr. Preacher, won't you set?"

I took a seat on one of the two battered kitchen chairs. The four of them—a little towheaded boy sat quietly on the bed—stared at me.

"If'n you don't want us to jine your church, jist what is it you do want?" asked the man.

Proud, the Ozarkian was also suspicious. It was one of the things that made him such a great trader. "Mr. Southworth," I said, "I don't want anything. Can't you believe that?"

"The Kath-a-lick preacher wus here before, he didn't give us hill country people nothin'," he said stubbornly.

"I guess he just didn't think of Christmas baskets. Now can I go out to my car and bring in the groceries? I've got a few toys for the youngsters, too."

They needed the food. The woman glanced at her husband, and I knew her look meant assent. But he compromised.

"You kin leave the basket here an' I'll ask my preacher if'n it's all right to keep it. If'n he says no, I'll take it kindly you won't mind if'n I bring it back agin to the church."

I left it at that and went on my way. When in the next week Southworth didn't return the basket, I forgot about it. But a few weeks after that he showed up at the church and asked what he could do to repay me. Knowing that refusal to accept repayment of some kind would be taken as an insult, I asked him to drive Mr. Baines, the master plasterer, home from the church for a while, and insisted on paying for the gasoline. We had words about that, but Southworth finally gave in. The only trouble was that when his Ford broke down twice in a row on the road out of town I had to go back to ferrying Mr. Baines myself. It was either that or paying fifty dollars to get Southworth's car overhauled at the Eureka Springs Garage.

Baines had started work at St. Elizabeth's when Boss Hawley gave the regular plasterer an ulcer attack and he quit. I'd heard that Howard Fancher, of nearby Berryville, was a good plasterer and approached him. Fancher started work, but wouldn't touch the delicate job of plastering the arches and double arches of the nave unless I got George Baines, a local retired master plasterer, to oversee the work.

We went to see Baines at his cattle ranch outside Eureka. "Nope," Baines replied definitely to my offer, "I'm retired, and this cattle ranch is enough to kill me. You'll have to get somebody else."

There wasn't another master plasterer with Baines's skills in the northern Ozarks. Racking my brains on how to get him, I consulted Lee Morgan. Lee thought a moment, then told me, "George Baines is a Protestant, but I think he's got a Catholic son-in-law."

"But does he like him?" I asked.

Lee grinned. "All right, I'll try to find out."

Two days later Lee had the information. It was adjudged a fair bet that George Baines got along with his son-in-law, who visited him most Sunday afternoons.

Next Sunday Lee, Fancher and I went out again to George Baines's cattle ranch. The son-in-law was there. When I took him aside he told me, "It's no use, Father. I gave up going to church a long time ago." But when I told him what I wanted, he was relieved and said he'd do what he could. Half an hour later Baines came up to me.

"You willing to let me work at my own pace?"

"Anything you say, Mr. Baines."

"My car's in the repair shop. Can you pick me up in the morning and bring me back to the ranch at night?"

"You bet."

"Can you pay a master plasterer's hourly wage?"

"It won't be easy, but I'm not haggling with you."

"Well, I heard about your Christmas Eve service with that guitar and those baskets you gave to the hill country people, not one of them Catholics. I like the way you do things. Different. I'm going to charge you half my regular rate."

Baines not only did a magnificent job with Howard Fancher, but reconstructed the arches on his own. I was careful to keep Boss Hawley out of his way.

While the plastering was going on I reinstalled the altar and communion rail, and put my mind to the problem of the choir loft staircase. Over the past forty years the rain coming in through the leaking roof had rotted out the six-inch diameter pole. I wrote Maurey Schafer in Washington asking him to send me a good six-inch pole from his father's timber forests. Meanwhile a carpenter came by and said he'd heard I was looking for a man to build a stairwell. He said he could do the job, and I told him I was waiting for the piece of timber. "Shucks," he said, "you don't need no six-inch timber. All I'm going to do is use a one-inch center pole."

"What?" I asked him. "I took a big *six*-inch pole out of here."

"You don't understand," he told me. "An equal number of steps on all sides will bind in the staircase and it's agoin' to hold itself up. That's a law of physics."

I didn't understand what he was talking about, but when he finished the well and staircase with its one-inch center pole, it worked. I could never figure out what to do with the six-inch, 20-foot pole Maurey sent from Washington that somebody had said I planned to use as a battering ram when I declared war on the Holy Roller church.

By Easter the church was complete except for part of the roof and dome. Ben Booth, a roofer from Little Rock, donated copper for the roof that he'd saved during the war years and that was worth a small fortune.

I had hired Henry Pond to put in the ceiling. Henry's whole family was Catholic but himself. His daughter Celeste was in a convent and his wife and three other children were regular communicants in Harrison. He asked me for a catechism, and studied it each night for six weeks; in the evenings I answered his questions while he was on the scaffolding doing his work.

"Just one thing I can't quite go along with," he shouted down at me one evening in the fifth week, "and that's the future life."

"Watch your footing, Henry," I shouted back at him. "If you fall off that scaffolding you're going to find out, but it wouldn't do the church much good."

Henry laughed so much he almost fell. After another two months of instruction he entered the Church, was baptized, and made his first communion.

Since Father Chinery had investigated stained glass for the church windows at St. Elizabeth's before I became pastor, he had to be consulted on the glass samples I sent from Little Rock. The Morgans and I agreed we liked the red, but there wasn't any assurance Harry would too, so we picked the two worst colors, purple and orange, to show him along with the red.

Harry picked the purple. Katy Morgan said, "Oh no, Father, purple's for a funeral home," but Harry still liked it. Katy excused herself and came back with Lee. Father Chinery asked what color he liked and, well coached, Lee answered, "Well, if you're asking me, I like the red." Harry pouted and said, "I guess it's three to one against me." Katy picked up the samples and hurried away with them, saying, "I'll get the coffee."

Harry turned to me with a reproachful look. "Wish you'd come to Harrison for dinner more often, Joe. Those string beans aren't getting eaten and I could use the jars."

In May, when the electrical work was completed and the stained-glass windows in, I had spent $9000 and was completely broke. There was only one thing for it—go to Chicago and raise more money. Yet it was only ten months since I'd received money and gifts from my friends and relations at my ordination.

In Chicago I went to the Salernos, Angelo and Rose, and told them it would cost $3000 to paint the church. Angelo thought the figure low; the paint job for his house had cost $5000. He asked me if I could come back to town in two weeks for a party he and Rose would throw for the painting of St. Elizabeth's. I didn't say no.

The party was held at the Salerno home in Skokie, Illinois. Half the aldermen and judges of Chicago were there, a hood or two who had lately become respectable, and all the Salerno family. After the coffee was served, and before the dancing started, Angelo got to his feet and said, "You've had the best food and the best liquor in Chicago. But you didn't come here just to eat and drink. Make your contributions to Father Joe."

Around eleven o'clock Angelo came over and asked me how I was making out. I showed him what cash and checks I'd collected. One check from a judge was for $25; another from a gangster, $30. "Father, come with me, will you?" Angelo asked, and I followed him over to the judge, who was deep in conversation with the mobster. Interrupting, Angelo said jovially, "Is this all you guys are giving? Hell, you ate and drank more than that, Judge, Augie. Put a one in front of the other digits."

Later I asked Angelo if he hadn't taken a chance on embarrassing the mobster, who was known for his touchiness. He smiled. "Not on your life. Neither of them wanted to look like a piker in front of the other. Not with a priest looking on. And not in Chicago."

I took $3500 back to Eureka Springs, and started looking for some painters who were known to be reasonable. There weren't any, it seemed, in the northern Ozarks—one outfit asked $5500, another only $500 less. When Boss Hawley woke me up at 6 A.M. one morning and offered to do the whole job for nothing, I realized it was time to look afield, and drove the 190 miles to Little Rock. There, through their sister Dolly Mitchell, a professional artist who agreed to do a mural for the altar, I turned up the Cole brothers. The Coles agreed to my price—part of the package deal was that they'd sleep on cots in the church basement and take their meals free at the Morgans'.

Dolly laughed when I told her how pleased I was to get the Coles. "The boys aren't so dumb," she told me. "For months now they've been trying to get away from their wives for a little vacation. And if you know what I mean, Father, they don't mind an occasional beer."

I couldn't believe that the quiet Bud, Larry and Johnny were rounders, and in any case Eureka Springs was far from being the Sodom of northern Arkansas.

It took seven weeks to paint the church and the Cole boys did a first-class job. For six of those weeks they were never a minute late for Katy's 6:30 dinners, and were always in bed by eleven, except for Saturday nights, when they'd bring back beer from downtown. I had borrowed a small refrigerator for their beer and snacks, and every Sunday morning a big paper bag full of neatly packed beer can empties sat outside the basement door.

The last Saturday of the paint job I came back to the Morgans' about 6:30 from a sick call in Green Forest. Only Katy was home. The Coles, she said, had called up to say they were getting haircuts and meeting a buddy for dinner in town.

I left to meet Lee Morgan at the Rotary dinner at the Basin
Park Hotel on Spring Street.

Leaving the meeting, Lee and I ran into the brothers coming out of the cafe across the street. They weren't exactly
sober. I said, "I see you got your haircuts, but where's the
buddy you were supposed to meet?" There was a silence, and
then Johnny said thickly, "Father, that was a *Budweiser*
buddy, and how about you and Lee getting to know him,
too?"

We declined and the boys weaved off. "You think they'll be
all right?" I asked with concern, but Lee said that anybody
in Eureka Springs was safe when under the influence if they
didn't drive a car.

At home Lee and I decided we might have hurt the boys'
feelings by not joining them in town, and about ten o'clock
we dropped down to the church with some crackers and beer.
The basement was dark. In one corner stood a crated statue of
St. Anthony that had arrived that day. Having nothing better
to do, Lee and I uncrated the statue and left it in a corner.
Then, inspired, we crumbled up the crackers in the boys' beds,
short-sheeted them, and poured a can of beer into each. We
left the empty cans on the floor with a note saying, "Here's
three cans in case you need a nightcap. If you want a Bromo
tomorrow morning, come to Katy's after mass."

Next morning, after mass, I was saying goodbye to parishioners at the church door when a dusty car pulled up the
driveway. The Cole brothers' three wives got out. I tried to
get the girls away from the church by asking them to the
Morgans' for breakfast, but Mary, Bud's wife, said brightly,
"Thanks, Father, but we want to have breakfast with the
boys. They must still be sleeping—we'll surprise them. Is the
basement this way?"

I ran.

The phone at the Morgans' rang an hour later. It was Bud
Cole. "Father Joe? You really fixed us. First of all, when the

girls woke us up this morning, the first thing I saw was that statue of St. Anthony in the corner, and I nearly had a heart attack—I thought I was dead and in heaven. But that's the least of it. The place smelled like a brewery and the girls cried and won't talk to us; they think we took the job here so we could carouse and raise hell every night of the week. We're on our way over. You better explain things to the girls good." Click.

The mess didn't get straightened out till dinner time. The wives wouldn't believe me when I told them the boys hadn't cut loose till last evening, and the boys wouldn't buy that I hadn't alerted their wives to come down from Little Rock and catch them in flagrante.

The Cole brothers finished and went back home. Three heavy scrub brushes on waxers were worn out scouring the rotunda. Terrazzo went down on the nave floor. This completed work on the interior of the church, and I began the landscaping. Flowers and shrubbery were put in, and fourteen stations of the cross, in white Italian Carrara marble, along the side and at eye level. In front of the church was a Fatima scene, also in Italian marble, donated by the Koch and Deusch families. At night floodlights installed along the stone wall made it a breathtaking sight. St. Elizabeth's was fast becoming a prime tourist attraction in Eureka Springs.

When I worked at the church, which was often, I wore overalls with the pockets worn through. One day while I was putting in the floodlights, a woman called at the church. "Is the priest around?" she asked me. "I know him quite well and I'd like to see him." I didn't want to interrupt my work and told her the priest was out at the moment but would probably be back after a while.

Next morning the visitor showed up for the service. Later one of my parishioners who had sat next to her told me, "Father, that woman was so shocked that the janitor was saying mass that she left after the Offertory."

CHAPTER

2

IN Green Forest, population about 800, 12 miles from
Eureka Springs as the razorback runs, almost everybody
worked in the chicken plant or was connected directly
with farming. Most of the people could trace their ancestry
back to the Civil War or earlier. They took their religion
seriously and there were a lot of churches in town, among
them the Baptist, Methodist, Church of Christ and several
Holy Roller denominations.

Green Forest, with its handful of Catholics, became part of
my parish in the fall of 1952. One Catholic family in town had
a daughter who was marrying the son of a Baptist hill
country family. Since this was a mixed marriage, I had to call
on the parents of the boy to find out if their son had had a
previous marriage or divorce. The river was up at the time
and the roads nearly impassable; when I came to the parents'
shack, a creek barred my way. I blew my horn and the hillman came out of his house to stand on the bank, a shotgun
cradled in the crook of his arm.

I got out of the Chevvy and introduced myself. I had to
shout—the man was a good twenty yards distant. There was
a rowboat tied to a stake on the hillman's side, and I asked if
he'd come across or mind ferrying me to the other side.

"No," he shouted at me, "you fire away and I'll answer you from here!"

I asked if he knew his son was marrying a Catholic girl.

"Don't 'prove of it," he shouted back, "but that boy of mine, Ludovic, looks like he's agoin' to do hit anyway!"

I explained that in the Catholic faith a priest marrying a couple had to make sure there had been no previous marriage.

"W'all, I kin tell you Ludovic ain't been married afore. I kin tell you thet."

"I've got to ask you at least thirty questions," I shouted back, taking out the list. "Don't you think it would be easier if I came across?"

"No!" he yelled. "I'll tell y'all what y'all want to know from here!"

I shouted out thirty-five questions to which he shouted back the answers. When we were finished I asked the hillman to come across to sign the paper. He started back to his shack, yelling over his shoulder, "Mister, I never sign *nothin'*. That's why I'm a happy man today!"

"Then I'll have to mail them to you registered!" I shouted as he disappeared.

I was hoarse when I got back to the Morgans'.

In the spring of '53 Carl Koch of Chicago and his wife Paula began to build a house a few miles outside of Eureka Springs. Carl was a wealthy man, with big real estate and business investments in the Midwest and the South, and Eureka Springs had never seen a house like it. Nobody built a home in these parts costing more than twenty thousand; Carl's would cost more than three or four times that much. Half the construction men in Eureka seemed to be working on it; when you went into the G. & J. Cafe, all you heard was talk about the Kochs and the magnificent chandeliers and furniture being shipped in from Chicago and New York for their showplace. Carl Koch must be going into Arkansas politics, it was said.

What other reason could he have for settling in these parts except to take over the state?

Actually Carl was building a house in Eureka Springs because his brother Albert, a retired dentist from Chicago, lived there and he had sunk some money into cattle. He had no intention of going into politics. "Smart man," Judge Anglin, the Berryville attorney and wit, commented. "When he moved into the Governor's mansion he'd find out he had two million people on his payroll whose names weren't exactly written down on it."

Unfortunately, the site of the Koch house was pretty dusty because of a lack of grass. Halfway through the construction Carl got discouraged and offered the house, when complete, to me for whatever purpose I could find for it. When I got over the shock I told him, "Thanks, Carl, but the only thing I can think of to do with your house is turn it into a gambling casino."

"All right, then, I want to help finance a rectory for St. Elizabeth's. They're talking about your church from here to St. Louis, and you've been living at the Morgans' too long. They tell me a rectory will cost about twenty thousand dollars. I'll match any contributions you get for it three to one. I just want you to promise you won't do all the work yourself. Hire an architect."

The five-room gray stone rectory was finished in 1954. I talked Carl out of an architect, but all I did completely by myself was chip the stone and mix mortar for Wayne Johnson, an excellent local carpenter and stonemason. Lawrence Putman of Eureka Springs was the contractor. The Morgans contributed funds. The rectory was valued at $17,000 and cost less than $8000. Carl dropped around often during construction, sometimes to pick up Paula, who shared the monthly scrubbing of St. Elizabeth's floors with the other women of the parish. A rumor got started that I'd been picked to run with Carl for Lieutenant Governor in the next gubernatorial election, and a reporter from a Little Rock newspaper called me to check.

"Why didn't you call Bishop Fletcher in Little Rock?" I asked him.

"You might not have told the Bishop yet," the reporter said, "and I didn't want to get him mad at you. This is the first time in state history I've heard a priest's thinking of running for public office. Let alone two Catholics on the same ticket."

"But I'm not running," I insisted. "Neither is Carl Koch."

"I hear this Koch gets what he wants," the reporter said. "Let me know if you change your mind, Father." He hung up.

While I was on the phone the soup I'd started on the stove had boiled over, making a sticky mess. I cleaned it up and began a new batch. After Katy's cooking it wasn't much fun doing for myself.

The phone rang.

"Father Lauro?" a voice said. "Has —— paid up yet?" There was a click on the other end and I replaced the receiver. This was the fifth nuisance call I'd had in the last two days, and therein lay a tale.

We had Bingo every Tuesday night in the St. Elizabeth basement. Lately the crowd had been substantial, and being substantial meant it was composed mostly of non-Catholics. Last Tuesday, by one of those freak coincidences that happen perhaps once in a decade, one individual had won five of the ten games played. This lucky player was Protestant. I thought nothing in particular of it until, when the evening was over, one of the non-parishioners said as she was leaving, "Well, Father, I guess you'll get a nice donation now from Mrs. ——." It didn't occur to me that she was implying the game had been fixed in Mrs. ——'s favor till next morning, when the phone rang and a male voice said, "What's she goin' to give you people in exchange, a couple of them graven images for your front yard?" and hung up. The other calls, most of them within the next few hours, were more of the same, all anonymous and more or less unpleasant. I knew better than to think it was a campaign against the Church by anti-Catholic elements in town; there was no such organized group. But the calls still hurt.

I asked Harry Chinery for his advice. No, nothing like this had ever happened to him although the crank calls were constant. He agreed the Bingo should continue; to stop it, if only temporarily, would have been an admission of guilt. I could just hope somebody else didn't win five games in a row and kill Bingo at the church. How about staying for dinner and a nice string bean stew?

The following week all ten games were won by Catholics. Some Protestants left grumbling, and next day one loser called to suggest that since all the winners had sat on one side of the room, the card distribution system be overhauled. Mind you, he wasn't intimating there'd been any funny business. I told him I'd look into it.

The week after that not a single parishioner won. One wrote a letter to the Eureka Springs *Times-Echo* recommending the prohibition of all gambling in Carroll County. But I noticed that she kept coming to the Bingo. Thereafter, in the following weeks' games, things returned to normal, with winners not confined to one religious group or another, and the trouble gradually blew over.

Frank Husnik was a retired steelworker of Polish ancestry from Milwaukee. Frank had lost a hand in a steel mill accident, for which he received a small pension. He lived about 15 miles out on the road toward Huntsville in a house he'd bought from a mail order real estate catalog. Though he had no car, somehow Frank got into town for mass every Sunday; when I asked him how he managed it, he just grinned and said I had more important things to think about. I'd already had a taste of his persnickity independence: when I told him to cut down on his contributions to the collection plate, he said, "Father, this is *my* business. Don't you tell me how much to give to the Lord."

I went out to see him in his house on the Huntsville road. His wife Muriel had died the year before and the place was in a terrible mess. When I asked him why he didn't clean it up he said, "Whenever I start Muriel follows me around, and tells me how to do things." He insisted she traveled with the Devil; every time he heard a noise in the house he said, "That's her and the Devil. She's down there and so is he. They travel around together, you know. Muriel always did like tall, dark, wicked men."

"You didn't get along too well with your wife, eh Frank?" I asked him. He only grinned at me.

I thought it would be a good idea to get Frank out of the house, away from Muriel and living nearer to the church, and I spoke to Carl Koch about it. Carl owned a little unrented house in town and said Frank could have it rent free.

When I told Frank about the house he grinned and said, "Now you never will find out how I got into town from the old house, ain't that so, Father Joe?"

The Morgans and other parishioners furnished the place and Frank moved in. He didn't hear his wife's voice anymore. "I guess all Muriel and her boyfriend wanted was that house of mine," he said. "Though I can't figure it out—they could have had the Kochs', or the Governor's mansion."

Free at last of Muriel, Frank took a new lease on life. He came to 7 o'clock mass every morning, helped out with the Bingo, and did other chores around the church. He started a small woodworking business on his own. It gave me a lift to see him, stocky and imperturbable, climbing the steep hill to the church every morning.

Occasionally Katy Morgan invited Frank to dinner. He wanted to give her Muriel's clothes as a gift, and asked me what I thought about the idea. Frank had told me Muriel weighed almost two hundred pounds, and I told him, "Well, Katy isn't Muriel's size. And she's got a lot of clothes."

"She don't have dresses like Muriel had," Frank said. "I tell you, my wife dressed for the Devil. They used to talk about it in Milwaukee."

"Frank, that doesn't sound like Katy's style. You know she's conservative."

"Well, you let her decide," he said in his stubborn way.

Next time Frank came to dinner he brought some of Muriel's dresses wrapped in newspaper. One of them was an ankle-length beaded dress from the twenties, at least thirty years old. "Ain't that something," Frank said admiringly, holding it up for us to see. "Katy, you'll be a sensation, wearing this one to church."

"No doubt about that," commented Lee Morgan, with a perfectly straight face. Katy had already fled to the kitchen.

Every time Frank ran into Katy or Lee at the church he asked if she'd worn the dress yet. "Guess she's waitin' for a special occasion," he told me. "When's that niece of hers gettin' married?"

When Frank came to dinner at the Morgans' again Katy told him she'd sent the dress to the cleaners. Frank noted she'd waited quite a while to do it, and asked which cleaners in town had the dress. Wardrobe Cleaners, Katy told him.

It was a mistake. The next week I dropped some clothes off at Wardrobe and the manager told me, "That Frank Husnik was in here asking when Katy Morgan's dress was going to be ready. Said he wanted me to do a good job."

"What did you tell him?"

"I said we always did a good job."

Frank cornered Lee at the church and asked if the dress had been returned from the cleaners. Lee told him the beads had come off in the cleaning. Next day I got a call from Wardrobe. "Maybe you can do something about Frank Husnik, Father.

He was in here raising cain because I ruined Katy Morgan's dress. Says he's going to get a lawyer and sue. I told him I didn't clean any beaded dress for her, but he called me a liar and walked out."

A moment later the phone rang again. It was Attorney "Judge" Melvin D. Anglin in Berryville. Had I told a parishioner of mine named Husnik to get in touch with him about a suit against Wardrobe Cleaners?

I explained the situation, and said that Frank must have heard me mention the Judge's name.

Judge Anglin brayed his harsh laugh. "All right, I'll tell him he doesn't have a case. Did you ever see so many crazy people in one place in all your life?"

Frank came to me with his problem. Could I get him a lawyer to sue Wardrobe? Judge Anglin had discouraged him from filing.

"If you can't win, Frank, I wouldn't bother with it. Lawyers cost money you don't have. Anyway, maybe Muriel didn't want you to give away her dress."

He was stunned by revelation. "You must be right! The Devil spoiled that dress! Any cleaner Katy would've sent it to would have ruined the thing. I'll buy her a new one to make up for her loss."

Lee wouldn't like that, I told Frank, but it took me almost an hour to convince him. Katy was so relieved she invited Frank to dinner and baked him his favorite cherry pie.

I first met Walt and Evelyn Koehler in 1952. The Koehlers ran one of Little Rock's better bakeries, and after picking up some candy for the Eureka Springs kids, I dropped into the Koehlers' shop on Main Street to buy some pastries.

Reaching for my billfold, I discovered I had only enough money to pay for gas for the 225-mile trip back. The salesgirl smiled, said, "Wait a moment, Father," and returned with

Walt Koehler, Jr. who had been baking in the back. He was covered with flour dust.

"No charge, Father," he told me firmly. "I'm a Catholic and those boys at the seminary could use a few sweets."

I explained that I was the pastor at St. Elizabeth's in Eureka and had nothing to do with the seminary now. Would he accept a check for the pastries?

Walt shook his head.

I handed him two boxes of candy. "Then I insist you take these in exchange."

"Father, I've got three boys, aged four to eight. They're not exactly underweight now."

I told him I never accepted anything from anybody without giving something in return. This had nothing to do with morality and was actually selfish in intent; I just didn't want to be under an obligation. A priest might be a beggar for the poor but he must not *beg*. Would Walt accept the candy for his employees?

By this time the salesgirls had gathered around. One said, "I'll take some, Father," and another grabbed a box from under my arm and ran away, giggling.

"Well, I guess that settles the argument," Walt said, and invited me to dinner at his home that evening. He wouldn't take no for an answer—it was almost five o'clock; the weather forecast was for heavy rain, bad driving conditions for the 190-mile trip to Eureka; I could stay at the seminary if I wouldn't accept his hospitality for overnight.

At the Koehlers' I met Walt's stunning wife, Evelyn, his parents and his three boys. Soon I was deep in conversation with the youngest, four-year-old Ralph. Ralph kept trying to tell me something but I couldn't make out what it was. Walt and Evelyn told me he couldn't speak too plainly yet; not even they could understand him. But I persisted, saying, "What is it, Ralph? What are you trying to tell me?" Ralph would just point at me and say something unintelligible.

"Let's forget it, Father, and go in to dinner," Walt said.

"One more try," I said, and with everybody looking on, repeated, "What are you trying to tell me, Ralph?"

Ralph pointed at my trousers and in tones as clear as a fox horn in a hollow, said loudly, "Your zipper is unzipped!"

Lee Morgan told me about the Crow children, three deaf-mutes living in the hills outside of town with their parents. The Crows were Protestants. Old man Crow, he said, drove a truck and did odd jobs in Eureka Springs. The children stayed at home and didn't go to school.

I drove out to the Crows'. Linda was five, Donald, eight, Kenneth, ten. They were bright and goodlooking children and it was terrible to think that the silence they inhabited now they would inhabit always.

The house was slovenly, as unkempt as its mistress. Mrs. Crow was a big, vital brunette with shrewd eyes who still had traces of past beauty; she sat in a wrinkled wrapper with curlers in her hair, smoking one cigarette after another from the carton on the table before her. No groceries in the house, I thought, but plenty of cigarettes.

While the children stared I told her about the Arkansas School for the Deaf in Little Rock. Would she agree to an examination of the children there? It was August now; if the school thought there was a chance to help the children, we'd be pressed for time to enroll them for the start of classes in September.

"We can't pay nothing," Maxine Crow said.

"You won't have to. The state takes care of all expenses."

She lifted an eyebrow. "You want these kids to turn Catholic? One soul to save's as good as another, whether or not it kin talk or hear?"

"No ulterior motives."

She expelled smoke. "Don't believe it. If you don't want these kids to become Catholic it must be you want your church to look good in these parts. Let me tell you somethin'—you're wastin' your time. You could hand everybody in this town a hundred dollars and if the Pope came through he still wouldn't get the time of day."

"I wouldn't argue with you. That being so, you must be wrong about my motives."

She shifted restlessly. "Well, Father, I got to talk it over with my husband. Could you come back in a couple of days?"

When I returned Mrs. Crow had questions. How would the children get home for the holidays? Could I get them some clothes? Linda needed work done on her teeth; did I know a dentist? I told her not to worry.

Puffing nervously on a cigarette, Mrs. Crow said, "You sure about the Catholic business? That's a real purty church you got up on the hill."

"So far as I know there isn't a single Catholic staff member at the School for the Deaf. And I promise you the kids will never see the inside of St. Elizabeth's if you don't want them to."

When I told Lee Morgan the Crow kids needed clothes for their examination in Little Rock, he took out his wallet and said, "I knew I should have kept my mouth shut."

Mrs. Crow was busy when it came to shopping for the children and Katy Morgan accompanied me downtown. My heart turned over at Linda's little guttural of joy when the clerk wrapped her new dress; it was the first sound I'd heard her make.

After the examination in Little Rock the doctor said Kenneth could read a little but couldn't write, and his speech was only a little better than that of the others, which was very poor. There was a chance to help them, but only Kenneth was old enough to enter the school in September.

We dropped in at Koehlers', and Walt, Jr. loaded the children down with so much cake and cookies that Linda had to sit on Kenneth's lap going back in the car. In Marshall I stopped at the Reeves' drugstore and Wilbur and Juanita gave the children chocolate ice cream. Linda cried soundlessly when she spilled some of it on her dress.

Next Saturday at the church the three Crow kids knocked at the rectory door. How they had gotten into town I never did find out. Kenneth's lips silently formed the word *work*. I set them to picking up paper scraps and mowing the lawn. When I looked out the rectory window there were the three of them on the mower, accomplishing nothing. I went out and gave them money for the movie show and ice cream.

The phone rang at four o'clock. It was Katy. The Crow children had dropped in on Lee at the electric company, she said, and he'd driven them home.

"I didn't think they knew about Lee," I told her.

"Oh, those kids know everything."

The phone rang again an hour later. "Father Joe? Lee. The Crows were sore you invited the kids to the church. They said you'd promised a hands-off policy."

"*Invited* the kids?"

"That's what they said. Said you'd given them money, too."

"Well, at least I didn't take it back for candles or the poor box . . . Lee, next time the kids drop in, and they probably will, let me know. I don't want them bothering you."

"No bother. Only thing was Mrs. Crow asked me for a cigarette, and when I was halfway back, and dying for a smoke, I discovered I'd left the pack. That woman smokes like a chimney. And she had the nerve to ask me to send her a carton of the Canadian cigarettes I get from Montreal. What's her address?"

I drove Kenneth up to Little Rock in September and drove him back and up again for Christmas. Next year Donald entered the School for the Deaf and the following year, Linda. For the next three years, at holiday time, I was on constant call as chauffeur. Not that I minded; it was a joy to see how the children gradually responded to instruction and therapy. By the second year they could all say a couple of words, and all of them eventually became good students. Linda showed talent at painting.

On the way back to school we always stopped at Reeves' drugstore. One time at Easter, as we were leaving Marshall, I felt a tap on my shoulder. I turned my head. In the monotone of the deaf the children chorused, "Who—what—thank you!" I felt I'd never been thanked for anything so well. How they must have rehearsed!

The good manners and neatness the children brought back from Little Rock had a beneficial effect on their parents. The Crows tried to keep a neater home, and after the house burned down from one of her carelessly discarded butts, they moved into the new little house Carl Koch bought them. Mrs. Crow cut down a bit on her smoking.

CHAPTER

3

FOR some time I'd been thinking of building a church in Berryville, but didn't know how to go about it: there was exactly $76 in my bank account. I didn't want to ask Carl Koch, who had been so generous, and there was no one else to approach. For all the faith I had in God and people, there wasn't any sense in getting started until I had a few thousand in hand with which the buy the land; the building I had in mind would cost about $120,000.

One day in March, 1954, the county nurse called me at St. Elizabeth's to say there was an emergency at the hospital in Eureka Springs—an infant girl born out of wedlock needed baptism. I called on the mother, who gave me permission in the recovery room; she said she'd planned to leave the child on my doorstep anyway. I baptized the infant and in three days it was dead. I buried the child and sang the Mass of the Angels for her. There were only three people at the funeral: Father James Burke, visiting from Chicago, Charley Nelson, the undertaker, and myself. Charley's bill, including grave and casket, came to $65. When I asked him if it was all right if I paid the following month, Father Burke took the bill from me and told Charley, "I'll take care of it. This is the first time in forty-four years I've been able as a priest to bury an angel and pay for it. This doesn't happen very often in Chicago;

normally Catholic charities take care of the burial expenses of Catholic illegitimate children."

I'd mentioned my plans for a Berryville church to Jim Burke. Three months later I was in Chicago. Father Burke handed me a check. I put it in my pocket and didn't look at it till I hit Springfield, 190 miles away, on my way home. I nearly ran off the road. The check was for $5000 and the note with it read "more to come for your new church."

I could hear the phone ringing as I put my key in the rectory door. It was Monsignor Lux in Chicago. "Joe? Forgot to tell you something," he said, coughing. "Got a five-thousand-dollar check for you here from *Catholic Extension* for your new church. Sending it out in the next mail." He coughed again, said, "Got to cut down on my smoking," and hung up. I knew better than to call back to thank him; he liked short phone conversations.

I started looking for land on which to build the Berryville church. It was a mistake to hunt for it myself—prices were suspiciously high, as much as $10,000 for a few acres. It was obvious some people in Berryville didn't want a Catholic church in town.

I asked Carl Koch to look for land but the prices they quoted him were little better. One man said, "Mr. Koch, you want to put up an *office building*, the price goes down by half."

John Torek, a Berryville accountant, had told me he owned a piece of land in town together with his attractive Baptist wife, Billie, and Homer Jackson. At first I hadn't been too enthusiastic about the land—a rock ledge ran through it and blasting would be necessary—but with every refusal John's land kept looking better. At first John's price was $5000; then he and Homer went down to $3500, cost. Billie said to her husband, "What's wrong, you're Catholic; why don't you give Father Joe your half? It's all right with me." So we got the land for $1750.

I had just hired my contractors, Lawrence Putman and Wayne Johnson of Eureka Springs, when Billie Torek showed me some anti-Catholic pamphlets written by a renegade priest that had been handed out by a school official the Sunday before at the Baptist church. They had upset Billie, and they upset me too, but when she asked me if I was going to talk about them on the radio, I told her no. "We expect hostility every once in a while—human beings are human beings. For me to throw stones at the Baptists would be useless. Radio time costs money and I intend to use it constructively."

But I was disturbed enough to pursue the matter. I showed the pamphlets to Homer Jackson, a member of the Baptist congregation and the building supplier from whom I planned to buy most of my supplies. I said, "I'd like to know why these were handed out at your church—they're offensive to the Catholic Church."

"Father," Homer said, "don't let it bother you. It's the exceptional member who does this kind of thing."

That was true. But it was no coincidence that the pamphlets had been distributed immediately after I'd bought the land, and that evening when I got back to the rectory, the phone rang and a voice said, "We hear you're planning to build a church in Berryville. Don't," and hung up. I wondered seriously if there was a place for a Catholic church in Berryville.

The first of the blueprints architect Frank Polito of Chicago would be drawing for the church at no cost arrived on the same day the county dynamiter was to blast the rock shelf on the church site.

I'd had trouble with the insurance company in Little Rock who had insisted that the dynamiter have a college degree. I couldn't find a local dynamiter who qualified, but finally I dug up a dynamiter who had quit Arkansas Tech in his sophomore year. The insurance company said he wouldn't do, but they were willing to insure everybody concerned except the dynamiter. I reminded them that he was the only one who was taking the risk, and hired a jackhammer man to take five feet off the rock ledge. Today one corner of the rear of the church sits on the rock ledge five feet higher than it's supposed to.

The day after the jackhammering, Harry Chinery called, disturbed. He'd heard rumors I'd started building a church in Berryville. I told him that for once the rumors were true.

"But have you got Bishop Fletcher's permission?"

"No."

"Joe, you're crazy! The Bishop'll never give you permission. I know for a fact he wants to go easy with the anti-Catholic elements for a while; he heard about those pamphlets that were handed out there and there've been a couple of other headaches in the diocese lately."

"I've thought it all out, Harry. The haters aren't going to win this one."

"Joe, the deck's stacked against you. Get out while the getting's good."

I told him I had a plan, but he wouldn't listen to me. "Remember, Joe. It's not only your neck; it's the Church's neck in Carroll County."

I didn't think I was risking the Church's neck because the way things were going now Berryville would have a Catholic church built mainly by the efforts of Protestants. And when I showed Bishop Fletcher proof of that, I knew he wouldn't want to stop me.

After the shock of the pamphlets and the anonymous phone calls—there were no others—the response of Protestants in Carroll County was heart-warming. The presidents of the Berryville and Green Forest banks each gave me $50 toward the church building fund. Hanby Building Supplies of Berryville offered supplies at cost. County Judge Arthur Carter was helpful. At the first bake sale, held at Legion Hall, the Protestant ladies of Berryville not only baked most of the cakes and cookies, but bought them, too.

And then the roof fell in.

Wayne Johnson was putting in the hollow concrete forms for the stairway when a man came up to him and said, "What are you going to hide under those steps—guns?" Wayne told him "Yes, machine guns," and the man went on, "You afraid of the nigras or the Commies?" Wayne allowed as we were mostly concerned with the Communists, and the man agreed we had to protect ourselves. Then he walked off.

Next morning I'd just arrived at the site when the Berryville police chief's squad car drew up to the curb. He'd had a complaint we were hiding guns. "Anything to it, Father Joe?" he asked, smiling.

"Look around, chief," I said.

"Some crank making more work for us," he told me before he left. "Please excuse the visit."

I'd just stepped in the rectory door when Judge Anglin called. Had I seen the Berryville *Star-Progress?* They had it I'd been accused of hiding revolvers, machine guns and a bazooka I'd brought back illegally from the U.S. Army. The police had cleared me but "Hear this," the Judge warned, "this isn't the last of it. My party line's buzzing like a queen bee with a hundred candidates after her, and I'll bet at least one out of three calls is about those guns of yours." He laughed. "You want to file any slander suits, let me know."

He wasn't far off the mark. For the next hour the phone rang constantly. Had I seen the *Star-Progress's* story? Did I think the Communists would get hold of it? The Negro organizations? And what would Bishop Fletcher say? That last one stopped me cold; it hadn't occurred to me that the Bishop read the Berryville paper.

The next to the last call was from Little Rock, from Monsignor Murray, Chancellor of Little Rock Diocese. A Berryville parishioner had called him with a fantastic story about my distributing guns from a new church site to an anti-Communist group in Arkansas that was probably the Ku Klux Klan.

"The story's only half-true, Monsignor," I told him.

"*Half*-true! Joe, what on earth are you talking about?"

I confessed and explained. Joseph Murray is a ruthlessly competent but an equable man. He didn't judge me for not having informed Bishop Fletcher I was building a church in Berryville. He didn't say I should stop work immediately. Nor did he praise my initiative. Bishop Fletcher would be back from a trip in a week, he said. I'd hear from him then.

After I'd put down the receiver the phone rang again.

"Father Joe? Boss Hawley. Hear you're buildin' a church in Berryville. Now you need any help there I'm ready to go. Bought me a new pair of overalls and a painter's billed cap. Only thing is, you want me there early tomorrow morning you'll have to pick me up. Car's in the shop. The wife had a little accident with some damn Yankee from out of state, got in her way in one of them big-duff Cadillacs."

I suppose it had to happen. Before Bishop Fletcher returned to Little Rock I was up to my Roman collar in exactly the kind of controversy the Bishop wanted to avoid at the moment. Nothing could have been worse for the cause of St. Anne's.

On a warm night in mid-September the Pendergrass Drug Store in Eureka Springs was broken into and entered. Change from the cash register was taken and the store ransacked as though a search had been made for narcotics. The following morning, returning to the rectory about 9 A.M., I surprised two young men trying to pry off the lid of the poor box.

One, whose name I later learned was Horace Hillar, was in his twenties, slightly built and timid-looking. The other, Ernest "Bluey" Bilyeu, was solid and tough. Tough enough to charge for the door, butt me in the stomach as I stood there trying to lock the door behind me, and, as I fell to the floor, escape out the door. By the time I'd scrambled to my feet and followed him, locking the door behind me, the red tail-light of his car was disappearing down the hill.

I went back to the rectory. Hillar sat palely in a chair smoking a cigarette. He said, "What you goin' to do with me, Father?"

I didn't answer but picked up the phone to call the sheriff. Sheriff Treat asked me for a description of the getaway car before he sent out a statewide alarm. I asked Hillar to describe the car, but he shook his head, saying, "You can't expect me to put the finger on a buddy." I noticed that his hands were trembling and his irises dilated. Drugs, I thought.

I told the sheriff the youth refused to describe his accomplice's car. He grunted. "He'll talk, Father. Just keep him on ice till I get there. Most likely these two burglarized the drugstore last night."

I asked Hillar if he wanted a cup of tea and he burst into tears. "What'll they do to me? I hear you don't come out of Tucker Farm alive. I ain't been in trouble before and my mother's got nobody but me to help her. Will you let me go?"

"The sheriff's on his way. I couldn't let you go now if I wanted to. That buddy of yours left you here to face the music in a pretty callous way. Don't try to save him at your own expense."

"Bluey'll kill me if I talk."

There wasn't much to say to that. I fixed him some tea. Sheriff Treat arrived before he was finished with it. As they took him away, the boy threw me a despairing look over his shoulder.

Sheriff Treat called next day. Hillar had identified his accomplice and Bilyeu had been picked up at his home in Springfield, Mo. He was one of Springfield's most dangerous criminals and had an arrest record as long as your arm. In his possession had been some religious keychains and a long-handled screwdriver. I was lucky, the sheriff said; if he'd hit me with that I might not be alive today. Would I go to Springfield tomorrow to identify him?

In Springfield I identified Bilyeu and called on Hillar's mother. The old lady pleaded with me to help her son. He was her only support and a good boy who only got into trouble when someone like Bluey came along. I said I'd do what I could, which wasn't much, to keep him out of Tucker Farm.

Judge Anglin called when I got back to Eureka Springs. The court had assigned him to defend Hillar and Bilyeu, who were being tried not for dope addiction but burglary at St. Elizabeth's. The drugstore had refused to prosecute out of fear of reprisal. Yet the presiding judge was determined to burn their addictions out of them at Tucker Farm. He felt so strongly about it he'd moved the trial up on the calendar to next week.

"Hope you understand I've got to make you look bad with the jury," Anglin said.

Of course, I told him, but hanging up, my stomach did a flip-flop. If Anglin made me look bad enough, Bishop Fletcher would hear of it. The Bishop wanted no controversy just now and might well order work on St. Anne's stopped.

I went to see the prosecutor and the judge. The prosecutor was willing to let up on Hillar, but not the judge. He had to go along with the law. When a man needed $30 a day for his habit it was a serious thing. Had anyone come into Pendergrass' Drug Store when Bilyeu and Hillar were burglarizing it they would have been knocked on the head. The men had to be rehabilitated.

I saw Hillar at Main Street jail. "There's not much I can do for you, Horace," I told him. "Anglin's a good lawyer, but he doesn't have anything to work with."

"He says he's going to try and get some jurors that don't like the Catholics . . . How many years do you think I'll get?"

"Three, probably. You might be out in a year and half if you lick the habit."

"It'll be easier to kick the habit than stay out of Bluey's way. I'm scared, Father."

The Eureka Springs Courthouse on Main Street is a three-story limestone building fifty or sixty years old. I'd never seen it so crowded with overalled country folk. Anglin tried to pack the jury with anti-Catholics, but the prosecutor, alert to what he was after, made several peremptory challenges. The final composition of the jury seemed a fair one.

In his cross-examination Anglin called me "Mr. Laura," which got titters from the jury. I could tell from his line of questioning that I was in for a rough time.

"Mr. Laura," he said, examining his fingernails craftily, "isn't it a fact that the Pope is considered by the Catholic Church to be the next thing to Jesus Christ?"

Before I could reply the prosecutor objected that the status of the Holy Father was irrelevant to the proceedings at hand, but the judge failed to sustain, and Anglin continued, "Isn't it a fact that the Pope can do no wrong?"

The prosecutor jumped up from his seat, objecting that papal infallibility wasn't the issue. This time the judge sustained him and warned Anglin that he stood in danger of contempt of court. Narrowing his eyes at me shrewdly, Anglin continued, "Now let's see if we can get to the bottom of this. First there's the Pope and then the Cardinal, and then the Bishop, and then the Monsignor, and then the parish priest."

"You left out the Archbishop," I said, to laughter.

"Now isn't it a fact that the Pope's trying to be Jesus Christ and you parish priests are trying your level best to become the Pope? Mr. Laura, you wouldn't like to be the Pope, would you?"

Before the prosecutor could object I said, "Yes, who wouldn't?" Laughter. For once I'd stolen the jump on him.

"Are you acquainted with the story of the Crucifixion?" asked Anglin.

"Certainly."

"Who did Christ die between?"

"Two thieves."

"Two thieves, for whom He had compassion. All right, Mr. Laura, there were your two thieves. Why then did you find it necessary to call the police? Where was your Christlike compassion?"

"These men were trying to rob the church poor box. That's hardly a Christian act. It was my duty to stop it and inform the authorities."

"As for the poor box, Mr. Laura," said Anglin, "let me say there's never been a preacher in the hill country who asked his flock for a single solitary dime."

"I hope you don't have anything against giving to the poor," I said to laughter.

The prosecuting attorney accused Anglin of trying to inject religious intolerance into the case. In rebuttal Anglin said he hadn't seen me preaching any funerals on cold days and that I wasn't the only man of the cloth who'd met obstacles in these hills where there existed many faiths, not all of which claimed to be the one true faith. As for the prosecutor, any minute he expected him to say a Hail Mary, pull a rosary from his pocket, and admit he was about to convert. Laughter. He just hoped a Jewish rabbi didn't get down this way, because if the prosecuting attorney wanted to embrace *his* faith, he'd have to go through a certain painful operation. Much laughter.

The jury was out for only twenty minutes. The verdict was guilty: Bilyeu got five years and Hillar two.

The *Times-Echo*'s report of the trial was routine and the whole thing blew over in a matter of days. I didn't hear from Monsignor Murray about it nor did he reply to the clipping on the verdict I sent for his files. Later Hillar wrote from Tucker Farm thanking me for the few dollars I'd sent him and admitting that the only way he was going to kick the habit was to sweat it out here at the Farm, bad as it was. Bluey, he said, had decided to let bygones be bygones.

Bishop Fletcher's reprimand, when it came, was mild. Actually he knew I'd started work on St. Anne's; Father Burke of St. Basil's in Chicago had told him some months ago. Meanwhile he'd been waiting for me to send him the plans. As for opposition to a church in Berryville, things would have had to have been a lot worse before he'd have ordered me to stop construction.

I went back to work with new energy and confidence. We bought and installed a used heating system from a Protestant church in Springdale, Arkansas. Charley Nelson donated the church doors. Jack Cadelli and his crew began work on the terrazzo floors. (Jack had not only lowered his price to rock bottom but made a $200 donation to boot.) I hired Carl Poorman of Huntington, Indiana, to paint a mural of Christ on the Cross. This was difficult because the sanctuary wall was curved; one arm of the cross seemed to bend and lent a surreal air to the scene. The stained glass windows arrived from Fort Smith.

The shipment of stone for the exterior came in cold weather. Everywhere I tried to chip it the stone would split, and it was impossible to work with. I wrote the company and explained the situation. They returned my check and told me to keep the shipment; it was too costly to return. In a few weeks it turned warm, and I decided to make another attempt at chipping the stone. This time, I had no problem. I mailed another check to the company. They were so astonished at my honesty that they returned the check as a donation.

In February the American Legion invited me to Texarkana, Arkansas, to give the address at their annual banquet. Texarkana was an eight-hour drive from Eureka Springs. Since I had to pick up some metal stripping for Jack Cadelli's terrazzo floors at his shop in Fort Smith, I decided not to accept Father

Pat Lynch's invitation to stay overnight at his Texarkana rectory, but left around nine o'clock, after the banquet, for Fort Smith. Going across the mountains, around midnight, I started getting sleepy, but at this hour all the coffee stops were closed.

I made Fort Smith about 4 A.M. and pulled up at Jack Cadelli's shop. As I put the key in the lock a cop poked his flashlight in my face. He wouldn't buy my story and we went along to the station house to check with Jack's wife.

A reporter on the late shift was curious about what a priest was doing at this hour in a police station, and offered me a lift to where I was going. Respecting the power of rumor as I did, I thought better of it and called a cab for the trip to Jack's shop.

I picked up the strips and after a couple of cups of coffee at an all-night diner, started for home. Driving through the Boston Mountains between Fort Smith and Fayetteville, the fog settled in and I had to slow down to 10 m.p.h. At this rate I'd never make Eureka in time to grab a few hours' sleep before my regular 7 A.M. mass at St. Elizabeth's.

At Fayetteville I pulled off the road for a nap and then continued on through Rogers, which put me about half an hour from the Springs. On one of the hairpin turns, fast asleep with my eyes wide open, I hit a guardrail, skidded across the road, and struck a rock wall. If that hadn't succeeded in waking me up I would have skidded again and dropped 150 feet over the mountainside.

Johnny Hunt's Steak House, a few hundred yards down the road, was open, I called the tow-truck to arrange for hauling the car into the garage and Johnny drove me into town. He dropped me off in front of St. Elizabeth's at exactly 7 A.M., just in time for early mass.

My next major problem was hanging the two-ton stone cross, 18 inches thick, 18 feet high and 15 feet wide, over the church entrance. The No. 1 and 2 pieces were fitted into their slots without too much trouble. But the only way we could get the crosspiece on was to derrick it up through a hole in the roof. Wayne Johnson, on the scaffold, guided the piece upward. The stone got hung up when the cable jumped the pulley and the only thing to do was clear everything below so that if the crosspiece came down nobody would get hurt. Some of Jack Cadelli's Italian terrazzo floor men were standing around, gaping, and Protestant Wayne snapped at them, "Listen, you guys, if you've got to watch, at least *pray* a little!"

I'd ordered the church altar from a well-known Italian sculptor who lived near a U.S. Army base outside Rome. When I heard that Dr. E.S. Moser of Eureka Springs was going to Rome to see his son stationed in the army there, I gave him the $1000 check due for the altar and asked him to hand it to the sculptor in person. Dr. Moser carried out his assignment and the altar, as per my instructions, was shipped to New Orleans. It would have cost more to ship it from there to Berryville than it had cost to have made, so I had to go down to New Orleans to pick it up. Wayne Johnson and I left for the city on the Gulf, in his truck. The trip was a disaster. What with the heavy load, coming back we had three blowouts. Uncrating the altar at the church, I discovered that chiseled at the bottom were the words, "In Memory of Dr. E.S. Moser," when the inscription should have read, "In Memory of Father James Burke." Dr. Moser laughed when I told him about it. "I guess the sculptor couldn't believe I'd come all the way over there to give him that check for nothing. Well, if those words are going to stay there, Father, you've got a five-hundred-dollar donation coming to you from me." When I wrote Jim Burke about the affair, he answered, "Let's look at it this way—you're $500 richer and that inscription won't come off, anyway."

One day, dressed in overalls from working on the church, I dropped in on a freight company sale of unclaimed articles. I saw a Sacred Heart statue that was perfect for the church, and asked the fellow in charge of the sale what was wrong with it. "That's an Eyetalian statue worth at least six hundred dollars," he told me. "There's nothing wrong with it; the crate just got banged around a little."

"How much?" I asked him, and he quoted a price of $175. I said I'd be back later and left. That afternoon I returned to the sale dressed as a priest. For some reason the price of the statue had gone up—to $350. "You've got competition," the man said. "There was a fellow in here this morning for that statue and he seemed to want it pretty bad." His jaw dropped when I told him, "As far as I'm concerned, the price is still one seventy-five, because I'm the man you were talking to this morning."

I got the statue for $175, plus delivery.

The church was nearing completion when I heard that half the girls in the Berryville High School graduating class needed formals for the big dance at the gym. I talked a Little Rock merchant into donating ten formals, but when I got back to town with them discovered they were all the same size. Since the dance was that night, I drove back to Little Rock to exchange the dresses. I arrived to find the store closed. After interrupting the merchant's dinner, I managed to get the correct sizes. On the way back to Berryville I was twice stopped for speeding.

When I got to the school gym the dance had been on for half on hour. Most of the girls, formal-less, hadn't shown up, and the stags sat around morosely. I got the chaperone to call each missing girl and talk her into coming to the dance, where they slipped into the formals and floated out on the floor. The dance proved a big success.

The evening before the dedication of St. Anne's, Archbishop O'Brien, Bishop Fletcher and Monsignor Murray arrived while I was putting on the finishing touches. Bishop Fletcher was frankly floored by the size and beauty of the church. "I didn't know," he said, "you were going to build a cathedral." I didn't remind him that when I'd sent along the plans for his approval I'd conveniently forgotten to include the dimensions.

Archbishop O'Brien said to the construction men, "I understand all you men are Protestants." They nodded. The Bishop turned to me. "Well, it seems to be a strong church. But couldn't you have hired a Catholic carpenter?"

That same day a car with two fur-swathed women drew up to the church. I invited the ladies to take a tour of the building. As they left I noticed the workmen were snickering. Wayne said, "There's no reason why you should know who that redhead and her girl-friend are, Father. Let's say they're on the town—the wrong side of town."

"Well, they've certainly got the right clothes for it," I said, to laughter.

St. Anne's was dedicated next morning, November 15, 1958. It was in the Gothic style and constructed of Carthage stone, hauled from Carthage, Missouri, 90 miles north. It had cost $60,000, raised by various contributors, and was completely debt-free. Seth Green, one of my contractors, said he couldn't have built it for less than $120,000. It was three times the size of St. Elizabeth's and the biggest church in Carroll County.

That afternoon the three visiting prelates were invited to Billie Torek's half-Catholic home for tea. In a dither, Billie had borrowed her friend Mattie Hambey's silverware and curtains for the occasion, but the Bishop and Archbishop put her at her ease by coming in smoking big black cigars. "We're so used to eating in Methodist Church basements," Bishop Fletcher told her, "that a half-Baptist house doesn't bother us a bit."

CHAPTER

4

JERRY Newton arrived in Eureka Springs in February,
1956, to take over the Mount Air Courts, a motel, as its
new proprietor. A Methodist, Jerry came to St. Elizabeth's for Sunday mass and afterward waited for a word with
me. He said his wife, Estelle, and adopted daughters, Sheila and
Kathy, would be arriving in town next month. All three were
Catholics. Sheila was seventeen, Jerry went on, and had recently had a serious operation for cancer of the neck. She'd
been unable to enter high school until next semester and would
have little to keep her busy. Could I introduce her to the other
girls at St. Elizabeth's? He turned his head aside and I saw he
was crying silently. After he recovered Jerry confessed he
hadn't told me the complete truth; Sheila wouldn't be going
back to school unless a miracle occurred—the Chicago doctors
said she had only a few months to live.

In the next weeks I grew to know and like Jerry Newton.
A native Missourian, he had gone to school in Kansas City and
at the University of Missouri. He had met Estelle in Chicago
and married her there. Estelle, born in Michigan, had gone to
the University of Detroit. After their marriage the Newtons
moved to Rockford, Illinois, where Jerry, in the depths of the
Depression, went to work for a cafeteria chain.

In 1938 the Newtons were living in Waterloo, Iowa. By this

time they were sure they were never going to have any children of their own. They adopted Sheila, born in March, 1949, from the Waterloo Hospital, when she was ten days old, and four years later they adopted another daughter, Kathy.

Estelle, Sheila and Kathy arrived in Eureka Springs in late March. I wasn't all that impressed by Sheila the first time we met; aside from good looks and warmth of personality she seemed ordinary enough. A pretty, petite blonde, her turned-up nose showed her Irish ancestry. She wore her hair long to hide the operation scar at the base of her throat.

Extraordinary charm is often deceptive; we don't know it has worked its spell on us till we lie gasping and flopping at the end of the line. For the next weeks Sheila was with me constantly; any time I had to take a trip to Rogers or Harrison she came along. Harry Chinery told me, "What an unusual girl," the Kochs said the same thing, and Estelle kidded that I wasn't introducing Sheila to the other kids but keeping her to myself. Suddenly I realized that all of them were right.

Then Sheila got her first bad headache and had to check into Carroll County Hospital in Eureka Springs for a couple of days. Estelle asked me not to take her on any more car trips. If the headaches started again she would need immediate attention and heavy medication.

One exception was a trip to Fayetteville for a Newman Club meeting at the University of Arkansas. On the way back, passing the strawberry patches at Rogers, Sheila said she'd never seen a strawberry field. I asked if she'd like to pick some and she nodded, her eyes bright.

"What a beautiful day, Father Joe," she said thankfully when I let her out at the motel later on. "I'll never forget it." I knew she meant this without qualification, as she meant everything she said. Her simplicity of response was a lovely thing. It extended even to the pair of obviously unmarried lovers ducking guiltily into their car at the moment: Sheila smiled at them and waved goodbye.

This proved to be the last day before she went into the hospital for good. That evening I ran into Dr. Van Pelt, who told me it looked as though the malignancy was developing on the other side of Sheila's throat.

I asked him what he thought her chances were now, and he said, "If the cancer's spread, I give her a month or two, at the most."

I was stunned. For me Sheila was so vibrantly affirmative of life that to think of her dying was to question the validity of affirmation itself.

The result of Dr. Van Pelt's tests four days later were shattering. The malignancy was spreading rapidly. The doctor hoped the Newtons would be careful to keep from Sheila the knowledge that her illness was terminal. After all, she was only seventeen years old.

I don't know when I became convinced that Sheila wasn't like other young girls, alive and well or dying. The feeling must have come over me gradually and imperceptibly. In any event, I was talking to Jerry and Estelle one evening when Estelle put down her knitting and said, "What's up, Father Joe? Why all this constant interrogation? This is the fourth time you've asked us about Sheila's life in Chicago. I've told you all I know."

I believe this child is a saint, I thought. *No, it's stronger than that. I know it.*

How did I know? What were the distinguishing characteristics of sainthood? Besides extraordinary goodness, an extraordinary evenness of temperament. An acceptance of trials and suffering in the spirit that they were given. Christ had said, "Come to me and take up your cross." The saint was the human being who took up his cross in near perfect emulation of Him.

The answer to my question was that although Sheila had not as yet demonstrated a saintlike acceptance of trial and suffering, I was certain she would. In the strangest kind of way, it was as though, in this moment, I could predict much of what would happen to her before she died. The feeling was so strong and so frightening that I fought it and returned to my questioning of Jerry and Estelle.

I'd learned that Sheila, in grade school, had been a very healthy child, so healthy that she complained she couldn't catch a cold that would keep her out of school. A very active child, she would be up at 5:30 in the morning, riding up and down the sidewalk on her squeaking tricycle. Once the noise awoke a sleeping neighbor, who threw up his window and cursed. Sheila lisped back cheerfully, "That's not nice, Mr. Smith. Now you'll have to wait till I'm good and ready to stop!"

Sheila, Estelle told me, would never lie, even though telling the truth meant punishment. She never had a hateful mood. There were some slight arguments with her mother while she was growing up into her teen years about whether or not to associate with certain young people she knew, but next day she would say, "I heard what went on at the party last night, Mother, and you were right."

She had a wonderful disposition; jealousy, so common in teenagers, was completely foreign to her, and she never gossiped. She liked best to be at home with a crowd of teen-age friends, yet she enjoyed reading, was talented in ballet, and could be by herself for days at a time.

Nor was she a priss. One day Sheila was building blocks in the living room. Her sister Kathy, adopted by the Newtons in 1952, was at the creeping stage, and every time Sheila built up her blocks Kathy would knock them down. Finally Sheila said, "Kathy, every now and then you make me so damn mad I don't know what to do!"

Estelle remonstrated with her: "Sheila, you don't hear your father and mother talking like that in front of Kathy. Remember, she's just getting ready to talk. She'll pick up your words and they'll be the first ones she'll say."

Sheila went over to the davenport and sat there for a while. Estelle was worried she'd hurt her feelings, but then Sheila said thoughtfully, "Mother, I've been thinking. I promise you I won't swear in the house anymore. But when I'm outside I'm going to swear like *hell!*"

Sheila had no particular problems. She was a good student; she had a normal interest in clothes and good grooming; she got along well with the boys. She wasn't especially religious, though from the age of ten, at her first communion, she had tremendous, unassailable belief that anything she wanted could be gained through the intercession of the Virgin Mary.

Although the family moved often, the dislocations involved had no effect on Sheila, who made friends wherever she went. The shy, introverted Kathy's relationships with friends were intense and exclusive, but Sheila never played favorites. She was so popular that in Oak Park the Newtons could never call the living room their own; it was always full of kids.

Sheila's first cancer symptom, at sixteen, was a stiff neck; it disappeared and the Newtons thought nothing of it. By August 1955 Sheila had developed a small lump at the base of her throat. The swelling went down, but Jerry and Estelle brought her to a Chicago doctor to see if she had a gland condition. Penicillin failed to bring down the swelling and Sheila was examined by a surgeon, Dr. Boyd. At first he discounted cancer because she had lost no weight and her health was excellent. He decided on exploratory surgery, and Sheila was operated on in September.

She was in surgery for six hours. It was found that cancer of the nerve fibers, beginning at her neck, extended down her spine. A good deal of the cancer was cut out but her case was judged a hopeless one. Yet she had lost no weight and none of her bloom despite a cancerous condition that had existed at least nine months.

Jerry faced the decision of whether or not to move to
Arkansas and buy the motel he was negotiating for at Eureka
Springs. He and Estelle decided to go ahead; it would be better for Sheila to be busy in what time she had left, and Eureka
Springs would be a change for her from Oak Park. As the time
for departure approached, Sheila seemed to improve, although
the pain at night was severe. One evening Estelle said, "Let's
say another decade of the rosary; maybe it will help." Sheila
replied: "We've just prayed for me, Mother. Now let's pray
for somebody else."

Dr. Boyd, Sheila's Chicago surgeon, was amazed at her "improvement." Sheila was in good spirits and gaining weight.
There was no swelling of the neck to indicate that the cancer
was spreading in the area. Dr. Boyd gave permission for her to
go out with her classmates.

The night before Thanksgiving Sheila and her friends went
to a Little Theater presentation at Northwestern University.
The phone rang at nine o'clock; Sheila had collapsed during
intermission and been taken to the hospital by ambulance. Jerry
and Estelle felt bad that she would be spending Thanksgiving
in hospital, but when they visited her they found all her friends
there sipping crème de menthe in a haze of cigarette smoke
and playing cards. When she left the hospital Sheila began
wearing her hair long to cover the scar of the operation.

In March Jerry asked Dr. Van Pelt to get in touch with Dr.
Boyd in Chicago for any information he might need on Sheila's
case. It was then that I arrived on the scene. When Sheila
entered the hospital in April she had exactly a month and a half
to live.

I visited Sheila at the hospital every morning and afternoon.
She wanted communion daily, and finally I told her, "Sheila,
you don't have to receive communion every morning. What
sins can you commit in a hospital?" She smiled, but asked for
daily communion if it wasn't too much trouble. I gave in.

Afternoons I brought her milk shakes, something she could swallow easily.

In the second week the pain began to be intense. I said, "I'm sorry you're suffering," and she gave me a look of genuine surprise. "Father," she answered, "it's God's will." There wasn't a trace of mawkishness or self-pity in her tone; she was as certain that her affliction was the will of the Lord as she was that I had come into her life to make it easier for her to bear it. I thought of St. Therese's, "I realize as never before that the Lord is gentle and merciful; He did not send me this heavy cross until I could bear it. If He had sent it before I am certain that it would have discouraged me." Sheila had so much in common with St. Therese; like her, she was dying young; like her, she had beauty; like her, she was strongly identified with the Virgin Mary.

One afternoon she was finishing a milk shake when I saw a moistness on her cheek. A feeling of dread came over me and I could have predicted what she was going to say to the tone, syllable, inflection. "I'm going to die," she whispered. "Isn't that so, Father Joe? There's no hope for me?"

At least these were questions and not statements. I told her, "There's hope as long as you don't lose weight, as long as your health stays good. There *have* been cases of complete remission. Dr. Van Pelt says he's amazed at your general condition."

"I know the cancer's spread," she said, and as I was silent: "It's spread and I'm going to die. It's as simple as that."

"Everything's simple, Sheila, when you come right down to it. Terrifyingly so."

She smiled and took a Kleenex to her tears.

The nurses told me the pain sometimes kept her up all night but that she never complained, although she cried often.

One afternoon I found her reading Proust, something I'd always planned to do but never found the time for. "I'm reading him for you"; she smiled, and I knew I must have told her of my intention of reading the Frenchman.

"What a strange book," she said. "So much evil made good." I never had a chance to ask her what she meant; one of her girl friends came in then and Sheila put down *Remembrance of Things Past* to chatter about clothes and hairdos.

I was at St. Elizabeth's one forenoon when Estelle dropped by to tell me one of the local ministers was at the hospital delivering a sermon to Sheila on sin and the beauty of the hereafter. I rushed over to stop him, but by that time he'd already left. Sheila laughed and said, "Don't bother about it. He didn't upset me. I just said my rosary while he was talking and didn't hear a word."

I could believe it. Her powers of concentration, especially in recent weeks, were startling. At times she'd been able to put herself asleep, despite her pain, by concentrating on various objects in the room. The child had so much will, I thought, yet what use to her was that will when she could not will not to die at the age of seventeen?

To keep her as far away as possible from noise, Dr. Van Pelt had put Sheila in a back room on the second floor; her condition was such that the slightest sound was agony to hear. Here she was almost completely insulated from the sounds of the hospital, yet every time Estelle arrived Sheila would say to her nurse that her mother was coming or that she'd just heard her step downstairs.

Sickness with Sheila hadn't made a world of its own; she never came to feel, even as death approached, that people not with her in the hospital were representatives of a different race, from another planet. Her parents, her friends were still her world, and how her face would light up as any of us came into the room! Finally she was playing favorites with those she knew and loved.

Abruptly, five days before the end, she began to lose weight alarmingly, although the loss showed in neither face nor body. The pain became so intense she had to have three or four shots of morphine a day. The nurses could find no explanation of why the weight loss didn't show. "My God, Father," one told me, "the child's lost eleven pounds in three days! Yet she still looks like an angel!"

When Dr. Van Pelt told me he didn't think Sheila would live through the night, I went to Estelle and Jerry and said I'd share watches with them. I took the 1 A.M. to 3. When I arrived at about 12:30, the doctor said, "There's something strange going on in there."

"Strange?"

"There's an atmosphere, a presence. An almost overpowering quiet. And a difference in the quality of the light. It's frightened the nurses and they're reluctant to stay in Sheila's room."

I saw what he meant the moment I entered the room to spell Jerry. The quiet was preternatural and the light around Sheila's face—only the bedlight was lit—had an indescribable quality that had nothing to do with electricity and bedlamps.

Jerry whispered to me, "The last thing she said to me, about half an hour ago, was 'Don't turn me this way, turn me that way, because the Blessed Virgin is over there.' And before that she said, 'Job 16.' Do you know what she meant, Father?"

I shook my head. "Get some sleep in the lounge, Jerry. You need it." He looked exhausted.

"You'll call if you need me?"

I nodded and after Jerry had left sat there, watching her lovely face. She'd had an injection at midnight that had put her to sleep and her face had an unearthly beauty. Like Therese, with whom she now had in common a vision of the Blessed Mother, was Sheila willing a delight in her own suffering? If, as with Therese, suffering had become a part of love, had it become her joy also? I began to pray for her, terrifically conscious of the presence in the room. The Virgin Mary, mother of priests! To each priest she bore two loves, that of the Life of her Son and that of the Death of her Son. In the Incarnation she was a link between Israel and Christ; at the

Cross and Pentecost she was a link between Christ and His Church. Now she linked this dying child and Him who interceded for us above.

I gave Sheila extreme unction shortly before 2 A.M. She opened her eyes and, looking at the ceiling, said, "Why are there so many people in Hell?" I wondered if she had been given a prevision of Hell; if Satan, in his tireless quest of souls, had offered her a glimpse of the interesting company to be found there. Five minutes later her face lit up and she said, "The Blessed Mother is so beautiful!" A trickle of blood started from her mouth and I jumped up to call Jerry and Estelle. When we entered the room together seconds later, Sheila was dead. The birds still chattered deafeningly from the courtyard. A moment after I had closed her eyes, they ceased.

I mention the birds: never before, said Dr. Van Pelt and the nurses, later, had the birds been heard from at such an hour; never had they been so loud. Sister Pauline of the Lisieux Carmel had written of the death of St. Therese in 1897: "During the long agony of St. Therese of the Child Jesus, a multitude of little birds took their station on a tree beside the wide open window of the Infirmary, where they continued to sing with all their might until her death. Never before had there been such a concert in the garden."

Bishop Fletcher, impressed by what I'd told him of Sheila, gave me permission to wake her at St. Elizabeth's. This was unusual; a church wake was usually limited to a nun or priest.

The body was brought to St. Elizabeth's next morning in an open casket and put next to the statue of the Blessed Mother in the nave. The many tourists coming through the church at the time were startled to see the body; they thought it a wax image and remarked on Sheila's beauty. The last six weeks of excruciating pain had had absolutely no effect upon her face, something noted with amazement by Dr. Van Pelt. Charley Nelson, the undertaker, said that in over twenty years of practice he had never seen a face that needed so little work done by the embalmer.

Katy Morgan sang in the Mass of Angels I offered for Sheila. In my sermon I stressed how even in death God speaks to us: He had permitted Sheila's mortal remains, despite her pain and illness, to show her purity and saintliness.

Afterwards, scenting a story, a reporter came by the rectory to ask me if I was claiming Sheila was a saint. Had I told her parents, as he'd heard, they could pray to her for help? Was I interested in giving him material for a story he could sell to a New York tabloid for a pot of cash?

I was tired and drained and sick of aggressive, prying newsmen. I told him to get out.

Glad to be alone for a moment, I fixed myself a cup of tea and thought of what Jerry had told me about Sheila's rising from her pillow during the last hours of her life and saying the words, "Job 16." I looked up the reference in my Bible: "What the Lord giveth He taketh away."

I understood, but still I wept.

CHAPTER
5

D R. VAN PELT was long past his retirement age and for some time now had wanted to go to Europe. In October, 1958 he closed down the county hospital he had taken over as a private clinic. The 28-bed hospital had been closed for six months when the City Board of Commissioners came to me and asked if I had any ideas on reopening it. Eureka Springs, they said, badly needed a hospital for its elderly folk. The hospital at Rogers was too far distant for emergencies, and in the last few weeks several elderly patients had failed to survive the trip there by ambulance.

I told the Board there might be a possibility of getting some nursing Sisters to staff the hospital and suggested they write to Bishop Fletcher about it. Their letter ran in part: "In addition to the reasons set out above, we would like to suggest that because Father Lauro—Father Joe to everybody—has done so much for the community through his many charities and civic contributions and his outstanding accomplishments in rebuilding St. Elizabeth's and St. Anne's Churches, endearing himself to all the citizens of the county regardless of denomination, that the operation of the hospital by the Sisters would be a well deserved tribute to his untiring service to the community."

The Bishop got in touch with the Benedictine Sisters in Jonesboro, Arkansas, who promised three nursing Sisters and others later on, if needed. Delighted, the Board said it would be glad to provide living quarters for the Sisters.

The Commissioners successfully floated a loan to renovate the hospital, but a problem soon developed with the operating license. To meet new license specifications we would have to widen doors, redo the operating and delivery rooms, put in new floors and ceilings, install new tile and repaint the entire hospital. It meant practically gutting the present structure and building a new one.

"When I told Ray Anderson at the bank what the situation was," said Lee Morgan, one of the Commissioners, "Ray told me, 'Hell, Lee, why not tear the place down and build a new hospital?' To which I said fine, if they'd give us the money for it. Ray grinned and told me, 'It would take a hundred years for the town to pay back that kind of loan. This way it'll take only around seventy-five.' "

Thirty-odd women showed up to scrub the hospital from stem to stern before alterations were begun in May, 1959. One was an out-of-towner who faked a fall down the stairs and said she'd sue the town for a million dollars unless we settled with her for a thousand, "cash on the barrel head." County Judge Carter told her for the Board, "Lady, you sound like you come from Chicago. Hear some pretty good flimflam games originate in Chicago. You'd better light out for there right now, because if you don't we're going to put you in one of those barrels you're talking about and roll you all the way down Spring Street." She lit, together with the cigar-chomping, whiskey-drinking gent she'd been sharing a suite with at one of the hotels. They left a big bill behind them.

The alterations were completed in December. One of our biggest problems had been the wiring of the operating room. The National Electric Code required special wiring for hospitals. Also special receptacles had to be operated from isolation transformers, and everything grounded; the tile flooring required metal flecks and copper stripping laid beneath it to eliminate static electricity.

The Code Inspector couldn't get over the quality of work Art Nichols, the electrician, had done. "Well," Art explained to him, "I'd never wired a hospital before and had to do it by the book. I didn't have the experience to cut corners."

The hospital doors opened in September, and they've been open continuously ever since. Irene Castle, of the famous dance team, died there in 1969.

Now I had to get busy on a place for the Benedictine Sisters. For a while I thought a nice frame house on Fairmont Street might do, but Wayne Johnson told me it would take too much money to renovate. The Board of Commissioners asked for bids on a nine-room stone convent and got two or three in the neighborhood of $30,000. After its expenses with the hospital, the Board wasn't up to approaching the bank for that kind of money, and I was feeling a little discouraged when Wayne took out an envelope, did some figuring on the back, and said he could build us a convent for $17,000, provided I was able to cut costs all around on materials.

Work on a convent to include five bedrooms, a chapel, kitchen, living room, utility room and two baths, began in March, 1960. MacKinley Weems, a Protestant, donated his expensive bulldozer for two days of ground clearing. While helping out with the rock work I fell 12 feet from an over-loaded scaffold. Wayne and the boys insisted I get X-rays at the hospital. It turned out I had cracked a kneecap and I limped around for a week.

Wayne made the altar and built most of the Sisters' chapel furniture. We bought the rugs in Fayetteville. At first the dealer was reluctant to sell. "You're buying rugs for a houseful of *women?*" he said doubtfully. "I don't like the idea of their coming in to tell me they can't stand the color and want an exchange."

One difficulty we couldn't have anticipated. The five kids

from across the street slipped into the convent at night. They
glued shut all the drawers and closet doors. They trailed soap
flakes over the floors and smashed the light bulbs. They went
down to the basement and got hold of the brace and bit and
bored holes in the cement sacks. Then they poured water into
the holes. Art Nichols fixed them by wiring his tools for a not-
so-mild electric shock. Next day the kids' mother appeared,
screaming bloody murder and saying she was going to the police with a charge that we'd tried to electrocute her kids and at
the very least inflicted brain damage. "I've got a feeling the
cops have heard of your little angels before," Art told her,
"and when I get through filling them in, they're going to come
for your little monsters and put them in the new juvenile wing
at the P-Farm." That night Art staggered into the rectory
weak with laughter. "Milly at the telephone exchange just told
me Mrs. Katzenjammer called the P-Farm long distance, all
shook up. She wanted some information on their new kids'
prison. The warden told her it was a good idea but that the
legislature would never vote the funds!"

The convent was finished in November. It had cost $17,026
and was worth $35,000. Word got around that Wayne John-
son was a miracle man and he was deluged with offers. Painfully honest to the end, Wayne told people it wasn't so much
him or his crew as the way Father Joe Lauro had of getting
materials at cost "or less." One night the phone rang at the
rectory. It was a construction company president who wanted
to give me a commission on every dollar I saved buying him
building supplies. I told him I had no objection to making an
extra dollar, but that Bishop Fletcher had a way of finding out
about such things.

Sister Benita of the convent called around Christmas time.
Somebody had broken into the basement, flooded the place
and torn up valuable records the Sisters had stored there. "You
think it's the Klan, Father?" she asked anxiously, and I told her
no, that I had an idea what the trouble was and thought I could

fix it. I dropped in on the lady with the five kids and spoke briefly and to the point. Later Sister Benita, speaking of the convent's neighbors, liked to tell the story of the five kids from across the street whose shyness was so endearing. They'd stand on the sidewalk and gaze wistfully at the convent, but when a Sister invited them inside, they'd run.

Before I left Eureka Springs for Russellville in late December to replace the ailing Father Kordsmeire, the town fathers held a banquet in my honor. One of the gifts was a $500 check. I tried to endorse the check over to a local Protestant businessman whose store had just burned down, but he wouldn't accept it, so a few days later I mailed the check to him. When I arrived in Russellville the phone was ringing in the rectory office. It was Bishop Fletcher. "Welcome to Russellville, Joe," he said. "I thought things were going to be quiet with you for a bit, but you're starting out in typical style. What's the story on this check for five hundred dollars I got in the mail this morning? It's torn up, but I can see it's made out in your name."

Russellville, Arkansas, is about halfway between Little Rock and Fort Smith and only a few miles from the Arkansas River. In 1959 the census counted about 12,000. Although located in one of the nine least populated counties of the state, Russellville was the seat of Pope County and the center of a trading territory that extended northward into the Ozarks and southward across the Arkansas Mountains through the Ouachitas. Its chief industries are coal, lumber, cotton and chickens. The population, aside from the settled older residents, was transient and seasonal; families would come and stay for six months or so and then move on.

The town's pride was Arkansas Tech, at the north end of town on State 7. Tech was a state-supported, coed college which offered a four-year course in agricultural engineering, home economics, music and the liberal arts.

The parish plant, St. John's Church, rectory, two classrooms and a small convent for the three teaching Sisters, was off Highway 7 and about a mile from the center of town. My first night was sleepless from the whoosh of the big semis going by all hours of the night.

The rectory bell rang at seven the next morning. Standing on the mat was a young man in bib overalls. He jerked a thumb toward a jalopy parked under the spruce tree and said, "Father, I'm a good Catholic. I need food, drink and gas to get my family to Fort Smith."

"Don't give him a damn *dime*," a voice said. I looked around. Sitting on the flower bed border was a little man in his middle fifties with a wizened face and, from the wheezing sounds he was making, evidently an asthmatic. "Don't do it," repeated the little man. "Take my advice and send this here feller on his way."

I didn't like to be told what to do by a stranger at seven in the morning. Ignoring the little man, I asked the caller to wait. I went to the kitchen, made up some butter and jelly sandwiches, put half a dozen cold Cokes in a paper bag with paper cups and a bottle opener, and returned to the front door with them.

"Thanks, Father," the young man said. "What about the gas money to Fort Smith?"

"Don't listen to him," the little man wheezed.

I gave the young man a few bucks and he and his family rattled off in their jalopy.

"Shouldn't have done that, Father," said the little man, shaking his head. "Now he'll spread it around that the new priest at Russellville's a mark, and you'll have all kinds of people stopping here with all kinds of stories. What you should have said is, 'There's the lawnmower. If you'll mow the lawn I'll give you food for your family and money for gas.' Now if he's willing to mow the lawn for half an hour or so you tell him he can stop mowing and you feed his family. If he won't mow you know he ain't honest. Bet that one weren't even a Catholic—looked like a Methodist to me."

"Who are you?" I demanded.

"Wiley Peeler. Come here to help you out like I helped out Father Kordsmeire. Take care of your rose bushes, that is. Count your collection money. Chauffeur for you in my car there, that is." He indicated a battered sedan at least eight years old parked on the driveway. "I work at the post office nine to three, but any other time I'm at your service."

I found out about Wiley Peeler from my parishioners later on. He'd been very helpful to Father Kordsmeir and had a green thumb. He was a Baptist who'd converted to the Faith and had recently lost his wife. Once he'd owned a little general store. Now retired, Wiley lived by himself and worked part-time at the post office.

Wiley Peeler proved invaluable. He was always there when I needed him and never underfoot when I didn't. On Sundays he took the collection from the ushers, left it in a safe place at the rectory, and on Monday morning, after mass, counted the collection, banked it and gave me the receipt. He kept records for the construction that started in April of the next year. If I needed him to take someone to Little Rock, he was there with his Chevvy, which despite its condition led a charmed life and never seemed to break down.

Once Wiley showed up for a chauffeuring job wheezing so badly from his asthma that I had to ask his intended passenger to drive *him* over to St. Mary's Hospital for treatment. A few hours later Wiley phoned: if that fellow still wanted to go to Little Rock, he was feeling better and could manage it now.

Wiley was right about the free loaders. For two or three weeks straight I got three or four carloads daily of people wanting food, drink and gas. The lawnmower trick was effective. One out of three non-Catholics refused to mow the lawn, and about one out of ten Catholics.

Once a trucker came through who wanted gas money to

Tulsa, Oklahoma. He described himself as a good friend of Bishop McGinnis of Oklahoma City. I took him into the rectory office and pointed to the phone. "All right," I said, "if you're a good friend of the Bishop's call him up long-distance. If he vouches for you I'll pay your way to Tulsa."

He looked at me sadly. "Father, you don't believe me."

"That's not the point. Go ahead—call the Bishop."

The fellow fidgeted and pulled at his nose. "Father, I don't think you trust me, and it hurts."

"Hurts me, too. I'll pay for the call. Go ahead, get the Bishop on the line."

"Father," he said, "I haul oranges and grapefruit up here during the season. I always try to help the poor. You should see all the fruit I give them free. Now *I* need help."

"I'm not saying I won't help you. Just call the Bishop."

The fellow started for the door, shaking his head. "This is the first time I haven't been helped by a priest," he said. "Makes me feel bad. It really does."

"Don't lose your faith in human nature," I said. I almost asked him to give my regards to Bishop McGinnis.

In January of the new year, 1960, enrollment at the school suddenly swelled, and I decided to build two additional classrooms and a church hall.

Raising the money for about $15,000 of construction was no problem. The men parishioners knew our need for it and were generous with their pledges. Frank Polito of Chicago drew the plans, but then I ran into some red tape problems with the Arkansas Building Code, which required the signature of an Arkansas architect on any plans drawn out of state. It was suddenly March with construction still not begun and the kids driving me crazy. Wayne Johnson told me that if I wanted him and his crew they'd have to start work next week; they were committed to another job in Eureka Springs in mid-November and they estimated the Russellville construction would take around eight months.

I hadn't yet asked Bishop Fletcher for permission to build because I wanted to show him the plans as yet unapproved by the state. Confident they would be, I made arrangements with Wayne to start. As had the Cole brothers in Eureka Springs, Wayne and his men put up at the rectory and took their dinners at various parishioners'. This way, with room and board supplied, Wayne could and did cut down on his costs and was able to quote me a lower price accordingly.

Every morning I served breakfast at six thirty sharp so as to be ready for early mass at seven. A parishioner had given me a big slab of home-churned butter that naturally lasted for a long time. One breakfast after I had said grace, Wayne fixed his sleep-gummed eyes on the hunk of butter and complained quietly, "This is the most prayed-over piece of butter I ever did see."

The foundations of the church hall were up to window-height with brickwork when Bishop Fletcher and Monsignor Murray drove by one day in May. They didn't stop. I waited for the phone to ring with some pointed questions from Little Rock as to why I hadn't asked permission to build, but for the next week my only calls were local. When state approval of my plans finally arrived in June I got a full night's sleep for the first time in weeks. Next day I went into Little Rock to apologize and explain to Bishop Fletcher. His pause was masterly in its length, weight and density. Then he said, "Well, fine, Joe. Just as long as you aren't starting another Notre Dame."

One day the following week we were unloading 100- and 150-pound stones from the truck when a ten-year-old colored boy, all knees, elbows and eyes, stopped and asked, "Y'all *slaves?*" Wayne, covered with dust and perspiration, burst out laughing and dropped a stone an inch from my foot.

The boy's name was Ulysses Grant Wilson. He hadn't gone

to school today, he informed us. He sat down in the shade of
the big spruce with the glass of lemonade I got him and
watched us work with mild interest.

At 11:15 the kids came out of school to get ready for mass.
When I started toward the rectory, Ulysses asked me where
I was going. Into the house, I told him, to put on my vestments for mass. "What dat?" he wanted to know. Katy
Westman was going by at the moment on her way to play the
organ for mass. I told her, "Katy, when you go up to the
loft, take Ulysses Grant with you, but make sure he keeps
quiet."

At the first *Dominus Vobiscum* I glanced up at the choir
loft. Ulysses' intent black face looked down at me from
between two slats of the railing. In his mouth was a big red
apple Katy must have given him. He was pointing to my
shoes under my cassock. I'd been wondering at the inattention
of the children and especially about a hard core of persistent
gigglers. Now, looking down, I knew the reason. It wasn't my
shoes. I'd changed them, all right. It was my pants. I'd forgotten to change my workpants, and the cuffs were stiff with
cement.

After mass it was lunch time. I was in the rectory kitchen,
watching Helen Pheiffer and Sybil Wesley fixing roast beef
sandwiches for the work crew when Ulysses wandered in.
"You fixin' on givin' me some lunch?" he said, and I allowed
as I was, now that he mentioned it. I made him a lunch-meat
sandwich and poured him a glass of milk. He examined the
sandwich without enthusiasm and said, "Don't I git any beef?"

I told him beef was only for the workers, and he suggested
I make him a worker.

"You don't have a union card," I told him.

He studied me for a moment. "You tell me where I kin go
fer it, and I'll git me a onion card."

"You have your lunch," I said. "When you're finished, go

out and play on the swings with the children. Here's an apple."

"Done had me an apple already," Ulysses said. "Ain't you got a pear?"

Coming out of the rectory, Joe Reilly, one of the work crew, pointed to the playground. "You sure are integrated here, Father. Look at that black Ulysses. He's on the swing and the white girls are pushing him. There'll be hell to pay, some of the parents happen to come by and see that."

"Let them. Might do their prejudices some good to see their kids enjoying Ulysses' company."

After he was finished with the swing, Ulysses sang for the Sisters and danced for the work crew. He finished up his afternoon by riding down the street tandem with a little blonde girl on the Gosnells' white pony. When the shadows began lengthening I told him he'd better go home now. He could come by again on Saturday.

The phone rang while I was having early supper. Helen answered and when she came back she didn't mention who had called. When I pressed her about it she said, "Wait till after your coffee, Father. I'm not going to tell you about it till you're finished with dessert."

I knew it had to be something unpleasant, and it was. A parishioner had seen Ulysses riding on the pony with the little white girl and hadn't liked it a bit. She was writing to the Bishop. She might even write the Cardinal, she told me when I called her back. I told her not to forget the Pope.

But there were two other complaints about Ulysses that evening and I went to bed with a headache, feeling like a damyankee for about the first time since I'd arrived in Russellville.

In my next sermon I made my position on integration clear. I said I'd told the Negroes in town—there weren't any Catholics among them—that they were as free as the white Protestants to enter their children in parochial school, and as free to come to St. John's as any Catholic. Ignoring the scattered gasps and assorted indignant rustlings, I continued, "There aren't any Negro children in school here for one reason— because the colored people feel, rightly or wrongly, that neither the whites nor blacks in this town are ready for integration. But I'll tell you this. Next Christmas, as I did last Christmas, I'm going to ask your kids to help me distribute the Christmas baskets among the colored poor. Not because I want to 'make trouble' but because it's good for the soul for them to see how Negroes live in this town, and to take part in some Christian charity. Anytime a Negro comes into this church he's going to be welcome here. Those people who are going to walk out when it happens might as well walk out now, so I know where they stand."

Two families got up and left the church. Since 98 percent of my adult parishioners were present, I thought the odds were good that they pretty much agreed with me on the subject.

I'd asked Marge Hinterthuer, head nurse at St. Mary's Hospital, to let me know of any cases she thought I could help with. There was one, she said, a young girl of thirteen with cancer of the foot in Omaha, Arkansas, near the Missouri line. When I asked Marge what she thought I could do for the girl, she said, "Drive her into Little Rock for treatment at St. Vincent's Hospital. The Sisters there have agreed to treat Etta free. But the undertaker in town wants forty dollars for use of his hearse."

"Hearse?"

"I didn't think that was a very cheerful way to bring a patient to a hospital, either."

The town of Omaha commemorated the Indian tribe of that name. Etta Flippo was a shy mouse of a child so racked by constant pain she couldn't go to school. She lived in a converted barn with her father, a farmer and part-time Holy

Roller preacher. Rats ran above the hayloft where Etta slept, and the "kitchen" was papered with the Sears catalog. Her father was an ignorant but decent enough kind of fellow with no serious objections to being helped by a Catholic priest. I told him I'd be back in a couple of days to take Etta in to St. Vincent's.

It wasn't a day too soon. On the way she began to cry with the pain. I stopped in Marshall, where Wilbur Reeves and his wife Juanita had a drugstore. They put ice packs around Etta's foot as a pain-killer and gave her a quart of ice cream. About every hour for the rest of the trip I had to stop for more ice.

Etta was at St. Vincent's for three days of tests. Sister Margaret Louise took me aside and said they'd have to amputate at the ankle. "Father," she went on, "this could be serious. We better find out if Etta's been baptized, and I'll have to have permission from her father. We should operate no later than next week."

At first Etta's father didn't want the amputation. If the Lord had given her cancer he didn't think she should live; cancer was the judgment of Hell. And what would he do with a crippled child who couldn't fend for herself?

"Cancer's the rioting of diseased cells," I told him. "It's no more the judgment of Hell than a heart attack or stroke. Would you let yourself die without a struggle if you got it? Etta's young and she deserves to live, crippled or not. And maybe the Lord's testing you with this affliction. Have you ever thought of that?"

He hadn't and agreed to the operation on condition that Etta be supplied with an artificial foot. When I asked him if she'd been baptized, he nodded.

"Explain what you did so we'll know if it was a valid baptism or not."

"Wa'll, I poured water on her head."

"The child could die," I told him. "Do you want me to baptize her? I need your permission."

He'd have to think about it. "Remember," I said, "this doesn't make Etta a Catholic. All I'll do is pour the water like you did, but I'll pronounce the words of baptism Our Lord instructed us to use. I'll say 'I baptize you in the name of the Father and the Son and the Holy Spirit.' These are the words that John the Baptist used."

"Ain't got much to say fer the Baptists. What if I don't want her baptized like you said? Will y'all still do the operation?"

"Of course. I'll be back in a couple of days for your decision."

He agreed to the baptism and operation and the surgeons at St. Vincent's took off Etta's foot at the ankle. She made a good recovery. I sat at her bedside, holding her hand. Strangely, she didn't cry but her voice was toneless. "I kin still feel my foot there, Father Joe," she kept saying. "It wouldn't be so bad if'n I didn't still feel it was there."

What could I tell her? That it would be a miracle if the cancer was arrested and that in a year, probably less, they would have to operate again? I thought of her father's God, the wrathful Jehovah of the Old Testament. He was also Etta's God. For a moment I lost hope that Christ the merciful was with her too. All I could do was send for some ice cream. Etta liked vanilla.

After the operation the hospital had planned to outfit her with an artificial foot, but because of technical difficulties this proved impossible. Still, Etta's father was dissatisfied with the crutches St. Vincent's had given her.

"She don't git around so good," he complained. "Always fallin' down."

"It's only a month since the stump healed. She'll need practice. Those crutches are the best they make."

"Don't see much sense in spendin' a lot of money on a couple pieces of wood."

I was glad Etta hadn't yet arrived at the dating age with all

its brutal demands of physical attractiveness and normality.
Actually, just after her operation she'd been a celebrity of
sorts for a while; all her friends and school acquaintances had
come out to the farm to visit.

"Oh Father Joe," she told me, her eyes shining, "even that
stuck-up Priscilla Peters, she's the purtiest girl in school, drove
out to say she was sorry. And when I was goin' to school she'd
jest pass me by with that turned-up nose of hers way up in
the air."

"Any boys come out to visit, Etta?" I asked her.

"A couple," she said matter-of-factly.

There was nothing to be done about the school Etta was
missing because of her almost constant pain; the county had
no facilities for private tutoring. I brought her some battered
textbooks scrounged from Russellville High, but they weren't
of much use. Still, Etta became interested in history and delighted in reeling off the names and dates of the English kings.

"She's gettin' snobby ways," her father told me. "Always
takin' on about them British."

When I got a letter from friends in England I sent Etta the
stamps. I brought her books by Scott and Barrie from the local
library and sent away to New York for a Liberty scarf.
Every time I took her to St. Vincent's for therapy she wore it.

The cancer spread and six months later the surgeons at St.
Vincent's amputated Etta's leg at the knee. While she was
convalescing at the hospital I asked her if there was anything
she wanted, and her answer surprised me. Her classmates were
graduating from grade school now, she said. More than anything else she wanted a diploma. I told her I'd see what I
could do.

I went to the principal of her school and said, "Won't you
give the child a diploma? It would mean so much."

"But Etta's been absent for most of the year. And she hasn't
taken any examinations."

"Some universities give honorary degrees to benefactors

who haven't even finished the eighth grade," I told him. "I didn't attend my high school graduation because I didn't have the money for the cap and gown." It took me a good half hour, but I finally convinced him.

I framed the diploma and brought it to Etta at the hospital. She began to cry and I said, "You've got the diploma. Now what's the problem?"

She tried to smile. "Father Joe, there jest ain't nowhere in that hayloft to hang it up, is all."

A year later they had to amputate Etta's leg at the hip, but the cancer was arrested there. I was away from Russellville at the time, but Marge Hinterthuer wrote that Etta was doing well with her artificial leg and enclosed a note from Etta herself saying she still liked to read, especially the English classics. Still later I heard Etta had married a young man named Jones and had two boys. One she named William Shakespeare and the other Walter Scott.

The Carmelite nuns are one of the strictest religious orders in the Catholic Church. These cloistered Sisters are called to a life of prayer in a special way, living in an atmosphere of retirement, silence and solitude in order to deepen and develop their own response to God in prayer. In this way, as a group, they become a symbol to others of what all Christians are called to.

Their Rule is a rigorous one. Their day begins at 5:30 A.M., and a prayerful silence is kept throughout the day. They have two recreation periods, one after dinner and one after the evening meal. At meals no meat is allowed except for the sick, and a fast is observed during a good part of the year. Carmelites sleep on hard mattresses in small, simply furnished rooms and own nothing of their own, not even their habits.

Vatican II has made many changes in the life of the Sisters, but at the time I first met them the prescription that no nun was to be seen, except by her fellow Sisters and her family, without a veil covering her face, was still of obligation. Also the nuns then assisted at mass behind a veiled grille, and even holy communion was received through a small sliding door in the grillwork. Now the curtain is opened for the eucharistic celebration and the sisters enjoy full participation in the liturgy.

In the summer of 1950 Reverend Mother Prioress Mary of Jesus led a group of six Carmelite nuns from Loretto, Pennsylvania, to Little Rock to begin a new Carmelite monastery.

The Sisters settled into an old frame house at 812 Louisiana Street in downtown Little Rock, next to a parish hall. The house had been entirely remodeled to serve as a temporary monastery, but the new quarters weren't very satisfactory. The grounds inside were large enough only for a small garden, and too restricted for the Sisters to get proper exercise. More important, cloistered nuns who concentrate on prayer need quiet, and the Sisters had all too little of it.

The grate and turn through which cloistered nuns communicate with the outside world were located in the middle of the house, near the choir, and often it was difficult to insure quiet for the Sisters who were at prayer. Every Wednesday night the nuns could hear the numbers being called out for Bingo at the parish hall. The station house of a hook and ladder company was located only a few blocks away.

Bishop Fletcher had asked me to help the Sisters get settled. I was impressed by the way they were making the best of a bad situation, but much more by the happiness that shone from their faces. The hearts of these nuns had been so warmed with the grace of God and His love that their sacrifice was easy and their penance a joy. Being around them was much like taking a whiff of pure oxygen at high altitudes; they were a sure pick-me-up.

And it was impossible not to be impressed by their spirit. Two of the Sisters were ex-service women, and one had served in the Marine Corps. During the several days of Open House at Louisiana Street a visitor said to the attractive ex-Marine, "I can see why the old ones are here, but how come you are? Were you jilted?" The goodlooking Sister smoothed her habit of coarse brown material and quipped in mock surprise, "Do you think I'm the type?" Another visitor, commenting on the grating, offered the thought that it must be there to keep the Sisters in. A Sister corrected him: "The grating isn't there to keep us in, but to keep the world out."

When the Open House days were over and the cloister established, I wrote and visited the Sisters as often as I could. My Christmas collection of 1951 was for their benefit. Since I frequently asked them to pray for one or another member of my flock, my parishioners soon began corresponding with them. Unknown to me, Katy Morgan had told the Sisters about my headaches. One scorching day in August, 1952, the Sisters were expecting me with a load of canned goods I'd collected for them from my parishioners. When I got out of the car, the extern, one of the Carmelite Sisters who is permitted outside contact with the world, was waiting for me with a dripping washcloth soaked in ice water. "Father," she said, "we know how long you've been traveling in this terrible heat. We've set aside a room for you to rest in, and there are enough cold cloths ready to cool off the Devil himself."

One Sunday in 1953, after I'd made another appeal from the pulpit for the Little Rock Sisters, Carl Koch asked, "Who are these Carmelite nuns you've been talking about? Why do you ask for help for them when you need it so much yourself?" I told Carl and Paula about the Sisters and later Paula began corresponding with them. One day she told me, "The Sisters must be praying for me. Some wonderful things are happening." "That's fine, Paula," I said, "but just to make sure, you better keep on praying yourself."

Two years later, in 1955, the Kochs were visiting their children in Mena, Arkansas. Carl suggested dropping in on the

Little Rock Sisters. Bishop Fletcher happened to be there at the time, and he invited the Kochs and me to dinner. During a lull in the conversation Carl said, "I don't see how the Sisters can get any sleep with those fire trucks coming and going and the traffic noises, let alone be able to pray. I'll promise them thirty thousand dollars toward a new monastery and ten thousand a year toward a building fund."

Bishop Fletcher turned to me. "Joe, I guess you're elected to build. How long before you can start?"

"About four or five years," I told him, "and a couple of hundred thousand dollars. The Lord must have the best."

In September 1959, dissidents against the integration of Little Rock schools planted ten sticks of dynamite in the school board building less than 80 feet from the monastery on Louisiana Street. The Sisters got the full effect of the blast; all the windows on their side of the house near the school board building were smashed and the walls of the house, already far from steady, were cracked and weakened. It was evident that the nuns would have to move soon, and although finances didn't exactly permit, Bishop Fletcher decided to get construction under way.

Bill Allen, a Little Rock architect, and I had worked out plans for a chapel and over the last few years, from Carmels on the West Coast and elsewhere, I had gathered useful information on what the Sisters liked about their monasteries and what they'd like to change if they had a chance. Friends had promised their time and labor. I had looked forward to working on the monastery with my own hands, as with St. Elizabeth's and St. Anne's. And indeed, in October Bishop Fletcher appointed another pastor for Eureka Springs and its missions and brought me into Little Rock to supervise construction of a Carmelite monastery on West 32nd Street.

God willed otherwise. Late in 1959 Father Kordsmeire, pastor of St. John's Church in Russellville, became ill and, short of priests, Bishop Fletcher sent me to replace him.

That didn't mean, however, that I forgot the Sisters. Mrs. Albert Schafer sent me a $5000 donation for them. Chicago friends whom I was able to inspire with my own enthusiasm for Carmel also contributed generously. I wouldn't let the Sisters settle for a plain cement floor in the chapel and insisted on terrazzo. "The Lord," I kept telling them, "deserves the best." Jack Cadelli and his crew donated their labor and gave us the terrazzo floors at cost.

The Sisters' first mass was celebrated at the new monastery in September, 1961. One of the most beautiful Carmels in the nation, the simple but impressive building had cost $320,000. It is in two basic sections, the chapel and the monastery area. In the monastery area the quarters of the cloistered nuns are separated from the externs' quarters by means of turns and grilles. On November 4th, as part of the Enclosure Ceremony, Bishop Fletcher stepped through an interior convent door, listened as a key was turned in the lock on the inside and then, testing to make certain the door was securely fastened, completed the ceremony. Henceforth only doctors, workmen and others whose services might be required could enter the enclosure. When the dedication and enclosure ritual was brought to a close, the cloistered nuns, listening from behind their curtained grille off the Gospel side of the sanctuary, were again behind convent walls, there to spend the rest of their lives on earth in prayer and meditation and work.

One evening in the fall of 1961 I rang the monastery turn. I had spent the day in Little Rock seeing the Bishop and visiting some sick parishioners at St. Vincent's Hospital. While there I'd slipped my last ten dollars to someone who needed it, and I was reluctant to drive back to Russellville without some insurance against a flat tire.

"Sister," I asked the extern, "can I borrow ten dollars? I'll send you a check for it tomorrow."

The Sister laughed. "That's just too much, Father. Yesterday Mother Prioress was saying that over the years you've given us over twenty thousand dollars from your friends, plus all the gifts you've collected for us. Now you come to us and ask to borrow ten dollars."

"All right," I told her. "If ten's too much then give me five. But it's getting late, so make it snappy."

Many of the stories the Sisters tell so good-humoredly about monastery life are, characteristically, at their own expense.

Two teen-agers were passing the monastery on their way home from school. One said to the other: "What do they *do* in there?" The other answered, "Well, my mother told me they *Exist*, and when they're not just *Existing*, they sleep in their coffins and dig their own graves."

An extern was showing a visitor around the monastery. Naturally none of the cloistered nuns was in sight. The visitor turned to the extern and asked, *sotto voce*, "Tell me, are all the inmates *incurables?*"

The Sisters try to support themselves as much as possible by their work, which includes the baking and sale of altar breads. But in the early days, when there was a big debt to pay on the monastery, they were often in straitened circumstances and always grateful for alms. Any group of religious who depend on alms must depend on miracles, if only minor ones, and the Sisters are no strangers to miracles.

In the monastery kitchen sits a little statuette of the Christ Child. When the Sisters have a request they write it out and leave a note in the little leather bag extending from the statuette's hand. On one occasion a Sister wanted "a small cabbage." Next day a whole crate of Brussels sprouts was delivered to the turn.

Another time, during novena, Sister Anne, the cook, was making fruit compote for dessert and ran out of certain essential ingredients. She dropped a note into the little leather bag. It so happened that at the time a visiting seminarian was shop-

ping in town for the Sisters. The seminarian met a young boy
with twelve cents to his name who wanted to give a donation
to the Carmelites. Since they were standing in front of a fruit
store, the seminarian suggested the boy spend his money for
an orange, a banana and an apple, which he brought back to
Sister Anne. These were exactly the ingredients she was lacking for her fruit compote.

Shortly after the Sisters took possession of the monastery,
a Sister of another Order in town came to the turn and asked
the extern what she needed in the way of food and groceries.
The Sisters happened to be low on everything, and the extern
said so. Accompanying the nun that day was a high-school
girl who told her married sister about the Carmelites and their
current needs. The married woman spoke to her husband, an
insurance man, who went to a wholesale produce company
and asked the owner if he knew about the Carmelites, and
how they lived to offer adoration of the Lord and to pray for
His own. "Frankly," the insurance man said, "I've come to
beg for the Sisters. If you're not interested, I'll leave now."

The produce man asked him to sit down. "I'm interested,"
he said. "I lost my faith during the war, and I've been un-
happy ever since. Even though I've joined the Methodist
Church, nothing seems to matter. Would the Sisters pray for
the likes of me?"

Yes, said the insurance man. In return the produce man
promised to supply the monastery for a year with fruits and
vegetables. As a result he regained his faith at the Methodist
Church and the Sisters' table was green again.

Along with their many very serious requests for prayers,
the Carmelites have been asked to pray for dogs, cats, turtles
and birds. Once a petitioner from out of town asked the Sisters
to pray for his sick parakeet at home, which he'd just about
given up for lost. Next day the petitioner dropped by the
monastery and told the extern, "I called my wife in West-
chester, and she says Max not only made a complete recovery,

he's got so much pep he kept her up all last night, talking in his covered cage in the dark."

Saint Teresa, founder of the Discalced, or "shoeless" branch of the Carmelite Order, prescribed the soft hemp sandal because they were worn by the poor of her day and enabled Carmelites to walk almost noiselessly, facilitating prayer in the monastery. This has led to some strangely addressed mail being received there. Among other things, the nuns have been called "Discarded," "Displaced," "Displeased," "Discharged," "Disabled" and "Discredited." Once a letter carrier appeared on the monastery route with a letter for the Sisters addressing them as "Disappointed." Looking at the extern's shining face, he returned the letter to his bag and said, "This can't be for you. You sure don't look disappointed!"

At St. John's Seminary Monsignor Thomas Keany used to tell the story of Catholic Little Rock College's (later to become St. John's) first football game in 1916 with the Russellville Aggies, later Arkansas Tech. In the third quarter Little Rock was ahead and had just scored a touchdown when the fans streamed out on the field and, taunting the Little Rock players with such phrases as "mackerel snatcher" and worse, followed them down to the railroad station, hurling both gibes and missiles.

Since World War II anti-Catholic sentiment in Polk County had abated, but there was more of it in Russellville than in relatively cosmopolitan Eureka Springs. Catholics who had settled in Russellville as late as the mid-50's had told me that hostility to them was so great in the town that some had actually felt impelled to pass as Protestants.

With the national election in 1960 the problem began to become acute. Some ministers in Arkansas were asking their congregations to swear they wouldn't vote for John F. Kennedy, and so did at least one Russellville clergyman. As the campaign gained momentum toward its close, the rectory phone began to ring with all kinds of associated information, rumors and complaints:

"Hello, you the priest? This is a friend. I want you to know I'm going to vote for Kennedy even though my minister tells me not to. Hey, didn't he just slaughter Nixon in them TV debates?"

"Father Joe? You better not invite the Methodist minister's daughters over for a while. The word is you're trying to convert them."

"Father? Ella Mae wants to announce her engagement to the Perkins boy, who's a Protestant, but don't you think we better wait till after the elections?"

"Listen, you tell your boy we don't want no son of Joe Kennedy in the White House. It ain't that we're prejudiced— he's a fine-lookin' young feller and as smart as they come. But we jest don't like his pirate of an old man."

"Mr. Preacher? Al Smith didn't win in '28 and Kennedy ain't a goin' to win in '60 either. That's a promise!" Click.

About this time three Catholic women of Russellville were asked to attend a PTA meeting at which the question of whether Catholic scouts would be invited to join the West Ward troop would be discussed. However, instead of taking part in the discussion, the Catholic ladies had to cool their heels till they were called in and told the vote had gone against bringing Catholics into the scout troop.

You'd have thought it was the end of the world, or at least St. Bartholomew's massacre in reverse. I was on the phone for hours with the three insulted women, their husbands and their friends. Finally I got an idea. I called up the scoutmaster, dropped over to see him, and within fifteen minutes had an invitation for the Catholic boys in town to join his troop.

"It's easy," I told the nonplussed ladies. "You just have to go to the top." I might have added that better interdenominational relations could be achieved merely by proceeding on the assumption that the other party was as well-meaning as you were, and wouldn't turn the hand of friendship aside.

A case in point soon developed. I'd noticed that the Russellville High cheerleaders had no sweater insignia. Remembering how important it had been to me to be a letterman in high school, I had some letters made up in Little Rock and asked Walt Koehler to bake a cake in the shape of a football field. All that I expected was a regular sized cake. Instead it turned out to be a huge creation two feet by three. I dropped the letters and cake, along with some Coke money for the cheerleaders and football team, off at the high school principal's office and forgot about it.

The principal called the newspaper, the newspaper sent a photographer to the high school who took a picture of the cake. The story was picked up by the wire services. One version had me donating a stadium to the football team.

But the incident did have some nice practical results. The high school principal offered to supply a school bus for the transportation of Catholic children into Little Rock for plays and other public events, and thereafter I was asked to deliver the invocations at football games and various other functions.

On the night Kennedy won the election I got two anonymous phone calls at the rectory. One I'd rather not remember. The other was from the man who had called before to say he wouldn't vote for John Kennedy because he didn't like his father. Now he told me: "Just wanted you to know me and the wife changed our minds at the last moment. We just couldn't send anybody else but John F. Kennedy to the White House."

I was working on the new classrooms when the stoutish woman dressed in a white sheet came by, the children jeering in her wake. The woman slipped and fell to her knees.

"Hey, you kids!" I yelled, "quit that!" and came after them. The kids ran off down Highway 7, one shouting back, "Crazy lady! Crazy lady!"

"You all right, ma'am?" I asked, helping her to her feet. I noticed the big red cross down the front of the sheet.

"Why yes," she laughed, "and thank ye. Those kids were beginnin' to make my heart skip a couple of beats." Cheerfully she asked me if I knew of a phone she could use. Her car had stalled down the highway and she wanted to call a mechanic.

She called the garage from the rectory. Then she introduced herself. Her name was Madam Pugh, she told me, and she ran the Haven of Hope Healing Home on the road to Conway. She took care of up to 70 old people at a time, pensioners on Social Security who otherwise would have had no place to go. Occasionally she did some faith healing.

I asked her how she'd gotten started in her work.

"Well, Father, for that I got to tell you the story of my own healing. For three years I was in a wheelchair. I couldn't walk. I had a rare form of muscle paralysis and high blood pressure, to the extent that it had affected my eyes, and sometimes I couldn't see, either. It seemed there wasn't anything the doctors could do. One specialist in St. Louis wanted to take out three ribs for two thousand dollars; I told him I didn't have the money. Another doctor in Little Rock charged me two hundred for a four-minute consultation.

"Well, I turned on the radio one night and I heard this voice saying, 'There's a certain woman within the sound of my voice. If that woman will come to the altar tonight, she'll be healed.' It was just like sticking a knife in my heart. Just then my husband walked in, and I said, 'Honey, get me ready. This is my night. I'm going to get healed.'

"I went to this faith healer at the Assembly of God Church. Father, I saw more than I ever saw before, and I felt the spirit and that's something I never felt before. I mean I felt the spirit of God. I promised God I'd be one of the best servants He ever had if He'd let me get well. Father, I touched the hem of the garment, and I rose up and walked. And I've been walking ever since."

A few minutes later the garage people arrived to pick up Madam Pugh. She left after we had arranged a time for me to drop by the Haven of Hope Home the following week.

That evening one of my parishioners phoned. Didn't I know the reputation of a certain visitor to the rectory that afternoon? This person she was speaking of was an ex-fortune teller on the rodeo circuit. She was constantly in trouble with the welfare authorities. She was planning to put up a 50-foot illuminated cross that would make her neighbors out toward Conway a laughingstock. Surely I didn't want to waste my time with a religious cultist and fanatic who wore a white sheet, claimed she accomplished faith healings, and was halfway round the bend.

I seldom get angry. This time I did. I spoke my mind and then slammed the receiver down so hard that the operator rang up to ask if anything was wrong.

I went out to the Haven of Hope Home at an inconvenient moment. That morning Madam Pugh had gotten bad news— at legislative hearings in Little Rock the Arkansas Welfare Department had announced it was cutting, by 60 percent, payments to pensioners in old age homes such as her own. When I arrived Madam was on the phone, trying to rustle up backing from supporters for a trip to Little Rock tomorrow, the last day of hearings, to plead her case. Her assistant, an ex-county nurse, showed me around the place, not disguising her concern and worry. Unless a miracle came to pass tomorrow the Haven of Hope Healing Home would have to close its doors and its old and sick would have no place to go but the poor farm.

Things were bad enough now, she told me. "We barely break even as it is. We couldn't manage at all if the Kroger supermarkets, and fine people like Hank Pheiffer in its vegetable and fruit department, didn't give us free food and people weren't generous with things like those baby carriages."

I'd been wondering about the baby carriages, which a number of old people of both sexes were pushing around a concrete apron outside the two barrack-like buildings where the pensioners lived. "Those carriages," the nurse answered, "help the patients to walk."

Not a bad idea, I thought, and indeed, as I learned later that day, Madam Pugh had a talent for putting cast-off articles to work. She'd found her generator in an army camp junk heap and much of her kitchen equipment was army surplus. The barracks had been moved from a nearby World War II training camp.

"Moved?" I asked, surprised. "How can you move a barracks from one place to another?"

"Madam didn't move 'em *whole*. She knocked 'em down, trucked 'em here in sections, and reassembled 'em. She's good at things like that, her and Mr. Pugh." Mr. Pugh, an electrical engineer, was out of town at the moment on a fund-raising tour.

He and a telephone man, I heard, had installed Russellville's first radio station in a stable on the premises, and it was from here that Madam had been broadcasting, on an irregular basis, for the past sixteen years.

I took a look at the old-fashioned but well-maintained equipment and auditorium that seated almost a hundred. "Doesn't this place involve some upkeep?" I asked.

"Oh yes," the nurse told me. "Every time Madam needs some money real bad she signs on with a broadcast. Couple of years ago a man in Texas happened to be listening, and two days later there was a check in the mail for five thousand dollars. It not only paid all the bills we had; we were able to buy some hydrotherapy equipment as good as any they've got in the state. Now I'll show you where the old people live."

The barracks were spotlessly clean. They had been divided

for privacy's sake into separate cubicles, each with its own cot, chair and bureau. The Pughs had installed an ingenious speaker system by which each patient had a microphone to communicate with the nurse on duty. The old people seemed as content as any one could reasonably expect. One, a bright-eyed old gaffer named Strang, shuffled up to me and whispered, "Ain't got no complaints, Reverend, but there's one thing I caint git here and that's Indian nuts. Love Indian nuts. Be mighty obliged you'd send me some."

Madam Pugh put down the receiver as I came into the living room of her two-room cottage. "Spent about two hundred dollars in long-distance calls," she announced cheerfully. "Guess we'll have to have another broadcast to pay for 'em."

She smiled at me. "Got some promises from people who said they'd go to Little Rock and speak up for me. And I left messages with some others. Looks like we'll have a turnout, but I'm goin' to pray all night just to make sure!"

The phone rang. It was a well-known playwright who lived part of the year in Carroll County. He said he'd help. When I asked Madam how she'd met the distinguished gentleman, she told me she had helped his daughter. Later the nurse told me exactly how: Madam had cured the girl, given up by the doctors, of a crippling nerve disease.

I wished Madam luck and left. Two days later the story was in the Little Rock papers. Madam Pugh's prayer had been answered. The morning before, sixteen carloads of supporters and well-wishers had driven to Little Rock, and two private planes, full of Pugh adherents, had landed at the airport. These people had spoken so movingly in support of Madam and the Haven Home that the Attorney General had restored the welfare cuts.

A few days later I brought a pound of Indian nuts out to Mr. Strang, but the nurse wouldn't let him have them. It seemed he used the nuts not for eating but to lob into his fellow patients' cubicles. "Oh, Mr. Strang's quite a pest," the nurse told me tolerantly.

The construction at St. John's was completed a short time after the national elections. Archbishop O'Brien of Chicago, 83 years old but hale as a Polk County seed potato, came for the dedication. I'd written asking permission to name the new church hall after him, and he replied charmingly: "Joe, here I sit with four letters from Bishops in four different parts of the world, asking for money. And I've got to help them all; that's what I'm a begging Bishop for. Now you write me begging to use my name. In my fifty years as a cleric I've never once been asked that. You have my blessing."

The Cole brothers made a special trip from Little Rock to gold leaf Bishop O'Brien's name over the church hall entrance. Watching them finish the job, the Bishop said, "Well, now I can die happy with my name in gold. That must be my reward; I've a feeling I won't get any in heaven."

I offered a high mass in St. John's, which was filled to capacity with many of our Russellville non-Catholic friends and colored people. In the sanctuary sat Archbishop O'Brien, Bishop Fletcher, Monsignor O'Connell and Monsignor Murray. Also attending were more than 35 visiting priests and 15 Benedictine Sisters from St. Scholastica's Convent in Fort Smith. Eighty children from the first through eighth grades at the school took part, and the children's choir sang the mass.

At the noon dinner in the new hall five men who had contributed their time and talents to the project—Wiley Peeler, Wayne Johnson, Hank Pheiffer, Eddie Wesley and Joe Jacimor—received wristwatches engraved with their names and a blessing from the Bishop. I overheard Wiley telling the Bishop he'd better cut down on the sweets if he wanted to avoid diabetes.

After dessert Bishop O'Brien turned to me and said, "Joe, you didn't ask me to help you with the hall and classrooms."

"No, Bishop," I told him, "I think we can swing things, even though it means a heavy debt."

"The beggar doesn't expect to see his name in gold. I'm supposed to be giving money away—here." The check he handed me was for $20,000.

I told him I couldn't accept it, and asked his permission to give the money to St. John's Seminary for a new building needed on campus.

"Provided you'll use at least five thousand from it to help your debt here," the Bishop insisted.

Later that evening, while I was entertaining my distinguished guests in the rectory living room, three callers rang the bell in quick succession. The first was the Russellville police chief. He had in tow a Tech student he said was claiming I'd lent him my car to take his girl out. It was true, I told him. The Chief sighed and asked me to alert him next time I lent the car to anybody else. The second caller was Madam Pugh, in sheet and cross. Madam just wanted to tell me she was sorry she hadn't been able to make the dedication ceremony because one of the pensioners had gone off her head, said she was Sarah Bernhardt, and threatened to knife anybody who tried to deny it. The third were Ulysses Grant Wilson's parents, in their Sunday best. Ulysses had said, they told me, I'd invited them to drop by the rectory that evening. When the Wilsons left, after a cup of coffee and some cake left over from the dedication, Bishop Fletcher laughed and shook his head, "Joe, did I ever say you'd have things quiet here in Russellville? Why, this is Grand Central Station. We'd better send you off for a couple of weeks' rest. I can't afford to have you breaking down—I just don't have a replacement."

I decided that now wasn't the time to tell him I'd made up my mind to apply to Cardinal Cushing's Society of St. James the Apostle, to do desperately needed work in the Latin American missions.

PART IV

ACTION PRIEST

CHAPTER

1

I T took me more than a year to get to South America. When I asked Bishop Fletcher to release me from my Russellville pastorate, assuming I was accepted by the St. James Society, he said he couldn't do so immediately, having no replacement. But he would see what could be done in the fall of 1962.

"Frankly, Joe," he told me, "I'm skeptical of your ability to measure up to this challenge. You'll be volunteering for five years, and that's a long time. Life in the missions is rough; less than half the men who attempt it succeed, mostly for reasons of health. And these are young men you'd be joining, most of them fifteen to twenty years your junior."

He had other reasons why I should stay home. I was fifty, a bit old to be undertaking the mastery of a new language when, if he remembered right, I had no aptitude for languages. The high altitudes of Latin America might increase the intensity of my already severe headaches. A drastic change in my way of life could add to my troubles here. Finally, missionary work required team effort, and I was an individualist, a maverick. Except for a few months with Father Chinery in Harrison I had never worked in harness with anybody else.

All true, I admitted. Yet I wanted to serve in the Latin American missions so badly that I believed all these obstacles could be overcome. I was interested in the worker-priest movement which had begun in World War II when the European priest, impressed into forced labor battalions and fighting with the Resistance, had discovered the outside world. No American Catholic organization was closer to the worker-priest tradition than Cardinal Cushing's Society of St. James the Apostle, which was trying to break down the old pattern of asking the rich to help the poor by getting the poor to help themselves. This was work, especially where it involved building and construction, to which I was ideally suited. If Bishop Fletcher would recommend me, even with reservations, I promised he wouldn't regret not standing in my way. Would he write Monsignor Edward Sweeney, the Superior of the Fathers in Boston, asking them, despite his hesitations, to accept me for service around the end of next year? If he found no one to replace me by then I'd continue on in Russellville until he did.

The Bishop laughed his warm laugh. "Joe, I'd call that graymail, although somebody else might call it black."

In November I went to Boston for the interview Monsignor Sweeney had granted me in response to Bishop Fletcher's letter. The Monsignor had only one reservation—I'd be the oldest missioner in the Society's history. I objected, "But Monsignor, the Society's less than three years old. And so far as my age is concerned, what about Cardinal Cushing's Pope John XXIII Seminary here in Boston for delayed vocations? Some people come late to what they should be doing."

Monsignor Sweeney glanced at his watch. "I should have been on my way to the Cardinal's for lunch five minutes ago. Will you join us?"

I wasn't meant to meet the Cardinal just yet. As so often happened, the press of work had obliged him to cancel his appointments and his Eminence was having a solitary sandwich with his dictating machine for company.

My acceptance by the St. James Society came through in

September, the month Bishop Fletcher found a replacement for me in Russellville. In October 1962, at the request of Major General Terrance Finnegan of the U.S. Air Force, I flew to Harmon Air Force Base in Newfoundland and to Goose Bay Air Force in Labrador for preaching missions to Air Force personnel. At Goose Bay, snowbound and desolate, thousands of miles from home and its amenities, SAC pilots and crews cheerfully kept their demanding round-the-clock alerts. By late October I was in Boston for three days' briefing on my new work in South America.

"Our business is to get out of business," Cardinal Cushing had said of the Society's secular role as missionaries to the poor of Peru, Bolivia and Ecuador. Moving into critical poverty areas at the invitation of local bishops, 135 priests of the Society of St. James served the poor—95 percent of the population, who would otherwise be without priests—and worked to counter Communism's increasingly persuasive appeals. The job of the Society was twofold: in its spiritual aspects to preach the word of God to the poor and to serve them spiritually; in its secular aspects, to get the people to cooperate in the building of schools and churches, clinics and hospitals, cooperatives and credit unions which they could take over and run themselves with Peace Corps or local government or professional help if needed.

In Boston I stayed at St. John's Seminary in Brighton. Passing the Cardinal's home on the seminary grounds and the beautiful white marble statue of the Madonna, I thought of how often she must salute the venerable priest as he passed daily on the Lord's work.

One afternoon I was talking with Monsignor Sweeney in his office when a priest wearing the Society's embroidered red cross on his shirt pocket dropped in and spoke with Monsignor for a moment. Half his face was covered with bandages, and after he left I asked what had happened to him.

"Oh," Monsignor Sweeney answered casually, "Bill Coen was

in the Ecuadorian jungle and picked up an eye infection nobody here can cure. The biggest specialists can't even diagnose
it. He's going to lose the eye."

On November 2 I landed via jet in Lima, Peru. Ahead of me
were three months of language classes at the Cardinal Cushing
Language School at Cieneguilla, 30 kilometers outside Lima in
the foothills of the mountains. Here, under the direction of
Father Fred Cameron, were trained in Spanish not only the
Society's own priests, but others from the U.S., Canada, Ireland, England and Europe who had come to Latin America to
work among the poor, along with American and European
Sisters of various Orders.

After the third week at language school, linguists were
separated from non-linguists; those who showed special aptitude were put in the accelerated course. Having my difficulties, I wasn't among them. Intense study, especially for the
afternoon quizzes, brought on my headaches and at times I
had to drop my course work entirely for a day or two. When
I told Fred Cameron I wasn't looking forward to the subjunctive, he grinned and said, "Don't worry. The subjunctive is
unreal, the people here aren't. You'll manage."

In the second month of school eight of us went to the beach
in Lima for a swim. While I was riding the rough breakers a
huge one caught and tossed me to the bottom on my neck. I
came to the surface barely conscious. At the hospital they said
it was a partial dislocation of a vertebra and a sprained back.
After a few weeks of traction and therapy I was back at
school, but the loss of time had been disastrous and I never
did quite catch up. In late January I graduated at the foot of
my class. Juana Tavara, my instructress, told me consolingly
that I should be able to pick up much of the language in daily
conversation and could always manage to get tutoring.

On Christmas Day Father Leo Mahoney, pastor of St. Richard's Church school and clinic and of the St. James Society's

only parish in Lima, took me on a tour of the slum area that
fell within his parish. In Brazil the slums and shantytowns are
called *favelas;* in Chile, *callampas;* in Venezuela, *ranchos;* in
Peru, *barriadas,* with the individual streets called *barrios.* They
are the result of population growth, the movement of peasants
to the cities in search of nonexistent opportunity. They are a
social illness caused by social inequality, economic chaos and
government instability. They are the illness that the Alliance
for Progress hopes to cure.

The stink of open drains and rotting garbage turned the
stomach. Four hundred thousand slum dwellers squatted in
Lima *barriadas.* Had their locust-like descent upon it from the
city on Christmas Eve 1955, in dumb protest, been an augury
of much worse to come?

When I tried to hand over to Father Leo, to do with as he
saw fit, my Arkansas bon voyage gifts totaling $13,000, he
refused and I had to talk him into accepting half. Next day I
left for my assignment in Ecuador.

On March 12, 1963, we debarked at Guayaquil from an
Italian liner. I was one of six priests headed by Superior Gene
Costello and including Fathers John Auer, Paul McGreevy
and Jerry Degen, who would be working in Guayas province.

In Guayaquil, Ecuador's chief port and commercial city of
600,000, only three of its twenty-two parishes were staffed by
Ecuadorian secular priests. (Nominally 95 percent Catholic,
Ecuador averages only one priest per 17,000 population, compared to one for every 700 in the U.S. Latin America as a
whole has 36,000 priests and needs a minimum of 200,000
more.) Our Inmaculada Concepcion parish had twenty thousand people with no school, clinic, church or rectory. We
moved into a rented house, formerly a naval officers' residence,
set up a mass schedule at the local Catholic high school chapel,
and started a parish census. During the day I worked on the
census in the *barriada* area. Three nights a week I took Spanish
lessons from a private tutor.

Three hundred thousand people, migrants from the *campo* (country) to the city, jammed the 4000-block *barriada* called El Cisne, on the outskirts of town. Its poverty was even worse than that of Lima. Bamboo shacks stood on stilts in seas of mud or water. A green scum covered most of the mosquito-producing pools that made outdoor life at night unbearable. Starving pigs, chickens, dogs and burros roamed the "streets" at will.

No electricity or sanitary facilities existed. Always a *toldo*, or mosquito netting, almost always torn. Bedding, sometimes a straw mat on the dirt floor, sometimes a hammock. For light a piece of rag burned in a beer can full of kerosene. There was only one water pump for every ten blocks. Seventy percent of the able-bodied males were out of work and had they been employed as unskilled labor, their daily wages of 20 sucres, or a dollar, would have barely sufficed to keep a family of four alive unless the children also worked in the rice fields outside of Guayaquil at 6 or 7 sucres a day. If a *barriada* family's income was less than three dollars a week it was eligible for U.S. Government food—flour, powdered milk, whole wheat, corn-meal and cooking oil—which we got through Caritas, the Catholic relief agency, and distributed to the needy. Since about 70 percent earned less than three dollars a week and were eligible, it was often food from the United States that made the difference between subsistence and starvation for the hungry of the city.

Yet, I asked myself, was bare subsistence much better than starvation when U.S. Government food could not prevent the deadly malnutrition we saw all around us in the very young as well as in the adults? Sixty percent of the population were undernourished. The diet of the vast majority was seriously deficient in protein and fats. Only a few vegetables—among them onions and cabbage—were cheap and plentiful. Thousands had only one meal a day. What a tragedy that for lack of roads and cheap transportation, foodstuffs available in one region, especially bananas, were left to rot on the ground.

I began to keep a casual day book or diary, making entries on the average of three or four a week. This one for Good Friday, was typical:

The equatorial sky looks different in this part of the world. Strewn with stars but you can't recognize a single familiar constellation, and a feeling of dislocation sets in. . . . Took my Easter gifts and pay check and revisited the worst of the poor and sick I had met during the census. Gave 45 families my $210. My more experienced fellow priests are going to say I'm setting a bad example but how can you refuse them? Young mother of sixteen abandoned by her "husband" lying on dirt floor with a high fever from malnutrition. Nearby, also on the floor, her new baby one day old. Seemingly endless stream of noisy, dirty-faced children rushing in and out the open door. No beds. A stomach-turning stench arises from a kettle of boiling intestines on the wreck of a coal stove in one corner. This "stew" the family's next meal. Weakly the young mother whispers, "*Padrecito, Padrecito* . . ."

Went to the bamboo hut next door where a barefoot housewife was preparing a somewhat more palatable meal for her own family. I gave her money and told her to call a doctor and to throw out the filthy mess on the stove and feed the girl and her child what she could. Said I'd be back tomorrow with U.S. Government food.

A typical example of one of the *barriada's* common-law marriages gone sour. The father had simply disappeared. *Machismo,* the mystique of male dominance and supremacy, makes a man unwilling to tie himself down, understandable in such a terrible environment. Scores of children are being raised by mothers in fatherless households who can scarcely provide them with a single meal a day. I understand from Father Paul McGreevy, who has served in the sierras, or mountain area, where the Church is more influential than here, that the number of common-law marriages is much lower there than on the coast.

Elsewhere in the *barriada* a legless woman who dragged herself across the dirty floor on an old rug. Brought her communion and gave her money for food.

11 P.M. Dying infant in candlelit room where eight children huddled next to their apathetic parents. Administered baptism. Infant would be dead by morning. Probably a casualty of unboiled water or unpasteurized milk; these people can't afford charcoal to boil water with. Intestinal parasites, from contaminated water or lack of sanitation and garbage disposal, are unbridled menaces among the Latin American poor.

On my way back home via 18th Street, the red-light district, was solicited by one of the 50 adolescent prostitutes outside her little stall. When she noticed my collar she said, with dignity, "Forgive me, Padre." The girl was little more than a child. The usual price is 35 cents. I gave her a few sucres and walked away quickly.

Gene Costello and John Auer have left to take over a parish across the river in Duran. Here in Concepcion parish, Paul McGreevy, Jerry Degen and I remain to minister to 20,000 souls abandoned by their mother church that can't get priests to pursue vocations because to be a priest in Ecuador means to assume a lifelong vow of poverty.

May 5. John Kennedy called Latin America the most crucial area in the world today. Almost a quarter of our foreign trade is with Latin America and more than a quarter of our foreign investments. Since the end of World War II, U.S. Government grants-in-aid to Latin American countries have totaled more than $500 million. Over four million American workers depend for their livelihood on Latin America. In an emergency we would be completely dependent on her for strategic raw materials and food supplies, and her land mass constitutes our southern defense.

May 8. Called to house in neighborhood to investigate "strange happenings." Every year at this time for a week rocks fall on the roof of the house and smaller pebbles *inside*. Went outdoors to check. Men of family were on guard on neighboring roofs; nobody could have been throwing things from the outside, yet when I returned inside three rather large rocks fell on the roof in rapid succession. The woman of the house took me to a closed bedroom with no windows. Suddenly two pebbles bounced off the wall and fell at my feet. They smelled strongly of urine. I phoned Paul McGreevy from the corner cafe and asked him to check my reactions. Paul said I must be crazy but came by anyway. A bastion of New England rationality, Paul was just as puzzled as I when three pebbles rolled to his feet in the closed room.

In mid-July we took over adjoining Holy Rosary parish with an additional 22,000 souls. We rented a small garage, with 75 capacity, as our first church, and began saying Sunday masses. Fathers John Connell and John McHugh moved into the house to help. Paul asked me to start work on a new chapel for Concepcion parish, my first construction work in Ecuador.

The chapel was formerly two small apartments. I knocked out the wall separating them and reinforced the zinc roof with a steel beam. Of course I made mistakes, including paying $100 for the steel beam which I later found out could have been bought for $40. At first I rode herd on the laborers, thinking they were lazy. Actually they just couldn't be pushed in the heat. All considered, you got a good day's work for 20 sucres or one dollar wages.

You had to watch the stealing, though. I kept count of the cement blocks; otherwise a surprising number, considering their weight, disappeared. Even old cement sacks vanished. They had a value of 2½ cents each; on a big project you kept and sold them to buy more cement. The Ecuadorians used the sacks to paper the walls of their bamboo shacks for privacy and insulation against the heat.

One workman, José, had a habit of walking off with the old sacks. When I noted that more were missing than he could use, I told him, "Look, you must be selling them. We can do that ourselves. Remember, we pay you regular scale. You work forty-four hours and we pay you for fifty-six."

"You are right, Padre," he said. "I will make it up to you."

José presented me with an expensive altar cloth for the garage church. I returned it, saying he couldn't afford to deprive his family, whereupon he began stealing the cement sacks again. I assigned another workman to watch him but finally gave up. I couldn't fire him without trouble: Ecuadorian Labor Board regulations were stiff and involved severance pay of two or three weeks' salary.

Aug. 18. Skeleton historical facts to remember about Ecuador. Its Indian tribes were conquered by the Incas in the late 15th century. In 1526 Pizarro landed and by 1534 the Spanish had conquered and executed the last of the Inca Emperors. Quito, founded in 1534, became the seat of a royal governing council. Ecuador gained independence from Spain in 1822 and joined Simon Bolivar's Confederation of Gran Colombia. In 1830 it seceded as a separate Republic.

Aug. 24. Two young *barriada* girls of fifteen and seventeen came to the rectory and said their baby brother was so ill they feared he might die. Asked me to baptize him. As what I had been promised was a five-minute walk stretched into twenty and thirty, and then into another parish, I said to the girls, "Senoritas, you live in another parish; why didn't you ask your own pastor? He would have been glad to come." They only answered, "Padre, we are poor," and I knew they were saying that an American priest would go anywhere.

We passed through the unevenly paved and pestilential but partly lighted area of stucco and adobe houses, and approached the swampy area. It was dark as we crossed the road over a bamboo bridge, the shoeless, surefooted girls guiding me through the darkness by the hand. Here the bamboo huts were on stilts over stagnant water. Somewhere a rat scampered and there was a low and constant hum of mosquitoes.

Inside the hut I baptized the infant by the light of a burning rag floating in a kerosene-filled tin can. When I finished the old *Madrina*, or godmother, offered me two sucres—10 cents. "No, *Mamacita*," I told her, "you keep this and buy your god-child a little toy." I thought of the terrible irony that many children remained unbaptized until their teens; the reason was that their parents hoped to find them a *Padrino* or *Madrina* who had influence and could help them in the world; but, living in the *barriada* as they did, they seldom, if ever, came upon such a person.

I reached for my wallet and gave the newly baptized infant my last fifty sucres. The girls knelt to kiss my hand, but drawing it away I told them, "Don't do that. Come tomorrow to the rectory for food. And bring the baby. We'll take him to the hospital for medical care."

Distributing food beyond parish boundaries meant stretching our supplies even thinner and encouraging those poor outside the parish to come begging. But impractical as it might be, I couldn't refuse these girls after they had walked five miles in the dark to bring a priest to their brother.

"*Dios se lo pague*, Padre, God repay you," said the *Madrina* as I left.

Aug. 26. I was asked to bring communion to an old woman who couldn't leave her hut. The child who took me to her place refused to go inside, telling me she was frightened. Entering the filthy bamboo hut I soon saw why: the woman's mouth was horribly eaten away by cancer. After communion she reached for my hand to kiss it. My involuntary reaction was to draw my hand away, but then I remembered that into this mouth I had placed the Sacred Host. If the woman's cancer-eaten mouth was a fit place for Our Lord to enter then I could not think my hand was too good to be kissed by what remained of her lips. Father Connell and I will take turns visiting her weekly.

Aug. 29. First visit to outlying mission territory in Boca de los Sapos, a small town of 7000 about 35 miles out in the country. Like a stage set for a Western with its single street, of frame buildings and hitching posts. There are brothels at both ends of town. The people in the bamboo huts clustering around both sides of the street are begging for a priest to serve them, and I asked Father Gene Costello, our superior, to consider stationing me here. Gene said he'd heard from a French priest who had served the parish briefly after Father Lopez, also a French priest, had founded it in 1951, that the water was so thoroughly bad, the rainy season so miserable, and the living conditions in general so difficult that an American priest wouldn't be able to survive. I couldn't hide my annoyance at what I took to be a slur upon American toughness, and Gene said he'd write Boston about the possibility of sending me to Sapos.

Dinner at the rectory in Duran with Gene and John Auer. Duran looks as much like a frontier town as Sapos; Gene says if you took away the banana trucks you'd have Dodge City. Told me about the Alvarado brothers who raise cattle and horses nearby. One of them is the gunslinger called "Tom Mix" who's been terrorizing the *campo* for years.

A couple of weeks ago the Alvarado brothers came into Duran to drink and got into a barroom brawl with two auto mechanics. The Alvarados lost the fight and left ignominiously. Last Sunday night they came back to town with what appeared to be two *rurales*, or marshals, from Milagro, the province's metropolis. The brothers flashed what they said was a court order from Guayaquil for the mechanics' arrest on a charge of assault. The townspeople were suspicious; why were the *rurales* dressed not in their distinctive uniforms, with sombreros, but in civilian clothes; furthermore, if the court order were genuine it should have come from Milagro, not Guayaquil. They refused to give up the mechanics to be lynched or "shot while escaping." Stones flew and one of the *rurales* was hit in the face, after which they fired tear gas bombs into the crowd. The Alvarados and the *rurales* were finally forced to run for their lives. The crowd broke into the jail, where the prisoners had been put for their protection, and burned it down.

As yet there's been no sign of prosecution; and it looks as though what the townspeople had suspected was true; the Alvarados had been working with the off-duty *rurales* to get revenge on the mechanics.

Sept. 3. My fourth visit to the Guardaria, the girl's orphanage in Guayaquil. Here eighty-five girls from three to sixteen live jammed into crumbling, ill-lit and ill-ventilated quarters for twenty-five. Meat is served only once a week; classes are held in shifts in the courtyard. Clementina and Rosa, the lay directoresses, are as shabby as their little charges. Many of these girls are, strictly speaking, not orphans but have one or both parents who can't take care of them for financial or emotional reasons. What window screens they had were torn. The kitchen stove often broke down and when it did they cooked over a fire built on the concrete floor. The beds were double-decker old army cots, many of them broken; the mattresses soiled and torn.

It breaks your heart when a *chica* takes your hand as you start to leave and begins to cry because she's afraid she'll never see her "new papa" again. I bought candy for the children and told Clementina and Rosa that I planned to do something about getting a new place for them. They don't believe me; rather, they're afraid to. "Don't joke, Padre," Clementina begs me.

Sept. 7. Passed Four Square Gospel combination church and

school in *barriada*. Seemed to be doing a good job. (Is Aimee Semple McPherson looking down with her irresistible and Pentecostal smile?)

Aside from several Seventh Day Adventist churches in Guayaquil, haven't seen many Protestant missions in Latin America, yet they exist. There are more than 50 Protestant seminaries and 150 Bible schools. Some Protestant missionaries do excellent work in setting up small businesses, youth clubs, camp grounds for retreats, mobile health units. In Peru Jehovah's Witnesses operate over 150 elementary schools among the Quechua Indians, and have thousands of well-trained followers. Many radio transmitters are owned by a group of churches or sects, among them the effective Voice of the Andes in Quito which beams programs for as many as twenty sects. Protestant missions stress preaching in meeting halls and in the open air, and much effort is devoted to distribution of tracts and books, especially the Bible.

Sept. 27. The cost of inequality in South America comes very high. Seventy percent of Indian infants in Peru die before their second birthday. Perhaps 80 percent of Bolivians are completely illiterate. More than one-quarter Chileans suffer from serious malnutrition. In Ecuador, 2 percent of the people own something like 75 percent of the national wealth, and 50 percent of all children die before they reach the age of two. The scrawny, stunted kid kicking the soccer ball in the Guayaquil street has one chance in six of surviving to the age of forty; the wife he marries at fifteen will be old at thirty-five . . . Ecuador, the second smallest country in South America after Uruguay, has the highest population density of any and is compounding the problem with a 3.2 percent growth rate.

Latin American families exist which own more land than that occupied by sovereign nations. In Argentina, Brazil, Venezuela and Chile, there are families or alliances of families each of which owns more land than several countries put together. This situation has no parallel anywhere else in the world.

Oct. 4. Alba Celeste Rubera-Zambrano is a pretty, bright and talented fifteen-year-old at the orphanage. Some time ago I saw she would make a crackerjack teacher. In Guayaquil she had completed the equivalent of a U.S. elementary school education and would need a good high school course which she could get only in the States. The arrangements I made with friends and benefactors in the U.S. took a couple of months. Today I called Alba in and told her, "*Chica*, it's all arranged. You're going to high school in the States at St. Scholastica's Academy in Fort Smith, Arkansas, one of our southern states. The Benedictine Sisters of Saint Scholastica's have given you a scholarship and the rest of the cost, including plane fare and clothes, etc., has been taken care of by Mr. and Mrs. Robert Beck, Mr. and Mrs. Carl Koch and Maurey and Marie Schafer. You'll be living with Mr. and Mrs. Lloyd Lyons of Fort Smith. Their daughter, Shirley, who's graduating next year from the University of Arkansas, will tutor you in English. Now don't get so excited! You won't be leaving till next summer for the beginning of the fall term at St. Schlostica's, in September."

Alba had fainted. Clementina had no smelling salts and we had to douse the child with cold water. It took several minutes for her to come around.

Oct. 5. Prices of imported American food are astronomical. Corn flakes $1.25; can of peaches, $1.50; small jar peanut butter, $1.00 A ham runs as high as $10. . . . Middle-class schoolgirls in Guayaquil all wear saddle shoes, something that went out in the States in the fifties. . . . Everybody in Latin America knows a gringo can't do without a fancy house, two toilets, a maid and a car. . . . It is a commentary on something or other that the electric refrigerator used in the little side-street *tiendas* to cool soft drinks and to freeze popsicles, is rarely if ever used to preserve the proprietor's own food. . . .

In *hora Ecuadoriana*, Ecuadorian time, everything starts an hour later than it's supposed to. Naturally I find it difficult to adjust to this leisurely pace and Paul and Jerry predict it's going to get me into trouble. . . . The people of the coast are mostly mestizos, a mixture of Spanish, Indian and Negro blood that accounts for about 40 percent of Ecuador's population of nearly 4½ million. Another 40 percent are Indians, concentrated mostly in the mountains. Bolivians and Ecuadorians have more than 90 percent Indian blood in their veins. Whites and Negroes, the latter brought over to build the railroads, at the turn of the century, make up the remaining 20 percent. . . . People here look upon the U.S. as the promised land and many of them think it has one state and city, New York. At the orphanage the other day Conchita, a five-year-old, came up to me and said, "Padre José, take me to New York for ice cream." . . . Middle-class Ecuadorians, about 4 percent of the population though growing, are hardly exploiters of the people, nor do they have money in foreign banks. The owner of a small firm makes under $4000 a year and has his headaches, chief among them an excess of paperwork spawned by an implacable bureaucracy. . . . In the civil war between Guayaquil and Quito, the capital, the port of the country pays most of the taxes, makes most of the money and doesn't get its just return. . . . Last night Jerry Degen and I were writing letters in the rectory living room when Paul came in holding a brassiere by one strap. "Found this on the closet floor," he said. "Can't for the life of me figure out how it got there." Seemed to us it could only have been an heirloom from the naval officers who'd lived in the house before us.

In November I left for a month's fund-raising trip for the Society of St. James to Arkansas, Iowa, Massachusetts and Pennsylvania. I was back in Ecuador in December, for Christmas, and then off again in early February for what was now an annual event, my preaching missions at U.S. Army Air Force bases overseas. This time, for five weeks in February and

March, I was at five SAC bases in England, including High Wickham and Wellesbourne, where 19 years ago I had landed Wimpies from raids over Germany. Now only the weather was the same; the super-runways were for Jets, not prop-driven aircraft, and compared to the new field tower the old one, carefully preserved out of British respect for the past, looked like a matchbox.

In December Gene Costello received permission from Boston to establish El Triunfo parish with Boca de los Sapos as its seat. At first Boston was reluctant. The parish, covering 900 squares miles, would need at least three priests, and at the moment the Society was shorthanded. The rainy reason, which began in January and continued through March, was no time to start construction. To counter these objections I had only the need of Sapos for a priest to help its people. Gene described this need in several letters, and he must have done it convincingly. Boston gave its approval on condition that I not settle in at Sapos till Gene had two other men to send with me. Meanwhile I could start construction of a rectory.

The rectory was begun in January 1964 and work on it continued while I was in England. It was completed in April, a second-floor suite of six rooms above the garage and storerooms of the original building.

Paul McGreevy was pessimistic when I drove him out in late April to look over the rectory, now about ready for occupancy. "For over a year," Paul told me, "I lived in a second-story hall in the mountains in Peru, completely isolated, two days from Lima, eighteen kilometers from the main road and two hours from the nearest settlement. Bad as it was it was no-where near as bad as Sapos, Joe. I just don't think you'll be able to take it—the heat, the rains, the bad food, the isolation—for more than a couple of months before you come down with hepatitis or something worse."

"Just don't let Gene Costello hear you saying that," I told him.

In May I moved to Duran until two other priests arrived

from the States to share Sapos rectory with me. My fifteenth anniversary as a priest fell on the 26th of that month. The Guayaquil orphans sang a touchingly beautiful mass in Latin and Spanish at the Duran church. The medical staff of the S.S. *Hope*, recently arrived in Ecuador on one of their medical missions, helped me serve the children hot dogs, ice cream, cookies, candy and pop from their ship's stores. RN Winnie Quinn, from Arlington, Massachusetts, correctly predicted, "Father Joe, you're going to have a lot of sore tummies on your hands."

I had arranged with three doctors and six nurses of the *Hope* to give polio, tetanus and diphtheria shots to 3000 children of Sapos parish over the four days of June 7th to 11th. They would return in early July and August to give the follow-up second and third shots.

The hospitality of the *campesinos* in the deep banana and cacao country, 25 kilometers out along the river Chimbo, was a touching thing. These poor and simple people had nothing; yet they offered their American benefactors what they could— an elaborate spread of cold drinks and fruits that were enough to feed an army. Plus, in the Ecuadorian fashion, painstakingly handwritten testimonials of thanks in Spanish to each of the medical personnel. Typically the *Hope* people brought other gifts besides their medical skills: a ton of baby food for children of two to ten months that weighted down my Chevrolet Apache pick-up truck so heavily that, outside of Vuelta Larga, we had a flat. While I fixed it the roadside gradually became alive with brown faces come to stare solemnly at the *Hope*'s attractive nurses, covered with dust from the road.

The *Hope* people were back over the July 4th weekend, giving up their own holiday celebration. In the village of Cone I offered mass for the first time at the little church my five-man crew and I had finished bulding only a few days before. Father Lopez, a French missionary, had started the church five years ago, but when he left the parish there had been no one to complete it. I had poured a concrete floor, built an altar and completed the two unfinished walls with concrete blocks made by the block-making machine contributed by the Disabled American Veterans, whose generosity was and would continue to be inexhaustible.

In Vuelta Larga the vaccination clinic had been set up in the bamboo school. As the children came in, some pushed, others dragged, most bawling, they avoided me and wouldn't say their usual *"Buenos dias,* Padre José!" Held responsible for their inoculations, I was distinctly unpopular at the moment.

Although they had seen polio in other Latin American countries, the number of cases in this village of 2200 made the *Hope* people grim. Life was hard enough in the *campo;* what bitterness that so many of these children should be cursed with deformity too. I wondered why the U.S. Government had no program to fly these children who could be helped to the States for surgery in American hospitals; surely something could be worked out with the airlines whereby their fares were absorbed.

A young girl of fifteen came in with a female child one day old, wrapped in a blanket. Dr. Mark Kuhn of Fort Lauderdale examined the infant and told me, "The child has only a couple of hours to live." I baptized her then and there and little Maria died before we left Vuelta Larga.

Riding back to Duran in the Apache truck the choking road dust turned my white cotton cassock brown. Winnie Quinn said, "Holy dust, Father, but if I were you I'd wear a darker color." I told Winnie she had something there and made a mental note to have some gray cotton cassocks made up that would better take the dust of the Sapos roads, so bad in May through January that during these months I'd have to travel by outboard up and down the two rivers of my parish.

Any day now Fathers Leon Robichaud of Canada and Ray Kirk of San Diego would be arriving from language school in Lima to share the work of El Triunfo parish with me. Currently I was busy building a school in the village of Estero Claro, interviewing for a housekeeper, picking up the last of the secondhand furniture we needed, and unpacking and sorting the clinic medicines donated by the *Hope*. Unfortunately, aside from some badly needed bandages, this consisted mostly of the *Hope*'s oversupply of tranquilizers, donated by U.S. pharmaceutical houses. There was nothing a coastal *campesino* needed less than a tranquilizer, although, curiously, among the mountain Indians, there is said to be considerable emotional disturbance.

July 21. Painfully clear already [my notebook ran] that our worst problems at the rectory are an erratic pump and generator (2 h.p.; lights from 6 P.M. to midnight only) and toilets which back up. This in addition to the racket, day and night, from the radio in the nearby cantina which plays nonstop not the beautiful slow Ecuadorian *pasillos* but tinny rumbas and sambas; and the hornblowing of the *colectivos*, the local buses (with such names as "Popeye" and "Mr. Roberts" and "South Pacific") which pick up and let off passengers directly beneath my bedroom window. I looked for a plumber in this town of 7000 and all I could come up with is Salamon Calderone, who lives in an adobe house with an outhouse. Salamon swears he worked as a plumber in Guayaquil at the Hotel Humboldt but I'm afraid to check and find out he's lying.

"Don't worry, Padre," he told me. "Any time the toilets they are out of order I am right here to fix them. Just send Oswaldo to fetch me." Oswaldo was the smiling twelve-year-old he'd brought with him.

"You mean you're willing to pay Oswaldo to stay here just in case the toilets break down?"

Calderone looked at me reproachfully. "Padre, do you think I would agree to be your plumber and not do a good job?"

I didn't take him seriously about Oswaldo, but sure enough, later that evening Leon told me Oswaldo had followed him into the combined lavatory and shower room.

"I hope you sent him away," I said.

"No, he was here all afternoon," Leon said. "He told me you'd hired him to 'watch.' "

Sapos was originally a loading station for the haciendas of the area and developed into a community of merchants selling to the hacienda workers. On week nights its single street is almost deserted, but on weekends everybody comes in from the *campo* to buy and sell, a reinforcement of prostitutes buses in from Guayaquil, and there is instant carnival from noon Saturday to 2 A.M. Sunday. We'll have to fence in the space between church and adjoining rectory; the drunken *campesinos* stagger in to use the place as a public urinal.

The cry *teniente politico! teniente politico!* went up from the street below. Dogs barked, pigs oinked and chickens squawked. I glanced out the window. A crowd was gathering around a shortish, dark-complexioned man in shirt sleeves wearing the national badge of middle-class status, the Panama hat, which is made in Ecuador and distributed from Panama. He was shaking a lot of hands even for Ecuador, a hand-shaking country. The *teniente politico* is the J.P. for the province who hands out the papers necessary for baptism and marriage, performs civil marriages, and signs death certificates.

Some minutes later the doorbell rang. It was the *teniente politico*, with entourage behind. The faces of the people of Sapos were happy—at last their *teniente politico* and Padre were meeting, things were as they should be, from now on they might even be better.

Senor Alfredo Guzman shook hands with me elaborately. Then, taking off his hat and fanning himself with it, he preceded me up the stairs.

I offered him iced tea and he smiled. "It is excellent that you have a new refrigerator. But Padre, you do not drink liquor?"

"No, Senor Guzman."

"Padre, you do not drink the very cold beer?"

I shook my head. His face fell so far I would have offered him sacramental wine if I'd had it; I was beginning to feel like a poor host.

"I suppose you do not smoke either, Padre?" Senor Guzman said, and when I told him I didn't, although my fellow priests did, he sighed and took from his shirt pocket a crumpled package of the cheap, inferior Ecuadorian cigarettes.

I told the *teniente* I'd lay in some beer against his next visit to Sapos, and he brightened. We talked for a while about politics and the discovery in Guayaquil only a few weeks ago of a cache of Communist arms and a Communist plan to take over the country.

I said I thought the threat of a Communist take-over was exaggerated, mainly because it was Communist policy not to seize a country that was so economically underdeveloped it would take billions to put it on its feet. In other words, the Ecuadorian plum must be riper before the sickle tried to cut it from the bough.

July 25. John F. Kennedy wrote of Latin America, "Those who make peaceful revolution impossible will make violent revolution inevitable." Some experts feel the Communists can never achieve revolution in Latin America because the natives are too individualistic and the Latin temperament too anti-pathetic to organization of any kind, including that of the Catholic Church. Some Ecuadorians feel the Communists haven't made their country a base because here the surveillance system isn't as tight as in other South American countries—agents can meet in Guayaquil or Quito in safety and then return to their own home turf.

Yet the wife of a Communist agent in Guayaquil told John Connell recently that a Chinese-backed revolution in Ecuador is set for 1974. Since Ecuador is, next to Bolivia, the poorest country in Latin America, revolution, when and if it comes, is likely to strike in both countries.

July 27. First regular monthly meeting with local parishioners at Sapos elementary school, a two-classroom affair which
pays its teacher $50 a month. (He sleeps in a cot outside the
boys' lavatory.) The meeting wasn't five minutes old before
I realized with horror that the townspeople thought that now
I was here they could literally have all the U.S. money they
wanted. It was "Padre, we need U.S. money for this, that and
the other thing"—a new electrical plant, garbage cans, a sew-
age system and street lights, until I had to shout for them to
cool it. The U.S., I said, was no Father Bountiful. Once it had
been in something like their own condition of development; at
the turn of the century American laborers were making a dollar a day. Latin America even had some advantages over North
America: a better climate, absolutely untapped natural resources, an all year round season for crops. Even today in the
U.S. not every child finished high school and only some young
people went on to the university. Of the four boys in my own
family, only I had gone to college.

The people mustn't look to the U.S. for handouts. We of
the Society of St. James would help them build schools. Then,
as the schools developed promising students, all the families
could cooperate in sending them to Guayaquil for high school
and perhaps college. As with the U.S. in its beginnings, the
future doctors, lawyers, politicians would come from the
country folk.

Simone Rodriguez, the teacher, got to his feet. A polio case,
he stood no more than five feet tall. His face had the wooden
impassivity of the Indian but his sensitivity, suffering and compassion showed in his eyes. Ecuadorian education, he said, was
doomed to waste human talent until something radical was
done by the government to improve it. Illiteracy was at least
50 percent and there were thousands who didn't even know
Spanish. Hundreds of thousands, at least 35 percent of all
children of primary school age, had either never set foot in a
school or withdrawn after a few years of sporadic attendance.

Only 12 percent of young Ecuadorians between thirteen and nineteen years of age were in secondary schools, and less than 2 percent of young men between twenty and twenty-six years of age were in universities and other institutions. Young men and women who graduated from the teachers' training schools couldn't find employment or exist on the low salaries; they had to moonlight or turn to other occupations. The few new schools being built couldn't remedy the situation because the number of children reaching school age was increasing in far greater proportion. In the *campo* there were two big problems. New students, or students who had been out of school, were readmitted every 10 weeks. As a result the teacher had to repeat the work missed and thus held up the class in general. Then, during the first six weeks of the regular school year pupils weren't in school but in the rice fields, earning the few sucres that kept their families from starvation. Couldn't the school calendar be changed so that school started in February, the rainy season, rather than in May?

An excellent suggestion, I said. In some areas of the state of Arkansas, students were in school in August, regularly the month of vacation, because they were out in April or May for the strawberry harvest.

A young man in a nylon short-sleeved shirt and heavy woolen suit trousers rose and identified himself. He was a cobbler at the local *Zapateria*. He had never finished high school because of his parents' poverty. He wasn't a Communist but surely I agreed with him that the curse of his country was the rich who had their money stashed away in foreign banks. Who wouldn't invest it in their own country but wanted it safe elsewhere in case of revolution. It followed that the American people could best help the poor of Latin America by leaguing with them against the rich. What did I, an American priest, say to that?

"Let me tell you a story," I said. "In Guayaquil recently there was a Spanish priest who started a strike to better the conditions of the factory workers. Nobody had ever dared to do that before. The factory owners offered a compromise settlement that wasn't fair but was still a big improvement; the priest refused to accept it. The owners offered slightly better terms and the priest refused again. The owners decided 'this gringo from Spain' had to be got rid of, and they had their way, because what the rich want in this country they get, and you aren't going to change that for a while. Now perhaps, just perhaps, this priest could have accomplished more for the workers by accepting the settlement and then working for a better one. Instead he was thrown out of the country. I ask this as a question. Think about it."

Senor Sanchez, proprietor of the *Funeria*, or funeral parlor, a stocky mestizo, raised his hand. Surely I wasn't serious about lack of American funds? America was the richest country in the world. Wasn't I joking with the people of Boca de los Sapos when I said they could expect no American money to help them make decent lives for themselves? For instance, he had heard that American capitalists were going to buy up the surrounding countryside so they could dig for oil, or was it diamonds?

Salamon Calderone saved me. He came into the classroom, a crisis with plumbing or generator writ large on his face for all to see. I excused myself and declared the meeting over.

July 30. A flat on the outskirts of Taura. I put on the spare and dropped the flat off at the tire repair shop in Boliche. A mile out another flat, and this time I was spareless. I'd been waiting for more than an hour for a car or bus to pass when two *rurales* pulled up in their blue and white coupe.

They got out languidly, tall men in boots and sombreros with a weary air of command. They shook their heads at me. A very dangerous business, Padre, being stranded hereabouts. The bandit "Tom Mix" was back in the area. Cassockless, in my work pants and blue St. James shirt with its inconspicuous red cross over the pocket, I wasn't easily identifiable as a priest. "Tom Mix," who had already killed eighteen people, would shoot me for my truck without a second's hesitation.

The *rurales* dropped me off at the gas station in Duran. A few minutes later the mechanic and I were on our way to Boliche with a spare. The mechanic had a revolver strapped to his waist; he was one of the two men whom the Alvarados, brothers of "Tom Mix," had tried to kidnap and lynch last August. He tapped the revolver significantly, saying, "Senor Mix, Senor Mix." I sighed, knowing the revolver would cost me double.

Rattled into Boliche two hours later but the people squatting near the bamboo church were still waiting for the U.S. Government flour I'd promised them. After distributing the flour it was confession time. Sitting on a rickety chair in the open while a tethered goat bleated nearby and the children knelt before me, I heard over thirty confessions. As usual the boys looked straight into my eyes as they made their confessions and one, a bright-eyed little ten-year-old named Pancho, put his hand on my knee. I said to him, "Well, Pancho, they're your sins and you're proud of them, is that it?" Pancho nodded, smiling brilliantly, "*Sí, Padre, sí!*" Some of the other waiting children were within hearing distance, and I told them to move back. "*Chicos* and *chicas*, you're not supposed to listen. You're bound under the same pain of mortal sin not to listen as Pancho is bound not to listen to you. A confession is private. If I wanted you to hear what Pancho's saying, I'd tell him to get up on the altar and yell." A gale of giggles in reply.

Returned to the rectory to find Calderone there working on the toilets which had backed up that afternoon. "One thing is sure," Ray Kirk said disgustedly. "This rectory will never be the center of social life in Sapos. I'd be afraid to let a *gringa* step in the door."

CHAPTER

2

I N August 1964 Richard James Cardinal Cushing flew in
from Boston on a month-long visit to his missions and
priests in Ecuador, Peru and Bolivia. Though we had
corresponded, this was the first time I had met the great Prince
of the Poor. During his two days in El Triunfo parish, Cardinal Cushing put up at the rectory. In his party were Doctor
Ed Wright, a brother of Cardinal Wright of Pittsburgh and
the Cardinal's personal physician, Monsignor Rossiter, his secretary, and Monsignor Edward Sweeney, Superior of the St.
James Society. To guard against midnight disasters with the
plumbing, Salamon Calderone slept downstairs in the clinic
on a cot.

The Cardinal spent two afternoons visiting four of our El
Triunfo missions. Commenting on the blue, gray and yellow-
striped chapel at Boliche, he grinned and rasped in his famous
gravel baritone, "Now that's what I call a colorful church."
At km. 32 the poor presented him with a half dozen eggs, a
chicken, flowers, oranges and bananas. The man who only the
evening before had given $150,000 to the Catholic University
of Guayaquil and had promised $90,000 for a new Mother
House for the Lauritan Sisters, who work primarily with the
destitute, received these simple gifts with quiet dignity.

Holding an egg in his hand, he turned to me and said, "Joe,

build a school here in memory of our beloved Jack Kennedy. God, how I miss him!" I assured His Eminence a school was on my agenda for the poor of km. 32 and thanked him for naming it; John F. Kennedy School would be a fitting gift to the memory of the man who had also loved the poor of Latin America. When we returned to the rectory Dr. Wright urged the Cardinal to take his nap, but he insisted on sitting down immediately at my desk and writing out three checks—$10,000 "as a starter" for a hospital in Boca de los Sapos when I "got around to it," and $5000 each for schools at kilometers 22 and 32. That started him off on some hilarious stories of fundraising in Boston, and he didn't retire for his nap for another hour, although his craggy face was gray and drawn and I could see he could have stood a session with the oxygen tent that accompanied him on all his travels.

When I apologized to Dr. Wright for keeping the Cardinal from his nap, he laughed. "That's all right, Father. If there's one thing that gives his Eminence a lift, it's writing a check for the poor."

Later the Cardinal told me, "So many times people want to know why I give so much for education here. You're a little older; you know that without education these people are doomed."

He spoke of the missions. There were stories that Richard Cardinal Cushing wanted nothing more than to offer mass and serve the Latin American poor as a humble priest, and I could see now that they were perfectly true. He envied me my happiness and my simple life.

"Your Eminence," I said, "we need you in Boston."

He sighed. "Yes, that's what two Popes have told me."

Later that week, before moving on to Peru, the Cardinal visited the S.S. *Hope* in Guayaquil harbor. He went from sick bay to sick bay, comforting the elderly, joking with the youngsters. Those few in casts, who couldn't be lifted, he took in his arms.

Everywhere he took delight in children. The girls at the orphanage had become so fond of him I feared there would be hysterics when he left. At the Guardaria he passed out the *Hope*'s excellent ice cream pops that he'd plotted with Monsignor Rossiter to pay for when Dr. Walsh of the *Hope* had refused his check. When a pretty little *chica* came up to him for seconds he frowned and told her in his halting Spanish, "Now this stuff costs money, and in my job I've got to raise a lot of it. So if you grow up to marry a millionaire, promise you'll introduce me to him."

His parting words to me were typical of the man who, in the emerging church of renewal, gives a judicious push to the future when and where he can. "Stay in tune with the times, Joe," he told me at the airport. "The older you get the worse the wrong notes sound."

On the way back to town Paul McGreevy told me the Cardinal had promised him a $15,000 rectory in Guayaquil. "And all because of a couple of chickens."

"Chickens?" I said, puzzled.

"You know the poultry shop next door to where we live now?"

I nodded and Paul said, "Well, the night before the Cardinal came out to Sapos he slept at our makeshift rectory. Next morning he came down to breakfast and I could see he hadn't slept a wink. 'Paul,' he said in his gravel voice, 'those chickens kept me up all night. How much do you need for a sound-proof rectory?'"

The S.S. *Hope* left for New York on September 4. The day before, I dropped by to say goodbye to Dr. William Walsh. As he saw me down the gangplank, Dr. Walsh gestured toward the jeep parked on the pier and said, "It's yours. Keys are in the ignition."

I told him I couldn't take it. The *Hope* people had done enough already for El Triunfo parish.

"That jeep's twelve years old," Dr. Walsh told me. "It's no bargain. Maybe I'm even trying to get rid of it."

I knew better. A jeep was worth at least a thousand dollars in Ecuador. I insisted on giving Dr. Walsh a check for $300, and he accepted it, but as I stopped at the gate to wave a last goodbye, I saw him, at the top of the gangplank, tearing something rectangular into bits.

Sept 17-18. Here in El Triunfo parish 6 months and only today did I learn of a church and five schools that had been abandoned in the Chimbo area, about 10 kilometers from Vuelta Larga, and which I had never known existed. Father Lopez had simply forgotten to tell me about them.

I told the people that three American priests were here to give them weekly the Holy Sacrifice of the Mass, to teach their children to know and love God, and to instruct the adults in the evenings. I would be visiting their poor with food from the people of the United States. They asked "*Y leche, Padre?* And milk, Father?" and I said, "Yes, and milk I shall bring tomorrow for the children of the five schools." "*Dios con usted y Estados Unidos.* And God be with you and the United States," they said. Next day, when I returned with the food, one of the local schoolteachers helped me unload it. He warned me that a Communist was in the village.

"A Communist?" I was surprised. I had yet to come in direct contact with any since arriving in Sapos.

"His name is Wilson Romero. He has been talking against the Peace Corps workers, and he will talk against you."

"Wilson? Where'd he get that name?"

"Padre, many Ecuadorians have the names of American presidents. I know of a Washington, a Jefferson and a Pierce."

I asked what this Romero was like.

"Oh, he is a mean hombre, Padre. He killed a man in Milagro who refused to pay for some used clothing he sold him. You had better be careful."

"Is he a Russian Communist, a Chinese Communist or a Cuban Communist?"

Unsmilingly the teacher said, "Romero is very fond of Chinese food. In Guayaquil he is always to be found at the Chinese restaurant." Guayaquil had no Russian or Cuban restaurants, whatever that might mean.

Romero turned out to be a powerfully built man of around forty in an Arrow sport shirt. He carried a shabby briefcase that was so flat I was sure it was empty. He waited till I started distributing food from the back of the truck, then appeared from nowhere to push his way through the crowd and challenge me with the question, "Rich capitalist, how will you make these poor people pay for this food?" That left me with two options. I could ignore him, in which case he would continue his heckling and disrupt the food distribution, or I could have it out with him here and now.

I jumped down from the tailgate, lifted up my cassock and pointed to the seat of my pants. Laughter from the crowd. "Look at these rich, capitalist trousers," I said. "They've got patches on them."

He jerked a thumb at the Chevrolet Apache. "You've got an expensive truck."

"That truck isn't for me. It's for your people, to transport them to school and to church and to haul U.S. Government food to the poor."

"Some food," he said contemptuously. "It's gone in a week. Your food salves American consciences for the way your trusts exploit our cheap labor."

"Do the Chinese or the Fidelistas or the Soviets give your people food?" I asked. "Each of these sacks is a gift. You call me a capitalist. Well, tell me what you've done for your country besides preaching revolution, and you're at least forty years old. I've been here for only two years. I've built six schools, with many more to come. How many schools have you built?"

He spat, not at my feet, but at his; still, we weren't stand-ing all that far apart.

"You capitalists are rotten. All you care about is profit," he accused.

"Is that so? When I leave here the schools will stay. They don't have my name on them. Where does my profit come in?"

"In having people say the Church built these schools. They don't discriminate between the American and the Ecuadorian Church. They think, 'Maybe there is something good to be said for the Ecuadorian Church.'"

"There is . . . Your logic is crazy. I can't reply to it."

"No, there is much to which you cannot reply. Why don't you build a school here?"

"I built your people six classrooms and a church in nearby Vuelta Larga. Your people go there, as you very well know. Your own government wouldn't or couldn't build those six classrooms."

He picked his nose. "Well, you've got a boat you go up and down the river on. What capitalist does not have a private boat?"

"That boat was built in Guayaquil for sixty dollars and paid for by American friends. Its motor was paid for by another friend. You'd call him a capitalist, but no one in my country would. I use the boat to get to the people when the roads are flooded from the rains. I buy Ecuadorian gas and oil for the motor. . . . But we're not getting anywhere, Romero. I hear you're a pretty tough hombre. Any time you're ready, I'll take this cassock off and fight you, and you're a younger man than I am. You're not going to call me a capitalist or insult my church or my country and get away with it. Before I leave here I'll have spent over two million sucres. And most of that will have come from American workers."

I moved forward an inch or two, and Romero moved an inch or so back.

He cleared his throat. "Your Alliance for Progress is not an alliance and certainly it is making no progress." Laughter.

"Very clever. But all that proves is that you know how to put words together."

"What about American morals?" Romero said, shifting his ground. "Your movies, magazines and fashions have a bad influence on our youth."

"I exchange holy cards for Marilyn Monroe calendars," I said. "I've got a big collection of calendars at the rectory. Why don't you come by some time and take a look?" Laughter.

"That's all very well, but you can't deny American racial discrimination. You treat your Mexicans and Puerto Ricans like dirt."

"The fact remains that I'm not discriminating against a Mexican in Los Angeles at the moment, or a Puerto Rican in New York. I'm here helping your people."

He made a face. "The U.S. befriends Latin American dictators and ignores democratic regimes."

"Very probably, but the Church doesn't. Since 1950 the Church has spoken out against dictatorial regimes. Ever since Pope John's *Mater et Magistra*, landowners have denounced Catholic priests as Communists because they're preaching agrarian reform."

"We Communists support the causes of other groups and parties interested in social justice."

"That's what you say. Your motive is to sow confusion and unrest. You're behind the demands of the *campesinos* for land reform, but you oppose the government land programs that hope to improve the situation. Or you'll lead a worker's strike for higher wages but oppose government legislation to correct economic injustice."

He moved back another inch. "We in Latin America are forced to spend 90 percent of your loans to us on U.S.-made goods and services. And what about your American general,

Smedley Butler, who once bragged he made Mexico safe for the American oil interests?"

"That was a long time ago," I said, guessing, hoping I was right. Who was Smedley Butler?

Romero went on, "Why is it that Latin America's three greatest artists—Siqueiros of Mexico, Neruda of Chile and Niemeyer of Brazil, are all Communists?"

"Some sensitive men are Communists," I answered. "That doesn't mean that most sensitive men are."

"The problem for a Latin American is not to explain why he's a Marxist, but to explain why he is not."

"And the Church has been among the first to recognize this. Come on," I taunted him. "Without a machete in your hands you're nothing. You talk against our Peace Corps workers. College kids who come to help you find a better way of life. Who dedicate two years of their lives to you. They live in your huts and eat your food. They're no more capitalist than I am or your street vendors whose goods, as everybody knows, are either stolen or smuggled in." Laughter. "Tell me one concrete thing you've done, Romero. Maybe you've translated some Marx into Spanish? I know you sell used clothing, but I know you've never given a hand with a school."

Maybe his throat was dry and he needed a drink. He turned on his heel and, shoulders squared and chin up, walked away, briefcase banging against his hams. The crowd tittered. I went on with the food distribution.

Oct. 1. Started school in Immaculata, a small village along the Chimbo River. The need was great: 5 grades in a collapsing bamboo shack on the dirty road surrounded by chocolate and banana trees and overlooking a soccer field. My Disabled American Veteran buddies gave me $400; and the Blind Veterans, $100; I added to this $500 from Carl Koch and $500 from Mrs. Schafer for construction of two classrooms, one for the older children, the other for the younger, with ample blackboards and good ventilation. At the rear of one classroom a CARE kitchen will prepare American Government food for lunches, this to be supplemented by what can be grown in a vegetable garden in the back with seeds from CARE.

With six volunteers working a day each week we turned out 8000 blocks on the block-making machine over a ten-day period; over 700 blocks daily. The government permits me to give each worker who devotes a day's work 5 lbs. of flour for his family, a good incentive.

Oct. 15. Came in dead beat and covered with dust; stomach in bad shape and a headache like the anvil chorus. Went to bed at eleven and next morning was so weak I had trouble getting out of bed. Ray and Leon told me it was about time I took a day off.

At about ten o'clock the rectory bell rang. The cook said it was an Indian from the mountains whose son was dying. I got dressed and went down to see him, feeling pretty weak. I asked the man if he was sure his son was in need of the last sacraments. "*Sí, Padre, muy infermo.* Very sick," he told me. While I finished getting ready he had a cup of coffee upstairs in the kitchen.

The *Hope* jeep was out with Father Leon and the Apache truck with Father Ray; all I had on hand was a two-ton, ten-year-old Alliance for Progress truck lent to us yesterday for the delivery of U.S. Government food.

Ahead of me lay an hour and a half of hard driving over the rough back roads to Barranco Chico in the foothills of the mountains, and, when we got there, another hour's climb on horseback up the steep trails. I wondered if I could make it.

The Indian's ten-year-old son was waiting for us a mile outside Barranco Chico with two small Ecuadorian horses. The boy kissed my hand and said, "*Padrecito, rapido! Rapido!*" We mounted and the boy guided us up the slippery, dew-wet mountain path. Several times we almost slipped and fell and the strain was doing my headache no good. When we reached the summit I glanced below and shivered; there was a sheer drop of several hundred feet.

Tin Kent cigarette ads were nailed to the side of the mountain hut to keep out the wind. Inside, on his wooden bed, lay a boy of twenty. He was dying of hepatitis; probably he wouldn't last the night. The nearest doctor was in Milagro, over 110 kilometers away, and no doctor would come up the mountain; the boy had been too weak to move. I heard his confession, administered the last rites and gave him holy communion. As I prayed with him the boy reached for my hand and held it to his cheek. The entire family of seven knelt and asked my blessing. I asked the Indian how many families were in the area and if they needed food. "Sí, Padre," he told me. "There are forty-six families and we have very little. Most of us eat but one meal a day."

I promised to come back day after tomorrow with U.S. flour and cornmeal. The Indian said he would have pack horses waiting at the foot of the mountain. "God has not taken the life of my Pedro in vain," he told me. "In a very short time the rainy season will begin and it will be impossible for the horses to get up the mountains with loads of any weight. If we had not met today, Padre, my people would have had to go without the food you will bring them."

By now the dew had dried and footing was more secure. The trip down the mountain, with its compana trees, like inverted lilies in bloom, would have been pleasant had it not been for the pounding in my head. Around the truck squatted four Indians in ponchos, derbies and sparklingly clean white ducks. Gravely they informed me they had been guarding it against my return.

Nov. 3. Douglas Hyde, an ex-Communist Catholic who has regained his faith, writes: "The Communist as a person is a challenge to priest and layman alike. Communism could spread across the world through Asia and Africa and Latin America until the West was perhaps bypassed. But that need not happen. If it does it will be much more because of the character and training of Communists as people and our failure to respond to their challenge, than because of the strength of Communist theories as such."

Nov. 12. Leon's mother is ill and he has been called back to Canada, leaving Ray and me to carry on alone. Today I offered mass along the river bank with four sacks of cornmeal as my altar. A blessing to have the blue sky my ceiling and the trees my walls with the clear river rippling by. After mass I asked the people to pray for President Johnson and a young woman asked me, "Padre, cannot I pray for the handsome Presidente Kennedy, who I loved so much?" An old man of great dignity told me later, "Our prayers are those of the poor, and God will hear them."

December, 1964, was a wild month with Ray and me trying to complete the five-month course of catechism classes in 52 schools as we examined and prepared over 1000 children for their first confession and holy communion. Jerry Degen came over from Guayaquil to fill in for Leon, but it was still 6 A.M. to 10:30 P.M. for us daily, with our lunch on the road, a few bananas or mangoes, now in season, washed down with a lukewarm Coke at one of the roadside cantinas. What with this exhausting pace, I had to cope with the Curandero, too.

The Curandero, or Healer, had come from the hills a few months ago with his wife and set up shop in a little wooden house down the street next to one of the two town bordellos. He was in his middle years, stocky and powerfully built. He had, I heard, been successful in "curing" some of the girls, of what wasn't exactly specified. I saw him at mass, ostentatiously fanning away with his Panama, but had nothing in particular to do with him till one day he came up to me after the service, handed me some papers and said, "Padre, these are some things I have written. They are divinely inspired—I wrote them from a vision."

I asked him to leave his writings with the cook and said I'd get to them when I could. He was hurt I didn't read them then and there.

A few nights later I glanced over the soiled pages. They were stilted and undistinguished and it looked to me as if they'd been copied from a Spanish prayerbook. When I told him so the Curandero walked away without a word and didn't come to church for a week.

When he and his wife finally did show up, it was with a vengeance. They arrived late and noisily, drawing every eye. From the Curandero's neck hung a big cross and around hers his wife wore rosary beads. Both carried big vases of flowers which they set down before the altar. During mass they prayed out loud.

I told them later, "The mass is the central part of worship for all the people. Pray in response to the priest's prayers, not on your own."

"But Padre—" began the Curandero.

"There's no buts," I said, ending the conversation.

Next day both of them walked into church dressed in white sheets with holy cards pinned all over them. During mass they were a complete distraction, and I was boiling mad by the time I was finally able to get them aside for an explanation.

"I had a vision, Padre," the Curandero said, smiling beatifically. "In this vision I was told to come to church dressed as a saint."

"Were you also told that your wife was one of the elect? I don't know if you think this is going to help your business, but it doesn't help you with me. Now don't come to church dressed like this again."

Two days later Ray Kirk had the seven o'clock mass. When I got back from the *campo* that night he told me, "I thought you'd cured the Curandero and his wife. When I came out to ring the bell they were down on their knees, dressed in sheets and holding flower vases. They had holy cards pinned all over them."

"I hope you didn't let them in."

"Are you kidding? They stayed outside, but when mass was over you should have seen the crowd they'd collected. The Curandero started giving me an argument about your having no right to keep them out of church."

I dropped over to the Curandero's house that evening. He was in Guayaquil, his wife said. I told her that if they continued making a spectacle of themselves I'd have to see to it that they did it someplace else than in Boca de los Sapos.

"Are you threatening you will make us leave?"

"I have good relations with the *rurales*. Let's leave it at that."

"My husband knows many important officials in Guayaquil."

"I'm sure he's worked wonders for them."

"Since his visions he has been a much better Curandero."

"He cures nothing. Only God cures. It's best the people go to the clinic."

"My husband says he will complain to the Bishop if you continue to persecute him."

I smiled, and she asked what I found amusing. "You remind me of my parish at home," I said, and left.

A few days later a delegation of three girls from the bordello called on me at the rectory. They had given thought to their appearance and were dressed simply, even severely; their mouths had only the slightest trace of lipstick.

"Padre," began Carmencita, the spokeswoman, "the Curandero tells us you do not approve of him and he is thinking of moving from Boca de los Sapos."

"I have no objection to his staying if he stops disrupting mass with his free commercials."

"He has been a great help to us," said Carmencita, and the other girls, Rosa and Marguerita, nodded shyly.

"In what way?" I asked.

"He cures our headaches."

"So could aspirin," I said.

"He helps with the nerves, with the melancholy."

"So could tranquilizers, or a good night's sleep."

Carmencita paused. "He makes it so that we do not become pregnant."

"Do you mean he gives you birth control devices?"

"No, Padre. When one of us misses our time of month he passes a hand over our stomachs and says we will be all right."

"And you are all right?"

Carmencita and the girls nodded.

"To that I can say only that there will come a time when he'll pass his hand over your stomachs and you won't be all right. How much does he charge for this?"

"Forty sucres, Padre."

"Forty sucres is a lot of money for a wave of the hand. How long does it take you to make forty sucres?"

"About an hour, Padre."

"It's still a lot of money. Why don't you come to the clinic, where it's free, for medical advice and assistance?"

"It is unpleasant for us to come to the clinic," Carmencita said. "People whisper and point and talk."

"You have just as much right to come to the clinic to see Doctor Chiquito as anybody else. The clinic is for all the people of Sapos. I promise you that nobody will make you feel uncomfortable. Now you must excuse me, ladies. It's time for mass."

A week later the Curandero and his wife left Sapos for Milagro. I heard they owed money in town. The bordello girls visited the Curandero by *colectivo*, but then two got pregnant and they started coming to see Dr. Chiquito at the clinic. Rosita, the clinic receptionist, had orders to put them right through and that made some people grumble that Padre José was favoring the *putas* because they paid more than the token two-sucre fee. I decided I didn't have time to worry about what the grumblers were saying.

For the first few months in Sapos we had no cook; none of us were satisfied with any of the applicants for the job. Since neither Leon nor Ray had any culinary skills, I took over the "cooking," which consisted of scrambled eggs and hamburger, in alternation. Sometimes I varied the menu with cheeseburgers or a Spanish omelet.

One day Leon pushed away his eggs and said, "You may be able to live on this stuff, but I can't."

"What's the matter with it?" I asked him.

Leon just looked at me. Ray laughed and I said, "Suppose I try some Ecuadorian dishes, like *llapingachos* or *empanadas?*"

Leon was doubtful. "You don't do much with hamburger, to begin with."

I asked Ray if he minded if I experimented, and he said to go ahead, so I got hold of some recipes. Unfortunately, my Ecuadorian cooking was a disaster. The *llapingachos*, a mixture of potato, boiled with cheese and then fried, and served with a sauce of peanuts, fried eggs and slices of avocado, looked all right and even *tasted* all right, but it made me sick. Leon consolingly suggested I drop the Ecuadorian stuff and go back to my original "simple" fare. The word *simple* stung me. I told him I was going to try the *empanadas*, meat pies with rice, cheese and onions, and *locro*, a soup of corn, potato and cheese.

Both Leon and Ray came down with a stomach ailment that kept them around the rectory for a couple of days. Neither of them would talk to me for a week, although Ray, noted for his sense of humor, broke down first.

Desperate for a decent cook, I hired, on the recommendation of a U.S. Army pilot who had finished a stint of photographic work for the Ecuadorian Government, his cook and helper, Maria and Lourdes. Maria was first-class and we were lucky to have her during Cardinal Cushing's visit.

But after a few months the two women began to get restless. There wasn't enough to do in Sapos and the men didn't come up to Guayaquil's standards. When John Connell asked if he could hire Maria and Lourdes for Holy Rosary rectory in Guayaquil, I was glad to let them go.

Blanca, a thirty-year-old mestizo woman with a year-old child, came to work for us. Not, however, without some second thoughts on our part; we had been warned she'd been fired from her last job for a missing radio. The first few months passed without incident; Blanca was a reasonably good housekeeper and a capable cook. When she found a boyfriend and began to sing at the stove we thought our housekeeping problems were over.

Not so. I found $20 missing from my desk. Leon said he was short 500 sucres, or $25. Ray wondered where the $30 he'd hidden in his bookcase had disappeared to. Reluctant as we were to suspect Blanca we had no choice: not only was she wearing expensive new clothes, but her boyfriend, Roderigo, had a new wristwatch and bicycle.

"Let's face it," Ray said. "Blanca isn't goodlooking enough to be moonlighting for Raquel at the Casa d'Amora. We'll have to fire her."

We called in Blanca and asked her to explain her clothes and her boyfriend's presents. She broke down and cried. Yes, she had taken the money but it was only so she could keep Roderigo, who was attractive to other women, at home. Besides, hadn't she been honest enough to admit she'd stolen the money?

Ray told her gently, "Blanca, we're here to help the poor. When money is taken from us it's stolen from the poor. We can't permit that."

"Oh please, Padre, I'll lose Roderigo," Blanca wept, and

promised it wouldn't happen again, but we stood firm and she left the rectory that afternoon.

At eleven o'clock the doorbell rang. Assuming it was a sick call, I went downstairs. The caller was Roderigo, drunk and demanding.

How dare we fire Blanca? Did we realize how this would affect his standard of living? He would be forced to sell his bicycle, perhaps even his watch. He would be reduced to the rank of peasant. We must take her back.

A certain amount of diplomacy was called for. Roderigo was capable of leaning on the doorbell all night, and there weren't any police in Sapos to make him stop. I told him we'd take Blanca back under one condition, that he marry and make an honest woman of her, in which case there was a fair chance she'd stop stealing.

He gaped at me. "Padre, you are joking! It is unfair to expect a man like me to spend the rest of my life with one woman! And you know Blanca looks not unlike a parrot. As one man to another, have pity!"

"Think about it," I said, and shut the door. Hopefully I waited, and was rewarded by silence; he'd gone away. I went up to bed.

Roderigo never did come back. I heard later he'd left for Duran. Blanca followed him there, but I had a feeling she didn't have too much luck tracking him down.

Dec. 12. "The Church . . . demands a deep social reform, and for an obvious reason: because present organization in many of its aspects is very far from being Christian. There are, in the present organization of the world, a great number of mistakes and injustices that a Roman Catholic must never accept. In the field of principles, Christian ideas on ownership and work have been forgotten . . . In the field of economy, there is poor distribution of wealth, a fact that has established misery as a normal product of modern society and has created in the social field the conflict of classes, rather than the Christian concept of cooperation and harmony. In a word: social order requires a thoroughgoing reform and it is the Catholic duty to fight for it."—Bishop of Talca, His Excellency Manuel Larrain Errazuriz, President Latin American Bishops' Council.

Dec. 18. Douglas Hyde has noted that a considerable number of Communist leaders and hard-core members throughout the world are baptized Catholics. Many lapsed or fallen-away Catholics are today leaders of Communist parties in the West and in mission territories. He tells a touching story of Luis Taruc, a Filipino Communist leader with whom he was in prison. Taruc, serving a life sentence, was a baptized Catholic. Hyde persuaded him to read a pamphlet on Catholic social doctrine. Visibly affected by it, Taruc asked why no one had told him about the Church's social teaching when he was a child. It was exactly what he was fighting for as a Communist.

Christmas Eve. Father Leon Beauvais of Boston arrived two days ago to replace Father Robichaud. I left Sapos 8 P.M. for Vuelta Larga. Two hours of confessions and my first Christmas mass at 10 P.M. in this church which has fluorescent lights that remind me of an all-night eatery on La Cienega and that attract so many bugs that some always fall into the chalice. At 11:15 arrived at Cone for an hour of confessions and began my midnight mass at 12:15 P.M. Started for home down the dust-choked road in my Chevrolet Apache loaded with 50 singing parents and children on their way from mass. Prayed there'd be no blowout from a tree stump in the road—we were two feet from the bank and would have tipped over into the river.

No snow or Christmas tree but the reflection of a full moon in the waters of the Chimbo and a peaceful and joyous evening. My passengers banged on the side of the truck as I came to their destinations and jumped off with a *"Feliz Navidad, Padre José!"* Home at 2:15 and set the alarm for 5:30 to be on time for the Sapos Christmas mass at 6. No sooner asleep than awakened by the cry, "Padre! Padre!" from beneath my window. The caller was a neighbor of Esteban, who ran the gas station. Esteban, he said, had shot himself and his widow was in hysterics. I dressed, picked up some tranquilizers downstairs at the clinic, and hurried over to Esteban's living quarters behind the gas station.

He had shot himself in the head and lay dead in a pool of blood. I gave the last rites and covered the body. His widow was carrying on, blaming herself that if she hadn't nagged him for his drinking he'd be alive today.

Esteban had had a fair education and read some books; there were several on the shelf above the bed, including some novels in Spanish. He had been a sensitive man; too sensitive.

I gave his wife some Equanil. Suddenly, whispers; standing in the doorway, half-dressed, were five girls from the brothel next door.

"This is no place for you to be," I told them. "Get somebody to stay with the senora and then go to church and say a few prayers for the poor man." They left, giggling.

"It is Christmas Eve, Padre," Esteban's wife kept sobbing. "My husband killed himself on Christmas Eve."

There were still plenty of people on the street when I went back to the rectory an hour later. "*Feliz Navidad! . . . Feliz Navidad, Padre!*" they called as I passed. At home I threw myself down on the bed but couldn't sleep; the dead man and the blood-stained room kept flickering before my eyes like a piece of torn film in a movie projector. Finally I gave up and went to the kitchen for a cup of tea.

Ray came in scratching his head and wanting to know what had happened; when I told him he insisted on taking my 6 o'clock mass even though his own mass schedule today was as tough as mine.

"But it's after three already and I can't sleep," I objected. "I might as well take six o'clock mass."

Ray grinned at me sleepily and lit a cigarette. "I'm insisting. If you can't sleep, spend the time counting your money."

At seven I was on the road for my first mass to be served at the church at Santa Elena, still under construction. Masses followed at Buenos Aires, Deseo, Deseo Dentro, San Mateo, Taura and Inmaculada. I got home at 10 P.M. so bushed I fell into bed without eating but glad to have celebrated my Christmas with the poor.

New Year's Eve. Pleasant dinner prepared by the cook and our dear friends visiting from Quito, Sisters Mary Raymond, Mary Aguilar and Mary Catherine of the Congregation of St. Agnes of Fond du Lac, Wisconsin. The Sisters have run a clinic in Quito since 1960. Picked them up at the Duran *gabarra*, the remodeled World War II invasion barge that operates as a ferry between Guayaquil and Duran. We spent most of the day together distributing food, candy and money to the poor in one section of the parish.

At 11 P.M. a telegram arrived from Maurey and Marie Schafer with word of Helen Shafer's death. She had passed away peacefully last evening. Helen had been in reasonably good health and I had been looking forward to seeing her on a forthcoming trip to the States in March. The blow hit me hard and I had to be by myself for a while. What a holy life she had lived, I thought, this unselfish benefactress of mine who, although she had servants, went down on her knees every Saturday to clean the little church in Montesanto, Washington, where she worshipped.

A while later somebody knocked on my door. It was the Sisters with Ray and Leon standing a little sheepishly behind them. "Sorry to disturb you," Sister Mary Raymond said in her high sweet voice, "but it's the stroke of midnight and we wanted to wish you a Happy New Year."

CHAPTER

3

ON March 26, 1965, at the invitation of General Edwin Chess, chief of chaplains, I flew from Guayaquil to Chicago on my way to preach a month of Air Force missions in the Far East. Accompanying me were Petita Alvarez and Sulie Alvarado. Petita was an enormous-eyed fifteen-year-old from the orphanage who would go to school at St. Mary's High School in Little Rock, returning eventually to Ecuador to teach at the orphanage. Sulie, an eleven-year-old polio victim who had been an S.S. *Hope* patient, needed a difficult series of operations. Surgeons of the Shriners' Hospital in Chicago had agreed to do the work without cost.

It was understood that Petita would stay with my brother Frank and his wife, Jean, until I returned from my Air Force missions and drove her to Little Rock. But when the girls and I landed in Chicago and I checked with the Shriners' Hospital, they told me they couldn't take Sulie for another month, at least. I was so busy getting ready for my next day's departure for Tokyo that the question of Sulie's immediate accommodations slipped my mind completely.

At O'Hare Field, waiting to board my plane to Travis Air Force Base, San Francisco, I told Frank and Jean, "Well, I'll be seeing you in about five weeks."

Jean nodded toward Sulie, dressed in one of her daughter
Gail's old coats; it was very cold in Chicago and the girls had
arrived (my fault) wearing their light Ecuadorian dresses.
"What about Sulie?" Jean wanted to know.

I explained about the delay with the Shriners' Hospital.
Frank looked at Jean and Jean looked at Frank. Then both
of them looked at me. Neither of them knew Spanish, nor the
girls any English.

I began edging away. "You've got two daughters," I said.
"You know what to do if the girls get sick—call a doctor.
Sulie can eat anything but rice. Petita isn't fussy." Then I
ran for my plane.

After five days of preaching at Tokyo Airbase, I moved on
to Okinawa. We had lost 35,000 men on Okinawa in World
War II; here my brother Frank, a Marine, had been wounded.
I saw the underground tunnels where the Japs had holed in;
the underground hospital where 138 girls had been put to
death because the Japanese feared their violation by the invading Americans; and Suicide Cliff, from which the generals of
the Imperial Staff had jumped into the sea below, followed
by thousands of civilians.

The last of the missions was held at Taipei and Manila. I
headed back home via Hawaii, where I was guest of General Hunter Harris, later Commander of the Pacific Air
Force, and one of the finest gentlemen I've ever known.

In Seattle I visited with Maurey and Marie Schafer. Maurey
told me of his mother's last bequest—a $25,000 gift to the
orphanage. He and Marie had ordered for the missions a new
Willys with 4-wheel drive. A badly needed addition to our
transportation system, the Willys couldn't have been more
welcome.

In St. Louis, at the National DAV convention, I was re-
elected national chaplain for a second two-year term. A letter
was waiting for me in Chicago from Ray Kirk and Leon, who
had returned to the parish in my absence. Jerry Degen had

come down with malaria and gone to Lima for treatment, they wrote. Heavy rains had flooded El Triunfo and there were three feet of water in church, clinic and rectory. "I asked Senor Sanchez," wrote Ray, "if he thought the rain was a Communist plot, and he told me with a straight face that he'd heard the Russian meteorologists in Moscow could do practically anything."

I had been corresponding with Mother Rosita of St. Agnes Convent in Fond du Lac, Wisconsin, about the possibility of her providing nursing Sisters to staff the Sapos clinic. Jay O'Brien, a student of Holy Cross College and currently on vacation, offered to drive me to Fond du Lac, and I took along Sulie and Petita for the ride.

The news at St. Agnes was wonderful; three nursing Sisters would join the clinic, hopefully in January of next year. That meant I'd have to start building a convent for the Sisters in May, as soon as the rainy season ended.

On the way back to Chicago I stopped off in Kalamazoo, Michigan, to visit with my sister Helen and her non-Catholic husband, Elmer Deichman. Helen and Elmer's son Frank was now a student at St. Martin's College in Olympia, Washington, my old alma mater.

During Holy Week, at the request of Father Ed Flannery of St. Rene's Church, my brother Frank's parish, I said mass in English, and at the request of Father Michael Cepan, celebrated high mass on Easter Sunday at Assumption Church, where my parents had worshipped. On Easter Monday my brother Walter and his wife, Ruth, drove the girls and me to Arkansas.

At Fort Smith, at the Benedictine St. Scholastica's Academy, we saw Alba Rubera, my fifteen-year-old protégée from the orphanage in Guayaquil who had arrived in Arkansas eight months before to attend high school at St. Scholastica's.

Weeping, pretty Alba threw herself into my arms. I told

her there was nothing to cry about, that the good Sisters had only praise for her hard work and dedication.

"I'm proud of you," I told her, "and so are the orphans and Senoritas Clementina and Rosa. A good student will be a good teacher, when you go back to the orphanage."

Alba looked up at me, eyes brimming. "Padre José, that will be in three years' time, and I like my life here so very much. Can't I stay here *four?*"

"Oh, you've met a boy, is that it?"

"No, Padre," she told me earnestly. "The Sisters watch me very carefully, and even if I did meet somebody, I couldn't understand his Southern accent."

We visited with the Lyons family, with whom Alba boarded. Lloyd Lyons, a disabled veteran who had lost a leg as a captain of infantry at St. Lô, and his wife, Dell, had made Alba a part of their family. Their daughter Shirley was now studying for her M.A. in social service at the University of Oklahoma. Shirley was the only Catholic in a Protestant family of five; she had converted when she was twelve. An attractive girl of great strength of character who had decided to devote her life to others, she had contracted polio at the age of eleven. I had first met her in 1961, when she was attending Arkansas Tech, in Russellville, on a National Defense Loan, with Arkansas Rehabilitation paying her tuition.

One evening as Shirley, another student and I were leaving the campus after a Newman Club lecture, Shirley's leg gave way beneath her and down she went. As I bent to pick her up, she smiled and said, "Oh Father Joe, I'm so clumsy." Such courage in the face of a difficult handicap impressed me, as had the wide circle of young friends who revolved around Shirley and were much influenced by her. I asked my benefactors to send Shirley to Lourdes and other European shrines, not in search of a cure but in hopes the experience would teach her to live with her affliction.

I succeeded better than I knew. When Shirley returned

from Europe, a more vivid personality than ever, she told me, "You know, Father Joe, when I left for France I was engaged to Jim. When I came back, I wasn't. If it hadn't been for the trip I never would have had the courage to break with him."

We dropped Petita off at the Morgans' in Eureka Springs, where she would be spending the summer before entering St. Mary's Academy in September, and drove to Little Rock. My classmates at St. John's Seminary and many friends had gathered at St. John's to celebrate Bishop Albert Fletcher's Silver Episcopal anniversary. Fifty archbishops, with Cardinal McIntyre of Los Angeles presiding, and over 400 priests, had gathered to pay their respects to Bishop Fletcher on his 25th anniversary as Bishop of Arkansas.

For two nights I got little sleep; former classmates were always knocking on the door for a little reminiscing. One anecdote connected with me had become legend; the story of Father Feeney, who, after I had responded with two minutes of complete silence to his request for a Latin translation, had urged me mildly, "Faster!"

I had mentioned chest pains to Sister Margaret Louise of St. Vincent's Infirmary in Little Rock, and she insisted I come in for a cardiogram. Dr. Frank Padberg, who had performed a spinal tap to help my headaches in 1958, read the cardiogram and recommended I see Dr. Ben Price, a Little Rock heart specialist.

I paled. "Nothing wrong, Doc, is there?"

"Not really. I just want somebody you'll listen to to tell you to slow down."

In no uncertain terms, Dr. Price told me to take it easier. My schedule was simply too much for a man of fifty-four. From now on I had to get at least seven hours of sleep nightly. If I didn't I might wind up with a heart condition within a year.

I left for Chicago to enter Sulie in the Shriners' Hospital. A day later I arrived in Boston to report at the Society of St.

James on Clark Street. I was talking to Monsignor Sweeney
when a familiar voice said raspingly, "Joe, why didn't they
tell me you were coming into town? Ed, bring him into my
office!"

What an incredible man; only yesterday Cardinal Cushing
had made his first appearance since his operation two months
before, when surgeons had removed three yards of his intes-
tines. Yet aside from loss of weight and a little pallor, he was
as vital and electric as ever.

He spoke of the missions; the children at kilometer 32, the
church he had dedicated in Sapos, the orphans were still fresh
in his mind. When was I starting work on J.F.K. school? On
the Cardinal Cushing school? Was the government giving me
any trouble with land titles? And was there anything he could
do? His grasp of detail was phenomenal; he forgot almost
nothing and what he did wasn't worth remembering. We
were talking shop when he interrupted me to ask when I had
last been in Lima.

"Not since language school," I told him.

"Joe," he rasped, "you should get away more often. Visit
with the fathers; it's good for you. Don't stick to the grind.
And how many masses are you saying Sundays?"

He had caught me unawares and I hesitated; I didn't want
to tell him I was saying as many as eight and nine masses on
Sundays when church law held me to three.

He laughed. "Joe, you're a rascal—you must be giving them
eight a day."

"Your Eminence," I said, "how can I deny the people when
as many as a hundred and fifty are gathered in His name to
hear the word of God? These people have been abandoned
but God gave them the gift of faith. What am I to do with
this gift—reject it?"

"What God has given to us, let us give to the people. Use
your judgment, but watch your health." He winked at me.
"All right, we won't tell Ed Sweeney about the eight masses."

When I left he gave me an autographed portrait I would cherish always. It was inscribed "To my good friend Father Joe—a dedicated missionary, a lover of the poor."

Sunday, May 30. Back at the missions now almost a month and if today is any indication it's as if I'd never been away. Mass at Santa Elena Church in Sapos at 6 A.M. Then packed the outboard motor, a tank of gas and my mass kit into the Apache pick-up and drove 45 kilometers to the Puenta bridge, where my 8-foot, flatbottomed fishing boat, donated by the girls and men of the Chicago Park district, is moored in the Chimbo River. Attached the outboard and was off down the fast-flowing stream, very high due to the rains. Mass at Cone with a half hour of confessions and 35 communions. Then upstream to Vuelta Larga, the first of five stops, for mass and confessions, watching out for floating debris and logs. My parishioners line both banks, some washing, some fishing, some waiting to receive a blessing as I pass. The sun is so hot that in order to avoid sunstroke I must periodically wet my head and face.

Back at Sapos 6:30 P.M. Parking the truck I saw a crowd across the street following a man staggering along and literally soaked in blood. When I went up to him he said, "*Ayuda me, Padre*. Help me, Father." He had a 15-inch machete cut across his shoulders, three others across his back and three on his scalp. Only the liquor his system had absorbed had prevented him from going into shock.

Taking him into the hospital at Guayaquil would have been a two-hour drive and he was losing too much blood to survive it. I got some clean towels from the clinic, sprinkled them with sulfa powder, put him in the pick-up and drove to Dr. Plutarco Chiquito's sugar plantation hospital at San Carlos, 15 miles away. I had to disturb Dr. Chiquito at mass; he rushed Julio Martinez, the victim, into the emergency room, ordered blood and oxygen, and began a two-hour sewing job.

At 9:15 Dr. Chiquito emerged, exhausted. He had, he said, given Julio two pints of blood; it would be five or six days before he was ready to leave the hospital. When I offered to pay him, the doctor put a finger to his lips, looked around conspiratorially and said, "Look, I'll put his name down and the bosses will assume he's one of the plantation workers. There are enough Martinezes on the rolls to start a revolution."

I got home at 10:15; then remembered I hadn't said my breviary. By eleven I was in bed.

Half an hour later the doorbell rang. It was Julio's wife. I told her when he'd be back and went back to sleep. The doorbell rang again at midnight; this time it was Julio's would-be assassin; he wanted to know if Julio was going to survive or not. Yes, I told him, thanks to Dr. Chiquito. He was disappointed.

It must have been around one in the morning that Ray's slow, grimly accusatory banging on the wall awakened me. I'd been snoring, evidently. I banged back twice to show I'd heard him, adjusted my mosquito netting, and hopefully turned over.

June 6. Dropped in on Senor Carerra at his Piladora, or feed store, and asked him to make a pledge for the convent. He said, "Padre, I can't give you more than twenty sucres a month for six months. I've got eight children." I looked him in the eye and said, "The convent will house the nursing Sisters who'll be staffing the clinic. If you've got eight children, you need the clinic more than I do." He grinned sheepishly: "Padre, I also have a sick wife." I went next door to the Almacen, or general store. Who should be at the counter but Carerra's "sick" wife. The adjoining shops were run by Carerra's three strapping sons, all in their thirties. By the time I was back to Carerra at the Piladora, the word had gotten out that I'd met his well-fed family. "Padre," he said, "I can't give you more than forty sucres a month for a year."

"I didn't come back for that," I told him. "I want to know if you can lend me a couple of grain sacks for my flour distribution." He blushed. Late that afternoon I got a note from him at the rectory pledging a decent contribution.

July 11. Trouble yesterday in Guayaquil. More than 20,000 demonstrators dispersed by tear gas by Ecuadorian soldiers and marines. They prevented political leaders from staging a mass rally in San Francisco Square. In the side streets demonstrators threw rocks at the troops.

This was basically a protest against the junta's plans to wait a year until elections are held and Guayaquileños' resentment against junta politics that both leftist students and bankers and planters agree discriminate against the coast in favor of Quito and the highlands.

July 14. U.S. Ambassador Wymberley Coerr and Richard Salvatierra, Consul General, their ladies and twenty other distinguished visitors due tomorrow on an inspection tour of the parish, and the plumbing had to conk out on us tonight. I literally ran over to Calderone's only to hear from his wife that he was at one of the cantinas in town. "Which one, Senora?" I asked with a sinking feeling, knowing there were at least ten of them. She shrugged. I told myself I couldn't afford to panic and started my search. He wasn't here and he wasn't there. I was coming out of my seventh place when a fellow with an *aguardiente* breath you could have lit with a match pulled at my sleeve and said, "Padre, Ramon [the cantina proprietor] did not want to tell you, but Calderone is at Raquel's Casa d'Amora. He left here half an hour ago." I thanked him and had started off for Raquel's place when it occurred to me I couldn't set foot in a brothel without causing a scandal. I needed the man's help. He said he was willing, introduced himself as Eduardo, and we left. I watched him disappear into Raquel's adobe house—one of the few in Sapos—with its red light glowing through the blinds. Fifteen, twenty minutes passed, but no Eduardo with Calderone in tow. Then a burst of drunken laughter and my heart sank. Maybe they were giving Eduardo free drinks because they thought he planned to stay. If he passed out, I was really in trouble. But the two men emerged a few minutes later. Avoiding my eyes, Calderone said, "It is the toilets again, Padre?"

"What else?" I said in belated triumph and relief, and bore my prize away.

Sept. 4. Had decreed for today that all people in town who were living together out of wedlock could be married free. Tremendous response and we were finished at midnight. One couple was in their seventies.

Sept. 5. After mass and catechism at Buenos Aires school heard that a woman down the road had just been delivered of a child who was very ill. The baby, three days old, had symptoms of tetanus. As I was examining the child a woman came in who said she was the *partera*, or midwife, who had delivered it; she was also the mother-in-law. I asked to see the scissors with which she had cut the cord and she showed them to me—they were filthy.

Went 20 km. into Milagro to the clinic and brought the doctor back with me. After looking at the child he said it had little chance but administered a tetanus shot anyway. I drove him home. He said that the *parteras* were a menace; it was impossible to get after them for needless deaths because their defense always was that the child would have died anyway. I asked if it wouldn't be possible to bring pregnant women into the clinic for an examination a month or two before term; then it would be easier to get them to come to the free hospital at Milagro for delivery. He shrugged and said, "If they can pay the clinic fees," throwing it right back into my lap. I'd go broke paying the clinic fees of every pregnant woman in the parish I brought into the clinic for examination.

Sept. 5. Social change here can't be achieved by any single agency of the government, the Church or a suddenly enlight-

ened elitist upper class. The Church is dragging its feet but has
the advantage of closeness to the people; it can instruct them
on how to cooperate with government. And the Church is the
only institution in the country that operates with continuity
when everything else falls into turmoil during a revolt or a
coup d'état. The Church must preach social reform to the
poor, that they band together against slave labor wages; to the
rich, that they plough their profits back into their own country; to the government, that it build factories and spend for
education and housing.

The poor must get into politics and change the Constitution.
Now the National Assembly is filled with the rich who won't
vote constructive taxes and pay none. The middle class must
scratch for a living so hard that it has no time for politics.

Sept. 6. Our Lady of Perpetual Help Orphanage will have
eleven individual houses or cottages with a capacity of 25-30
girls each, housemother facilities and flower garden.

Next to the dining hall a large laundry and ironing room
and adjoining that a basketball court. On the other side of the
laundry a playground for smaller children. Adjoining this the
Carl Koch School for 70 children of the first three grades.
From fourth grade on the children will go to Guayaquil's
nearby Regina Pacis School. The older girls will attend Regina
Pacis Trade School to learn typing and shorthand, dressmaking
and hairdressing. This way they'll be mixing with the outside
world in which they'll be making their way. The DAV has
already promised sewing machines and sweater-making machines for the trade school.

There will be a chapel on the grounds but for mass I want
the children to go to their nearby parish church, Inmaculada
Concepcion, and take part generally in parish life. The stigma
of "orphan" is a cruel and limiting one to begin with.

A low three-foot wall surrounding the orphanage will have
an iron-work metal gate. The gate will be open all day; the
girls are not to consider themselves prisoners. At the top of the

gate not the name of the orphanage but the words "Through This Gate Pass God's Loved Ones." Inside it a mosaic in rock work of Christ with the little children and the legend, "Suffer the little ones to come unto me."

Also an administration building with clinic, offices and living quarters for the Directora, Clementina and Rosa, her assistant. Here the records will be kept. No one will have access to them but Clementina. When I told her she would have the only key to the archives she blushed and said, "Padre, you do not trust human nature?" I laughed and said, "Clementina, let's say I trust a lot of human nature but not necessarily all of it."

I think I've found my second generation Directora! She is Carmen Periera, a goodlooking, capable, very intelligent girl of seventeen who is just finishing high school from the orphanage. Carmen will go to the States to study, work in U.S. orphanages and get practical experience in social work on the American model. Clementina approves my choice of her eventual successor. But she warned me, "You send a girl who looks like Carmen to the States and she'll never come back, she'll get married. Can't you send her to study social work in some place like *Switzerland?*"

Sept. 8. Ray and I went into an area of the parish where eight schools are asking for catechism and mass. At Los Alamos the Apache entered a rough dirt road, badly rutted. Ahead of us was a long black object that looked like a piece of rubber; as we approached I saw it was a huge cobra about seven feet long. I drove over the snake with the right wheels as Ray, noticing it for the first time, yelled, "Joe, stop!" I stopped about ten meters ahead and looked back. There, in the center of the road, seemingly unharmed, was the cobra, standing about four feet high and weaving back and forth hypnotically. I told Ray to close his window and backed up to get a better view. As we came abreast the snake lowered its head and slithered off into the tall pampas grass. Later I asked the people at Los Alamos if they knew of the cobra and they said yes, last year it had killed a man and a child. "Why don't you get the *rurales* to hunt it down?" I asked and they shrugged and said that would do no good, the snake was evil and thus impossible to kill. Several attempts had been made. Once it had been left for dead by the best machete artist in the area and on another occasion a man had emptied his rifle into it.

Driving back that night I told Ray what I'd heard about the evil snake. Drowsily he said, "Let's talk about it tomorrow. I'm too damn bushed just now for a theological discussion."

The girls at the orphanage were getting impatient for their new home. After the city of Guayaquil had donated land to build on, in September, I had drawn up plans for the eleven dormitories, dining hall, technical school and other buildings. Now, every time I visited the crowded, odorous old Guardaria, like a Goya ruin, the girls would crowd around asking, "Padre, where is our Girls Town? When are you going to start?" Senorita Rosa told me how little Elsa had come up to her and asked how old I was. Why did she want to know, asked Rosa, and Elsa replied somberly, "Padre José is not a young man any more and we want him to start the new place while he is still alive."

In early October there was a fire at the Guardaria, nothing serious and nobody hurt, but it was an indication that the overloaded electrical circuits could lead to a real disaster. I decided to get started with the new construction.

I needed at least $45,000 to get it under way with any assurance of paying my first batch of bills. I had $40,000—$25,000 from Helen Schafer, $10,000 from Carl Koch, and $5000 of my own donated by friends. Recently the sucre had gone up in value from 16 to 18.50 to the dollar. If I put my $40,000 into sucres and the sucre climbed to around 22, I'd make enough profit to buy materials and start work.

I went to Jorge Sotomajor, a banker who was on the board of Cardinal Cushing's new university. "I have no money in your bank," I told him. "I'm merely asking, for the orphanage's sake, how high you think the sucre will go."

"Father," he said, "you've been honest with us and we'll be honest with you. This depends entirely on the man on the street. When they demand the American dollar we've got to get it for them."

I asked what made the American dollar scarce.

"The banana industry. The banana industry in Ecuador needs American money at the moment. When the banana men demand it, we buy the American dollar. Just now I think the sucre could go up to twenty-two or even twenty-five."

"What's the highest you've seen it?" I asked, and he told me twenty-three.

I thanked him and left. During the next two weeks whenever I was in the city, which was often, I made it a point to check on the four o'clock market closings. I raised more than one boardroom eyebrow, and an exquisitely dressed young aristocrat approached me and asked politely, "Father, what are you doing here? Are you in trouble, and can I help?" He invited me to dinner that night at the Jockey Club with him and his stunning, German-born blonde wife. Later I found his check for $300 in my pocket.

The sucre went to 20½, then 21. Senor Sotomajor warned me it might begin to fall and that I had better be cautious. I watched the board for another week. When the sucre hit 21½ I went to Sotomajor and told him I wanted to invest $20,000. If it continued to climb in the next week or so I'd put in the balance of my $40,000.

He paled. "Padre, this is your decision, of course; I would not want the responsibility. Perhaps you should reconsider. You are, after all, gambling with orphanage funds."

I wrote out a check for $20,000. At the orphanage I told the children, "It's up to you *chicas* to pray these next few days that the Lord let me know whether or not I should buy in before the downswing starts. Please pray as you did for the city to give us the land. If everything turns out all right you'll have ice cream and cake."

In two days the sucre went to 21.60. I had made $4000 profit.

I invested my second $20,000. Within 48 hours the sucre went to 22.50. I had made 15 percent profit or $6000, enough to start construction. When I told Jorge I was pulling out he smiled and said, "I am so glad, Padre. Perhaps now I can begin to sleep again."

Next day the sucre fell to 21.50. Within another week it was below 18.

A week later I got a letter from Carl Koch. It was routine except for the P.S. which read: "Found another $25,000 I'm sending you to start work on the orphanage."

I thought of asking the girls if any of them had prayed for the $25,000 but decided to let well enough alone.

CHAPTER

4

NOV. 2. Feast of the Poor Souls at cemeteries in Taura and Inmaculada, with Fathers Ray and Leon taking care of ceremonies at other local graveyards. Touching to see how the people clean up their plots the week before and paint the wooden crosses. Most cemeteries are on a hill or mound in order to keep them above the flood-stages. People spend the night of November 1 at the graves of their departed and coffee and food is prepared during the night on portable charcoal stoves.

I thought of the Guayaquil cemetery with its elaborate marble mausoleums and crypts on the lower level and the makeshift graves of the poor with their little wooden crosses dotting the hillside above.

At each graveyard I sing a requiem mass and bless the graves, reciting the Prayers of the Dead as I go from plot to plot. Some may call it old-fashioned and sentimental but I find warmth and beauty in this custom of respect for the departed. Young men and girls sit in silent prayer at the graves of their parents and as I approach they lift their heads and greet me softly. I say with them the Lord's Prayer, then intone the responses for the dead.

Home at 8 P.M. to spend an hour in the beautiful Santa

Elena Church praying for my own departed. Year by year their number grows.

Later Ray told me how Senor Sanchez, proprietor of the local *funeria*, had made several circuits of Sapos cemetery, pointedly stopping to talk with those people who would most likely be needing his services by and by but skillfully avoiding those who under no circumstances could afford him.

Nov. 6. At eight thirty on this Saturday night Ray, I and Sister Julia, one of the Fond du Lac nursing Sisters, were finishing dinner when Leon dragged in from his mission rounds on the Estero Claro run. He washed up and sat down gratefully at the table. He'd taken his first sip of V-8 when Ray, with a catch in his voice, said, "You know it hurts when the *campesinos* come into church and ask for another priest to baptize their children. I finished mass at 7:45 and this baptism was waiting. I said to the parents, 'All right, let's take care of the little one,' but they said if it was all the same to me, they'd prefer Father Leon.' Leon choked on his juice, blinked and asked if they were still waiting for him. "Yes," said Ray, getting up from the table, "but you have dinner. I'll take care of it."

"No, no," Leon insisted, putting down his unfinished V-8. "I guess they're people from my section of the parish, from La Paz, probably." He went to his room for his cassock and a moment later we heard him going down the stairs. "Oh, Father Ray," Sister Julia chided, "you will have your little joke!" and we laughed. Five minutes later Leon came back, sat down at the table and finished his juice. "What's the matter?" asked Ray. "Didn't your admirers wait for you?"

"No," Leon told him, "but two baptisms just came in and I told them you'd be right down."

"You're kidding," Ray said, looking at him closely.

"Listen," said Leon. "You offered mass this evening and any baptisms tonight are your responsibility." Ray shrugged and got to his feet. Leon waited till the door closed below, then exploded into laughter. "That'll cure him, that California Cutie and his practical jokes!"

"Father Leon," Sister Julia reproved him mildly, "you didn't send Father Ray down there knowing there were no baptisms!"

"Yes, Sister," Leon told her with satisfaction, "and I'd do it again."

We expected Ray back momentarily, but he didn't show for almost another hour. "Good they brought that child in," he told us, shaking his head. "Advanced hepatitis. Won't last the night."

Leon stared at him. "Come off it, Ray. You're putting me on. You didn't have any baptism. That church was empty when I left it."

"It wasn't empty when I went back down," Ray said. "If you don't believe me, check out the records." He disappeared into his room to change back into his chinos and T-shirt.

Leon checked the baptismal records, as I knew he would, and found two baptisms listed for the night of Nov. 6. He wouldn't speak to Ray for a couple of days. When I asked Ray about it he laughed. "No, of course I didn't forge the records. What I did do was hunt up in a hurry two unbaptized infants I knew of in Sapos and tell the parents they'd better bring them in with witnesses. You think I was going to miss an opportunity like this with that Boston wiseacre? Chalk up another one for San Diego."

Christmas Eve, Dec. 24. Three days of heavy rains with the rivers rising and the river roads thick with mud. Two masses at the new church, Reina de los Cielos, "Queen of Heaven," at km. 22, constructed with donations by Major General Terry Finnegan, former chief of Air Force chaplains, and Brigadier General Monsignor Edwin Chess. After seven o'clock mass at Taura, returned home to a quick bite with Ray and Leon while Ray played Bing Crosby's "White Christmas" over and over on the vic. Finally Leon accused him: "You're trying to drive me crazy with Bing Crosby's 'White Christmas.' You know I can't stand Bing Crosby's 'White Christmas.' It's almost as bad as Joe's 'Grand Canyon Suite.' "

Tossed the mass kit into the Apache and started off on my rounds. As I turned off the main highway at the bridge that spans the Chimbo, I knew I was in for a muddy ride. What had once been deep dust holes now looked like mud-filled shell craters. If I hadn't known by heart every rut and hole in the road, and especially the narrows, where there was only three feet between the road and a six-foot drop into the river, it would have been the end of my Christmas masses. As it was, I had to slide and slew around them carefully in low gear.

I bogged down about two kilometers out of Cone. Soon *campesinos* were prying me out of the mud hole with bamboo poles. Arrived at Cone Church to find it beautifully decorated with the crib scene complete except for the infant Jesus. Heard confessions for two hours and at 10 P.M. the Christmas procession began with the beautiful Spanish Christmas hymns ringing through the still night air. We marched through town, singing the Christ Child's praises, a little girl of nine carrying Him on a white pillow. As I blessed the crib, she placed the statue in the manger, completing the scene. I began mass and five minutes later a heavy rainfall. Over 50 received Our Lord in holy communion.

At 11 P.M. off for midnight mass in Vuelta Larga. Today's rains had added to the hazards and passing a stretch of road where the river ran only a foot from it my heart was in my throat. Arrived at 11:30 and said mass in one of the classrooms under construction. The church, also under construction, has no roof as yet.

After the Christmas sermon the heavens, as if in reproof, opened and the rain came down in sheets. Almost 50 received Our Lord in holy communion and the singing was beautiful as the young voices raised in song with the rain on the roof as steady obbligato.

After mass I sought lodging in a nearby bamboo hut. Three planks with a white sheet was my bed for the night. At 5 A.M. I awoke with the roosters. The water had reached new levels in the early dusk. I washed hurriedly and was off on the road upriver. After three bog-downs I made it to Cone, reaching the bridge at 6:30. Now to cross and continue upstream for Inmaculada, where during the past year I had constructed a new church and Carl Koch School. In Inmaculada the Christmas hymns of the *Serranos*, or hill people, were more sentimental than those of the *Costenos*, or coastal people, of Cone and Vuelta Larga.

Thirty *campesinos* asked for a lift to the main road. They proved mighty handy later on when I bogged down again to help push the Apache out of a mud hole. Then, a quarter mile farther on, the motor spluttered and died. I checked the spark plug wires and dried them out, but no response. I took off the distributor cap and dried it with my handkerchief; then set fire to some newspaper and dried out the distributor completely. Onward.

Confessions outdoors at Buenos Aires while the people prepared the DAV School, constructed with funds from the Disabled American Veterans, for mass. A table was used as an altar and over it were placed, as altar cloths, three empty U.S. Government flour sacks.

Mass at Deseo Dentro at 1 P.M. in an old school building with one wall of homemade brick, a dirt floor with mud puddles and a thatched roof of banana leaves that leaked in the intermittent rain.

Despite the rain the children came with flowers and their little statues of the Infant to be blessed and placed on the altar during mass. Raindrops still clung to the petals of the freshly picked flowers.

Another mass at Villa Carmen at 3 P.M. after a 7-Up at a cantina on the main road. The children begged their *Pascua* or Christmas gift and I told them American clothing would be arriving in January. "*Ropa para mí, Padre?* Clothes for me, Father?"

"*Sí, chica, para usted y su familia.* Yes, little girl, for you and your family." If only we could see the joy a promise brings to the poor!

Returned home at 7 P.M. and after a sandwich and a Coke, hit the hay. At midnight Ray's banging on the wall awoke me. I rapped out "Sorry" in Morse code and went back to sleep. But did Ray?

New Year's Eve, 1966. Quiet celebration since a heavy mass schedule starts tomorrow at 6 A.M. Ray, Leon and I turned in at eleven after popcorn and soft drinks with the Sisters. About an hour later the strains of Ferde Grofé roused me and I went out to the living room. Ray sat in the armchair by the vic, in candlelight, sipping a beer and smoking. "The new young priest of the emerging church," I said. "A drink in one hand, a cigarette in the other, and listening to racy music." Ray made a "V for victory" sign with two fingers. A moment later Leon emerged, rubbing his eyes. "Have a heart with Grofé, sadist," he groaned. "Wouldn't 'South Pacific' be bad enough?"

Ray gave him his deadpan stare. "After 'Grand Canyon' it's 'South Pacific,' and then I'm playing Bing Crosby's 'White Christmas.' It's New Year's Eve, Beauvais, and we're going to tie one on. Have an Ecuadorian beer."

We didn't get back to bed before twelve thirty.

Jan. 2. Leon has left for Holy Rosary parish and been replaced by Mike Diehl. During the war Mike flew for the Navy in the ferry command and served on anti-submarine patrol duty in the Atlantic. After discharge he entered Notre Dame and post-graduation, Conception Seminary in Conception, Mo. In 1965 he joined the St. James Society.

Mike, forty-five, is reserved and ascetic-looking with pepper and salt hair cropped short. He had quite a first day. In his jungle parish outside San Martin, he married an Indian man of ninety-five and his seventy-year-old bride. The bride wore white and the couple's eight sons and four daughters were present. On the cable car crossing the Suga River, the wheel took off three of the operator's fingers. Two and a half hours later Mike got him to the hospital. The doctor said, "Who's going to pay for it?" and Mike said he would, with his entire first month's salary. Driving back to Sapos in the station wagon, he was sideswiped by the *colectivo* "Popeye," driven by a madman who claims to have once raced in the Indianapolis 500. No damage except to the *colectivo*'s fender. But who should happen to be a passenger but a *transito*, a local traffic policeman. The *transito*, a friend of the bus driver, decided the accident was Mike's fault.

"I'm due in court next Tuesday," Mike groaned. He looked at the grinning Ray. "You want to exchange parish routes with me?"

"Not on your life," Ray told him. "As they said of Willie Loman, in *Death of a Salesman*, 'That New England territory always was rough.'"

Jan. 4. Due to take the jeep into the *campo* today, Ray discovered its battery was missing, stolen. He went over to the convent to borrow the station wagon we had presented to the Sisters. Station wagon's battery was missing, too. We were lucky the Apache was in the repair shop.

Two weeks later Ray and Mike went on a five-day retreat outside Guayaquil. The following morning I got up feeling weak and nauseous and by nightfall was running a fever. After taking a couple of aspirin, I broke out in a sweat followed by chills. Had I come down with malaria? These were the same symptoms Jerry Degen had had before he left Sapos.

Next day Dr. Chiquito examined me at the clinic. "Padre," he said, "you have the 'big H'—hepatitis."

"I had jaundice when I was in Africa with the RAF," I told him. "But I've been pretty careful in Ecuador."

"You've been here four years and its about time it caught up with you. Better go to Guayaquil Hospital for treatment. You could die out here."

I asked him if I could hope to recover by late February, when I was due to fly to Germany for a month of Air Corps preaching missions. "Only if you get plenty of rest and start eating decently, with plenty of protein," he told me. "You don't, the disease will become chronic."

I wondered if I should write General Chess, calling off the German missions, but decided against it. I'd take my medicine on schedule, cut down on work where I could, and see what happened.

Ray and Mike returned over the weekend. On Saturday morning Isabel Burgos, a four-year-old, was brought into the clinic with first-degree burns on her face and hands. Three of the fingers of her right hand had become fused together.

There were no plastic surgeons in Guayaquil, but Sister Julia knew of one in Quito. We drove to Duran where she called Quito and made arrangements to bring the child in.

I'd planned to take Isabel to Quito, but then Gene Costello ordered me to move to Rosary parish for a month to be treated at the hospital. Sister Julia flew Isabel to the capital for surgery.

When I asked Ray if he'd informed on me to Gene, he started whistling "Grand Canyon Suite."

By the end of February I had recovered. On the 25th I arrived by Pan Am jet in Frankfurt, Germany, and for the next five weeks preached missions in Weisbaden, Sembach, Ramstein and at Etain Air Force Base, France. I took a side trip to Cologne to see the Cathedral; part of the town was still rubble. It was a strange feeling at first to be speaking God's name in a country over which, twenty-two years before, I had rained death and destruction as an enemy bomber pilot. On April 1 I flew from Frankfurt to New York and landed at Guayaquil on the 2nd.

Julia brought little Isabel to meet me. The surgery had been successful and she would eventually be pretty again.

April 4. The government program in agrarian reform, by which the *campesino* was given enough land to start farming for himself, collapsed last month "for lack of funds." Is it too much to ask of the U.S. Government that it had recognized the danger of collapse in time and lent the Ecuadorian Government enough money at a low interest rate to forestall it?

In Bolivia and Chile the huge estates have been broken up and these countries finally projected into the 20th century. For the last twenty years the Church has been in favor of land reform on a large scale which would require expropriation by the government of the large plantations and their parceling out to the *campesinos*. In Ecuador 0.4 percent of the landowners hold 45.1 percent of the arable land, while 73.1 percent of the landholders subsist on 7.2 percent of the arable land. Failing expropriation of the great haciendas, the Church has been in favor of cooperatives which finance the *campesinos* in the purchase of four or five quadros of land. (In Sapos there's no sense in starting a cooperative because the people don't make enough money to save. Paul McGreevy has begun one in Concepcion parish with 1 percent per month interest charges.) Farming his quadros, and also working for his hacienda owner, the *campesino* can make a better living than he has so far done, raising enough to feed one cow to be sold for $50, a lot of money for these parts.

April 12. Taking the outboard down the Chimbo when a submerged log overturned the boat. Had to dive in seven feet of water to recover my mass kit. I dried out in a bamboo hut on the river bank and, an hour later, arrived on foot in Inmaculada. The people were lined up along the bank, waiting for their Padre. The women took my soaked vestments to their huts and put their charcoal flat irons to work. A short time later I had them back, and no valet shop in any exclusive hotel around the world could have done better. Fortunately the Host in its plastic container had stayed dry as a bone.

April 21. Yesterday Ray took the Apache to nearby Boliche to have its headlights and springs repaired. Last night the mechanic and three of his friends, fueled by plenty of *aguardiente*, took it out for a joy ride. At 1 A.M., coming round a curve, the Apache left the road and ploughed a path over 70 yards of trees and boulders. The mechanic was killed and the other occupants seriously injured; the truck was wrecked completely.

Senor Guzman came to tell me of the accident. He had given deep thought to the problem and come to the conclusion that it would do no good to try to collect from the garage for the truck; as for the hospital charges involved, he would see to it that I wasn't billed for them.

I didn't know whether to laugh or cry. He took my silence for approbation.

"Of course, Padre. There is no reason why this affair should be more expensive to you than it has already been. Perhaps I could trouble you for another bottle of beer?"

Last night, coming back from Barranco Chico about 9 P.M., Ray saw a light in Sapos cemetery and went over to investigate. Senor Guzman was doing an autopsy at one of the graves with a 12-inch knife. Ray said, "If that man wasn't dead when the *teniente* started, he was certainly dead when he finished!"

Sunday, April 24. There was an Indian sleeping in the church doorway when I rang the first bell for 6 A.M. mass. As he moved and stretched the church door swung open and I saw the lock was missing. "How long have you been sleeping here?" I asked the Indian. He shrugged. "Padre, I do not remember. I think all night."

I put on the lights and began to investigate, expecting the worst. The tabernacle veil was disordered, but the lock secure. In the sacristy the chalice was missing, along with a small crucifix from the altar. What was most frustrating about the theft, along with the thought that anyone could be capable of it, was the fact that there was no sense in reporting it to the police. It would only have gotten into the newspapers, brought St. Elena Church more publicity, and led to more thievery.

May 12. Infant mortality figures from the government: total deaths for the year 58,989. Less than one year old, 20,608; one to four years, 13,403. 34,000 deaths out of 59,000 are below four years of age, or 58 percent. At the clinic these statistics are seen in terms of young children with malnutrition, beri-beri, anemia, tuberculosis, malaria, gastroenteritis, tetanus, pneumonia. Primitive midwifery accounts for many fatalities. What should be most heartrending are the endless cases of malnutrition, little potbellies staggering around on pipestem legs; yet they are not, being too familiar. What sticks in the mind is a case like that of the little three-year-old girl with a cleft palate and harelip, brought in by her mother. Probably the mother had measles during pregnancy. The child's father beats her because she cries, and she cries because the cleft palate makes it difficult to feed her. The Sisters feed her now by improvised gavage and Dr. Chiquito prescribed sleeping medicine, but not so much the father would be tempted to give the child the entire bottle in hopes of killing her.

I told the mother that the child, very pretty except for her deformity, must have an operation and that I'd see to it. Sure enough, at the end of the day Dr. Chiquito told me, "All right, I'll operate at Guayaquil Hospital. If I don't I'll have nightmares about your dropping everything to fly the little angel to the States."

Aug. 18. Roused around 11 P.M. by a pleading voice beneath my window. *"Padre, un accidente encima de la puenta.* An accident at the bridge." Dressed hurriedly and learned downstairs that the bus that made the Guayaquil to Riobamba run had gone off the road at the bridge. Awakened Dr. José Mancero, the young Cuenca medical school graduate who has taken over at the clinic, and we were off in the station wagon to the bridge, 30 km. away.

Traffic was tied up for about 100 yards on the bridge approach. I parked the car on the roadside and the doctor and I hurried up to the bridge on foot. *Transito* police and *rurales* were directing traffic and rescue operations, their patrol car headlights providing illumination for the nightmarish scene. A *rurale* told me there had been no guard rail on the bridge approach, and the driver, new to the route, had been driving at excessive speed.

The bus was on its side in three feet of water. On the hillside lay three bodies, a child of twelve, and a man and woman in their thirties. I anointed them with holy oil and gave conditional absolution. Dr. Mancero and I started down toward the bus.

Police and volunteers were working to extricate the last of the dead and injured. Doctor José crawled into one window and I into another. I comforted an injured woman as the rescuers worked to free her. Four more bodies were found which we helped bring to road level. Then Dr. Mancero attended to injured survivors resting in the police cars.

It was 2 A.M. now. The police captain asked me to take the six bodies into Guayaquil morgue. We arrived in the city to find the press, police and ambulances awaiting the *gabarra*. The radio had broadcast news of the disaster and friends and relatives were waiting. It was 3 A.M. before we left the morgue and 5 A.M. before we arrived back in Sapos. I was half-dead with fatigue yet sick with anger. Why was it the poor who always suffered so much in disasters, accidents, fires? The answer was simple: because they had no money to protect themselves, and because they had no money, no one was interested in protecting them.

Aug. 28. Stuck between the two front cushions of the

station wagon, I found the shoe of one of the women who had died in the *colectivo* accident at the bridge ten days before.

Towards the end of the month Mike was brought in by truck from his area with a gall bladder attack. After they had operated on him in Guayaquil he developed a lung infection, and it was decided to send him to St. Elizabeth's Hospital in Boston for further treatment. At the first sign of real danger, Cardinal Cushing wants his missioners home.

Ray, I and Sister Peter rearranged our schedules to cover Mike's area, and the pressure was on. My headaches came on again and one afternoon I fainted in the dugout canoe that ferries over the Boliche River at Taura. Segundo, the boatman, told me when I had revived, "Padre, please don't do that again. My boat almost tipped over."

In mid-October John Auer came out from Duran to help with First Communions. One hundred and twenty received communion in Vuelta Larga alone. Here, only three years before, only five had received Our Lord.

On October 30 I turned the parish over to Ray and John—Mike was to return in December—and moved into Paul McGreevy's Concepcion parish in Guayaquil to concentrate on the building of the orphanage, where construction had started in May. In addition I had construction work in the *campo* to complete: six classrooms and a church in Vuelta Larga, a combination classroom and chapel in Las Pampas, and a classroom and chapel in Nuevo Recinto.

On the 31st Sapos honored me for my five years' service. The procession, led by the Transito Band from Guayaquil, started from the bridge and ended at the rectory, where Ray and John had sweated over a wooden platform and dais for more than two weeks. Last but not least marched Carmencita and her senoritas and the girls from Raquel's Casa d'Amora. Only three pigs, five chickens and one lean pariah dog got in the way; the dog, perhaps resentful of John's comfortable girth, tore a strip from his cassock. The route was decorated overhead with palm fronds at intervals of every 50 feet. The *teniente politico* m.c.'d the ceremony and made the major address. Senor Peño, the town tailor, also addressed the crowd. There were no disturbances by the Communists. I received a gold medal from the Ecuadorian Minister of Education, a commendation in script from the President of the Ecuadorian Senate, and various citations. My gifts from the people included woodcarvings, bookends, a Panama hat with a brim so wide it could have been from a Bogart movie, homemade crossed Ecuadorian and U.S. flags, a scrapbook of Ecuadorian leather, marble ashtrays from Cuenca, and artificial flowers.

Later Ray, clutching his aching temples, complained, "All this stuff and the tears that went with it isn't worth the headache Guzman's speech gave me. Oy!" He looked at John. "You got any aspirin?"

John grinned and shook his head. "Only had three tablets left and I gulped 'em down before the ceremony. Wasn't taking any chances."

I hadn't been back at Concepcion parish for a day before I had visitors, two Sisters from Los Sagrados Corazones School in Guayaquil. The good Sisters had gone out to Sapos to see me and heard I was in Guayaquil. "Padre," they said, "help us with a school for the poor in El Cisne." El Cisne was a section of the Guayaquil *barriada* and could certainly use a school. I knew I didn't have the money for it, but in a week I'd be seeing Carl Koch, and I told the Sisters I'd see what I could do.

I flew to Cincinnati to dedicate the new DAV home and factory, where disabled veterans would manufacture Identotags to support the DAV program in 50 states to help veterans' widows and orphans. Then I moved on to Chicago to visit family and friends. The surgeons at Shriners' Hospital had done wonders for Sulie, who was still living with Frank and Jean. I asked my dear friends Bud and Marge O'Brien to get me a decent price on fixtures needed at the orphanage.

They did and hunted me up a new benefactor besides. Adam Riffle, an acerbic Chicagoan with a heart of gold, was especially generous even though his wife was ill. He said he'd pay for the ranges and refrigerators to be bought at cost, and asked how many washroom fixtures I needed.

"Forty sinks and forty toilets," I told him.

"For how many kids, you said?"

"Three hundred fifty."

"That's one toilet for every nine kids," Mr. Riffle said doubtfully.

"You don't understand about South American youngsters," I told him. "Especially girls. They're not used to flush toilets, and when they have one, they use it a lot."

Typically, Bud and Marge O'Brien insisted on buying them all.

The last day of my six-day trip I spent with the Kochs. Carl not only offered me $4000 for the school at El Cisne, but upped his contribution to the orphanage $20,000 more, and asked me if there were any other projects I might want to add to my list.

"Thanks, Carl," I told him, "but my enlistment with the Society is up in March, when I'll be coming home to take up my old parish at St. Elizabeth's. As it is, I'll be lucky to finish the orphanage and all my other projects by then. I'm not looking for anything else to do."

By mid-November I was back in Guayaquil and deep in a mess of trouble, labor trouble.

Before leaving for the States I'd had difficulty with a construction worker at the orphanage. This man, Rafael Ortiz, after producing 30 cement blocks a day, had left the job and gone home. When I called him on it he said 30 blocks was his quota. I told him he had no quota and that he could have gotten out 50 blocks if he hadn't gone home early; however, I'd give him another chance. He produced 30 blocks and went home. I told him, "You must have heard about how they do things in the states. You're fired."

"You cannot fire me," he said. "I am Segundo's brother." Segundo Ortiz was my construction supervisor.

"Well, let's put it this way—there won't be any more pay checks for you," I said, and walked away.

When I returned from the U.S. there was a notice waiting for me to report to the Labor Board for a hearing on Rafael. After an hour of cooling my heels in the anteroom and enduring Rafael's reproachful looks, we were called inside and the hearing began. The Labor Board was composed of five men, each of whom had a moustache, slicked down hair and a briefcase.

Rafael's lawyer opened the proceedings by saying I had fired his client without just cause. In addition, his mother was sick. The lawyer produced a physician's affidavit to that effect.

The Board chairman asked me why my counsel had been delayed in getting to the hearing. I told him I had no counsel.

That got me a few black looks. Didn't I realize, the chairman asked, it was an insult to appear before the Labor Board without counsel? An insult to whom? I wanted to know. To the Labor Board, was the reply. I said I hadn't realized I was insulting the Board when I thought I could plead my own case. With more than a trace of impatience, the chairman told me to say what I had to say in my own defense.

"I moved this man up from common laborer," I said. "His conduct was extremely bad for the morale of my work crew. Finally, he's my supervisor's brother."

Rafael's lawyer shot to his feet. "That has nothing whatsoever to do with the matter at hand!"

"Oh?" I said. "If I let him get away with it, what do you think the result would have been?"

"Were his blocks satisfactory?" asked the lawyer cannily.

"That's not the point," I replied. "If he was turning out fifty blocks a day, I'd still expect them to be satisfactory."

"Norte Americano efficiency," said the lawyer senten-
tiously, "is not Ecuadorian efficiency. When in Rome we
must do as the Romans do."

"I thought this was Guayaquil," I said. "I'm building an
orphanage, not for me, but for you, for this city. I should
think you'd want it built as efficiently as possible."

"Gentlemen," the lawyer addressed the Board, "we request
two hundred and fifty dollars damages."

"That's foolish," I said. "This is orphanage money. You
press me too hard and I'll get Senor Rocha, the best lawyer
in town. I'll fight this and you won't get a penny."

"Are you willing to give this man a week's salary?" asked
the chairman.

"I'll do better than that. Because his mother is sick I'll even
take him back, but I'm warning him again in front of you that
if he doesn't produce this time he's out for good."

Rafael came back to work next day. He produced 55 blocks
the first day and 45 the second. On the third and fourth he
fell to thirty again, although he stayed on the job till quitting
time. I told him, "You remember what I said. It's up to you."

"Padre," he whined, "my mother is sick."

"Funny, your brother told me she's better."

"Segundo has a very large mouth," Rafael said, but he
started producing 50 blocks a day from that time on and I
never had any more trouble with him.

Nov. 21. Clementina told me about the rich lady who
brought the orphans a five-pound bag of rice as a donation.
I told her she shouldn't have accepted it. "Don't accept from
the rich any donation less than 500 sucres—$25. Keep your
head high, Clementina. God will provide as long as you're
sacrificing for these children. Their prayers got you our new
building site when I couldn't. Their prayers got the money to
start construction. No, don't humble yourself to the rich. Our
Lord didn't have much use for them."

"What should I do, then?" she asked me.

"Here's a formula for you. If the donation's a small one, say the children haven't had meat for two weeks and would they make it enough to buy meat? If they refuse, say you'll do without. They'll say to themselves, 'What did I do wrong? I was refused by the orphans today.' You'll never reach these people unless you open their eyes and their hearts. You've got to stop thinking you're content to be as you are."

"Oh Padre," Clementina said, "you're talking like a revolutionary!"

Rosa came in then and told me of the rich lady who had boasted to her of giving 150,000 sucres to the Guayaquil church for a crypt to be used as a family mausoleum. "And what did you say to that, Rosa?" I asked her. "Nothing," she answered. "Well," I said, "you might have told her, 'Senora, give a tenth of that to something living, like the orphans, and you can boast all you please.' "

Dec. 21. Having fair success trying to bring young women of Guayaquil in to lecture the older orphan girls on what is needed to do secretarial, dressmaking, hairdressing work in the city—skills, deportment, dress, etc. I want to equip the girls so that they have something better to look forward to than working as a housemaid for next to ñothing, getting pregnant by the son of the house, and being thrown out on the streets.

It would help if the lights weren't always going out at crucial moments. Last night Senorita Fernandez was talking to the girls about office work when the room was plunged into darkness. She had the presence of mind to add, "And if you're working late and the lights go out, make sure the boys' hands stay where they belong!"

Jan. 5. Narciso Lopez, a fine craftsman, makes iron and grillwork and installs aluminum doors and windows. His metalwork shop is at 301 Avenida Machala. I asked him to do the iron gate and dining hall doors and windows, but at first he was reluctant. "Padre, I have no capital to buy materials with. I can't get a bank loan. I have no collateral. The banks would rather work with the big outfits and they'll give only short term loans at 15 percent interest. Then, I have a hard time collecting from people I subcontract for; they know I can't afford to sue."

"All right," I told him, "I'll give you an advance. How about five thousand?"

He looked at me. "You will do this for me? Why?"

I laughed. "You'll see when I get on your tail. I'm a fair man but a hard taskmaster, and I'll press an advantage where I can."

Narciso, a Venezuelan in his sixties who once lived and worked in the States, is a sophisticated man, a philosophical pessimist, a kind of gently cynical Claude Raines marooned in Ecuador. "Well," he said, "frankly, that doesn't sound so good. I was afraid you were a kind of Vince Lombardi in a Roman collar. But if you're willing to take a chance on me, I guess I'm willing to take a chance on you."

Feb. 29. This week spent checking with Customs on entering orphanage supplies. Ecuadorian duty so high I couldn't pay it, and items had to be sent to storage. Got the bright idea of calling President Arosemena Gomez in Quito and asking him for an appointment to discuss the matter. Could I fly in tomorrow for a talk at the Presidential Palace? asked his Excellency. Next day we spent half an hour together. President Arosemena was most gracious and wrote me out a duty-free pass for any and all orphanage imports.

Spent the night at Perpetuo Socorro Hogar, the old Quito girls' orphanage run by Senorita Leonora Heinert. When I told the girls about speculating on the sucre for the orphanage in Guayaquil, one moppet asked, "Padre, why don't you go to the casino at the Hotel Quito and win some money for us?" I told her I had no luck with roulette. When I mentioned to the girls that the orphanage would be finished in March a *chica* of nine said, "And when will you build us a new home in Quito? This building is so old, Padre, and so damp and dark."

What could I say? I couldn't refuse her so I answered, "I would love to, Manuela, but I must finish the one in Guayaquil, and in the meantime you pray to God that we can start yours one day."

By "we" I didn't mean Joe Lauro, but she threw her arms around my neck and said, "*Gracias, Padre José!*" In minutes it was all over the place that I was going to build them a new home.

March 2. Asked Hanibal Santos, chief engineer of the Empress Electric Company, pointblank if he could lay out the electric wiring for the orphanage at cost. He looked at me thoughtfully and said, "Let me call Mr. Capwell, our president." Santos not only recommended to Capwell that a company crew install the orphanage wiring but suggested that the company donate the materials, too. Mr. Capwell said fine. Just one sour note in all this. As I was leaving, Santos added, smiling, "Oh, by the way, Father Joe, you're in luck. Caesar Reyes, our senior man, will be doing your installation. He did the Guardaria, you know, over twenty years ago."

In April, 1968, I left for the U.S. to resume my pastorate at St. Elizabeth's in Eureka Springs. My five years in Ecuador had been up in January, and I was looking forward to a good rest among old friends from whom I had been away too long.

Missioners of the St. James Society remain under the jurisdiction of their own bishop. When I was recalled, this was the bread and butter letter Father Gene Costello wrote to Bishop Fletcher:

Your Excellency:

For me, as Superior for Ecuador of the Society of St. James, it is both an honor and a pleasure to write this letter in regard to Fr. Joseph Lauro, a priest of your diocese who has spent five fruitful

years here as a missionary. Father Lauro came here in March
of 1963, after language training and some brief assignments in
Peru, so I know him well.

His work here has been distinguished by unflagging zeal and
devotion to the poor. He leaves behind a most remarkable record
of construction both in his parish of Los Sapos and in the city of
Guayaquil as well. In addition to completing the parish plant at
Los Sapos, consisting of rectory, church, convent and dispensary,
he built also a large number of chapels and public schools throughout the four hundred square miles which were his pastoral charge.
His accomplishments in this regard have been recognized by the
Ecuadorian Government as attested to by various decorations and
testimonials. No one individual has ever done so much in so short
a time to bring the blessings of religion and education to these
people.

When he began as pastor of the parish of Los Sapos, he found
an enormous area with more than thirty thousand people, an
area which for at least four years had been without a priest.
Within a year or two, thanks to his unbelievable efforts, the time
lost had been made up, with more than a thousand Baptisms and an
equal number of First Communions. In each of the 63 public
schools of the area, religion is now taught on a regular organized
basis. American nuns have been brought in for catechetical and
dispensary work, and so on. None of the spiritual or corporal
works of mercy has been neglected under his direction.

He will be missed. We thank your Excellency most sincerely
for having loaned this truly remarkable priest to us.

Sincerely and respectfully,
(Rev.) Eugene W. Costello

With the orphanage more or less complete now, I felt I
could cope with its affairs by long distance. Leonora Heinert
had moved from Quito to take it over, much easing my mind.
But no sooner was I back in Arkansas than Leonora was writing me almost daily about various problems and difficulties.
The power failures were constant. A washing machine had
broken down and needed a part not obtainable in Guayaquil.

The toilets were flooding. The painters weren't only watering the paint, but stealing it in rubber medical bags they wore strapped around their waists. Prices were going up and she was running out of money.

On a rainy day in April I received two letters from Ecuador in the morning mail. One was from Leonora saying that the orphanage was down to two sacks of cornmeal. The other was from the orphan girls in Quito. All 58 of them had signed their names to a one sentence petition reading: "Padre José, you promised to build us a new home."

I picked up the phone and called Bishop Fletcher in Little Rock. I told him I had to go back and why. He listened and said, "Joe, you can't take another five years of it. It'll kill you."

I told him: "Bishop, I don't have to sign up for another five years. Nor would the Society want me to—they can't take on another parish. I'd be freelancing under Archbishop Mosquera of Guayaquil for as long as it takes to finish my commitments. A year, two at the most."

He sighed. "I'll look into a replacement and call you back."

He called back within the hour. He had a replacement for me. When did I want to leave? As soon as possible, I told him.

On May 18 I landed at Guayaquil airport. There wasn't anybody to meet me. When I arrived at the handsome orphanage with its elegant wrought-iron gate made by Narciso Lopez, I learned that the telegram I'd sent announcing my arrival had never been delivered.

"It's all right," I kept reassuring the upset Leonora, Clementina and Rosa. "I don't care whether you had a reception committee to meet me or not. I'm here, I'm home."

" 'Ome," said a small voice with a Spanish accent. I looked around. A wandering three-year-old stood in the doorway, listening with thumb in mouth. She took out her thumb to parrot again, uncomprehendingly, the unfamiliar English word.